ENCYCLOPAEDIA OF INDIAN WOMEN THROUGH THE AGES

ENCYCLOPAEDIA OF INDIAN WOMEN THROUGH THE AGES

Volume—3
Period of Freedom Struggle

Simmi Jain

KALPAZ PUBLICATIONS
DELHI-110 052

ENCYCLOPAEDIA OF INDIAN WOMEN THROUGH THE AGES
(Sociology, Women Studies)

Rs. 3600 (Set)
Rs. 900 (each volume)

ISBN: 81-7835-116-1 (Set)
ISBN: 81-7835-174-9 (Vol. 3)

Published in 2011 in India by
Kalpaz Publications
C-30, Satyawati Nagar,
Delhi-110052
E-mail: kalpaz@hotmail.com
Phone : 9212729499

Printed at: G. Print Process, Delhi

Contents

Preface

The status of women in our sub-continent passed through a most intricate and complex socio-economic terrain. The male-dominated society was indeed a glaring phenomenon and had always edged over their social and domestic environments. Being the earning member in the family, he considered himself fairly superior in terms of his status. But women could maintain their identity and emerged as useful partners and bread-earner for her household affairs. Undoubtedly she did not shirk to meet any economic challenge with dignity and respectable disposition. The volumes on *Encyclopaedia of Indian Women Through the Ages* have been diversified into four categories and cover the themes in a fairly comprehensive and analytical way which are as follows.

The volume on Ancient India deals with a detailed description on social status of women in the Vedic period and in the Mahabharata Era. Emphasis has been laid on their marital status, numerous duties of household affairs, basic rights enjoyed by them, sexual life in practice, social status of a widow and the way of life she had to lead, ideology of motherhood, divorce and remarriage, property rights, the sati ritual, the views of Swami Vivekananda, and foreign accounts of marital arrangements.

The second volume lays emphasis on Medieval India. It includes social position of women, female slaves, women in politics, religious education and practices, observance of purdah, and divorce, *mehr* practices, nikah-marriage, valid marriage, irregular marriage, the sense of equality, women in administration, dissolution of marriage, dower, social customs like birth ceremony, naming ceremony, selection of marriage partners, women education including higher education, their academic contribution, particularly of Gulbadan Begum, Hamidah Bano Begum, Zeb-un-Nisa, Jahan Ara and others, fairs and festivals, games, mostly indoor games, playing cards or *Tash* or chess, pigeon flying, kite flying, female costumes including cotton, silken and golden clothes and a detailed study of Khanzada Begum, Ayisha-Sultan Begum, Zainab Sultan Begum, Maham Begum and Bibi Mubarika.

The third volume has deep thrust on women and freedom struggle. The role of eminent women has been a glaring phenomenon in this volume. In fact these women have become a significant part of our history. Commencing from the historic role of Begum Hazrat Mahal, Rani Lakshmi Bai of Jhansi, Rani of Ramgarh, the theme lands us comprehensively into various social Acts, viz., mobilisation of sati, 1829; Widow Remarriage Act, 1856; the role of Consent, 1891 and the prohibition of Child Marriage Act, 1929. The volume has also highlighted the role of foreign women in our freedom struggle, i.e., Sister Nivedita, The Mother, Mira Behn, and Annie Besant. Mrs. Besant was elected Congress President in 1917—during the crucial period of the first global war.

The emergence of Mahatma Gandhi on the political stage of India in 1915 generated a new spirit of sacrifice for the attainment of *swaraj.* Such women were Kasturba Gandhi, Bee Amman, Parvati Devi, Sarojini Naidu, Kamaladevi Chattopadhyaya, Durgabai Deshmukh, Margaret Cousins, Sucheta Kripalani, Hansa Mehta, Mridula Sarabhai, Usha Mehta, Rajkumari Amrit Kaur and several others. They courted arrests in the Gandhian movements along with numerous women satyagrahas. Even after the attainment of Independence, their role in several fields of development including education, medical, defence, politics and administration is quite laudable.

The last volume gives us a comprehensive analysis on historical perspective and legal review. It deals with the changing social status of women, Gandhi and his contribution for the emancipation of women in economic and political sphere, Dalit women in politics and their changing socio-economic status with new awakening, vision of Annie Besant for generating patriotic spirit among women, role of the regiment of Rani Jhansi as a significant part of the Indian National Army, women and family welfare having deep bearing on sincere initiatives shown by women rather than men to plan their families despite their law position and lesser sex ratio. Other significant aspects on women in this chapter deal with their pitiable plight as labourers in a factory, field or road work, life of working women, regional status of women, particularly in Punjab, Haryana, Madhya Pradesh, sensible findings of a survey based research on women in a slum in Mumbai. Last but not the least a chapter has been well-written on Kerala nuns and nurses in terms of their working status and social difficulties. A few significant case studies on the two categories have been well-analysed.

I feel much beholden to several eminent scholars whose writings have been used in these volumes in order to fill up necessary gaps. The consistent academic support and help of several institutions of higher learning including the members of prominent libraries deserve my respectful acknowledgement. But for sincere support from these categories of scholarly and institutional help, these volumes probably would not have seen light of the day.

With this comprehensive academic survey, it could be judged with the remark that these volumes would be certainly welcomed by eminent social scientists, researchers and students in India and abroad.

Simmi Jain

Introduction

The mutiny of 1857-58 was the first organised armed efforts by the Indians to achieve emancipation from the English political grip. The time was one of great tribulation for the Indians and the English alike, because both experienced unmatched convulsions in the history. The British won, but the Indians gained too, because the movement became a symbol of courage and sacrifice for the subsequent generations. The first symptoms of unrest were experienced in the first quarter of the year 1857 when the soldiers at Berhampore (five miles east of Nowgong), Barrackpore and Ambala, revolted against authorities. The Indian Regiments were disbanded and the criminals punished. But this did not quieten the situation and proved only a prelude to the open resort which followed in May.

The leaders of the outbreak were not only men but also women, including *Begum Hazrat Mahal, Rani Lakshmi Bai, Rani of Ramgarh* and *Rani Tace Bai.* Some of them participated in battle while others endured the sufferings and privation, imprisonment and death.

Reform movements against 'social evils' affecting women started in British India in the early 19th century and have been usually attributed to external factors such as the impact of English education, missionary activities and liberal views from the west, as well as to internal expeditions such as the nationalist agitation against imperialism and the religio-cultural resistance by Indians to the challenge of Christianity and western culture. The subjects handled by the reform movement—such as *sati,* widow remarriage, polygamy and women's property rights—were troubles of a certain strata of society, such practices being mainly confined to the higher castes and classes. They were matters raised by bourgeoisie, male social reformers from urban areas who planned to idealise female role as wife and mother in the context of patriarchy. Whether like the orthodox reformers they looked back to a Vedic golden age where women were believed to have possessed a high status, or whether they looked forward to a new fundamental based on liberal principles which negated the 'barbaric' heritage of the past—the male reformer's fundamental assumptions were the social reform and female education would revitalise and preserve the patriarchal family system, produce more companionate wives and better mothers and hence have a stabilising effect on society. The reformists felt that middle-class family structures were being threatened by the prevalent social vices.

From the very inception of the Indian National Congress, its membership was welcome to women. At its first session Allan Octavian Hume asked political reformers of all shades of opinion never to forget that unless the elevation of the female element of the nation proceeds *pari passu* (with an equal pace) with their work, all their labour for the political enfranchisement of the country will prove vain. Ten women attended the fourth session of the Congress at Bombay in 1889. Like the males, females participated from Calcutta and Bombay including Swarnakumari Devi, sister of Rabindranath Tagore. She had abandoned *purdah* and together with her husband, edited the Bengali journal, *Bharati* having thus achieved the name of being the first Indian women editor. In 1886, Swarnakumari began *Sakhi Samiti* (Ladies Association) to infuse among Indian women an active and enlightened interest country's welfare. From Bengal, also came Kadambini Ganguli, a graduate of Calcutta University and the first woman doctor from Bengal. Other women included Pandita Ramabai, Mrs. Shevantibai Trimbak, Mrs. Shantabai Nikambe, Mrs. Kashibai Kanitkar and Miss Manekjee Cursetjee, and they developed into famous educationists and social reformers.

Besides hundreds and thousands of Indian women who devoted their lives for the sake of their country, there were a large number of noble and courageous foreign women who witnessed in India—its religion, its philosophy and its culture as a whole, hope for the redemption of the universe. They felt that in India's spiritual death, universe shall find its grave. Women like Annie Besant, Margrate Cousins, Sister Nivedita were great source of inspiration for Indian women who had started coming out of their home to play the bigger role in achievement of freedom.

Gandhiji commenced his historic march to Dandi on the sea coast near Jalalpur on 12 March 1930, and formally inaugurated the propaganda and was arrested on the 6th of April. His arrest was the long awaited indication and the campaign began with countrywide strikes. It specially electrified the patriotic enthusiasm in women which not only gave a two-fold courage and support to the cause but also invited attention and appreciation from the outside world.

At first, women had not been permitted to participate as Gandhiji had felt they would complicate matters. But the females of the land, coveting a place of equality with men, could not sit silently at the call of the country. They protested that in these crucial days there should not be any watertight compartments of services. They demanded that no conference, no congress or commission dealing with the welfare of India should be held without the presence of their kind. Similarly, they asked that no marches, no imprisonment, no demonstrations organised for the welfare of India should prohibit women from a share in them. Subsequently they were permitted to participate in all phases of the campaign.

The status of women in the traditional Hindu system was not an enviable one. They had been reduced to the status of second-class citizens by laws formulated and introduced by men. According to Gandhi's basic principle of the essential oneness of humanity men and women cannot be regarded as different in essence; they share the same soul, the same life, and the same basic human feelings. Yet although they complement one another. Gandhi maintains that men have tended to dominate women with the result that women have developed an unfortunate sense of inferiority and have come to believe that they are inferior to men. It is true that there are vital differences between men and women and that the basic purpose in life for women differs from that of men, but this does not mean that women are in any sense inferior. Gandhi's argument is that women require different qualities than men in order to fulfil the obligations of motherhood, for example, and in many ways it is a sad reflection on society when it encourages women to forsake their customary duties as custodians of family life to take up duties normally performed by men, such as taking up arms in defence of one's country. In Gandhi's view, the duties involved in maintaining moral standards and a good home in the midst of bad social influences require as much courage and fortitude as those involved in defending one's country against an aggressor.

After achieving independence in 1947, India had a tough job of social reconstruction, economic progress and political consciousness to be able to ensure justice and equality to all its citizens. The makers of the Constitution of India, which amongst others, had distinguished women like Sarojini Naidu, Hansa Mehta, Durgabai, Renuka Ray and Malti Chowdhry as its members, were conscious of the prevailing social infirmities and inequalities offered constitution to the nation which bestowed equal rights to all its citizens and that all of them are equal before the law. This resulted in framing of a constitution that is a rare document and covers all aspects of human dignity and good citizenship.

But some aspects of Constitution remain written and are not practiced in real life. One of them is the right of equality, specially with regard to the women. They remained as discriminated as ever and continue not to have equal opportunities. They have been the unequal citizens since time immemorial and though things are changing for better, they are not as rosy for the rural and downtrodden women of our times.

1

Mutiny of 1857

The mutiny of 1857-58 was the first organised armed effort by the Indians to achieve emancipation from the English political grip. The time was one of great tribulation for the Indians and the English alike, because both experienced unmatched convulsions in the history. The British won, but the Indians gained too, became the movement because a symbol of courage and sacrifice for the subsequent generations.

In the century preceding the outbreak, the Indian political map was radically changed. Lord Dalhousie had intensified the process of absorption through a vigorous application of lapse policy. The years of his regime (1848-56) witnessed the absorption of eight states meaning a quarter million square miles of territory was added to the East India Company's territorial limits. The period also saw the missionary activities opposing early marriage, *purdah* system, the passing of the Widow Remarriage Bill in 1856, activities of some English officers involved in proselytising, the introduction of railways, telegraph and the greased cartridges. National environment, especially of northern India, was wrapped in vague doubts. The British authorities, not satisfied with mere annexation of the States, also wanted to intervene in their religious affairs and put an end to the caste system.

The first symptoms of unrest were experienced in the first quarter of the year 1857 when the soldiers at Berhampore (five miles east of Nowgong), Barrackpore and Ambala, resorted to incendiarism. The Indian Regiments were disbanded and the criminals punished. But this did not quieten the situation and proved only a prelude to the open resort which followed

The leaders of the outbreak were not only men but also women, including Begum Hazrat Mahal, Rani Lakshmi Bai, Rani of Ramgarh and Rani Tace Bai. Some of them participated in battle while others endured the sufferings and privation, imprisonment and death.

On April 24, 1857, at Meerut, C. Smyth, Commandant, 3rd-Light Cavalry, ordered a procession to test the loyalty of the soldiers. Out of ninety sepoys present, 85 refused to accept new cartridges. As a consequence they were court-martialled and sentenced to varying terms of imprisonment extending up to 10 years. The sentence passed was announced on May 9, 1857, in the presence of a gathering to create a consternation and fear. The soldiers were stripped of their uniforms and then were handed over to the smiths for fastening shakles around their arms and legs.[1] The scenario might have been picturesque for the English Commander but distasteful to the Indians gathered there. "There was a good deal of murmuring in our ranks," says Gough, "and had it not been for the presence of the British troops it is impossible to say what might not have taken place."[2]

On the same evening, the 'women of *bazar*' jeered at the sepoys. "Your brethren have been ornamented with these anklets and incarcerated and for what? Because they would not swerve from their creed and you cowards as you are, sit still indifferent to your fate. If you have an atom of manhood in you, go and release them."[3]

The taunts inflamed their hearts. "The spark which fell from female lips, ignited at once and the night of the May 10, 1857, saw the commencement of a tragedy never before witnessed since Indian passed under British sway."[4]

The flames of fire broken out at Meerut, on May 10, spread fast over a large part of northern India.

Begum Hazrat Mahal

While the women of Meerut were partly instrumental, in accelerating action on the part of sepoys, situation in Lucknow, a place not very remote from Meerut, was motivating Begum Hazrat Mahal to monitoring the leadership.

Hazrat Mahal, a dancing girl, later became an acknowledged wife of King Wajid Ali Shah of Oudh by *'Motah'.* The annexation of Oudh in 1856 came as a heavy blow to the royal family, chiefs and the people. Hazrat Mahal, unsatisfied as she was, decided to stay back in Lucknow, while the deposed king made his abode in Calcutta.

The queen mother could not tolerate this injustice and left for England. "An aged queen brought up in all the pomp and luxury of the East, the soles of whose feet were scarcely allowed to tread the ground, laying aside the prejudices of travel, and undertaking a journey of some ten thousand miles, appealed to the people of England for justice." Her efforts proved fruitless.[5]

The frustrating factors were : (a) the absorption of Oudh into British territory made 60,000 people jobless and artisans and craftsmen lost their only means of livelihood; (b) Jackson, the resident at Lucknow, had converted Chatar Manzil, a palace for the royal family, into his residence; (c) Qadim Rasul, a building of sanctity, was converted into a storehouse; (d) new revenue settlements provided no relief; (e) judicial system remained cumbersome, expensive and lengthy; (f) some of the old taxes were replaced by the new; and (g) the payment of pensions, according to the pension list, prepared at the time of annexation, was unduly delayed.

In the early part of April, Dr. Wells, a British medical officer in Lucknow, tested the quality of medicine by applying the bottle to his mouth before giving it to patients. The soldiers refused to take it lest the taint of a Christian should degrade their caste. Commandant of 48 Native Infantry reconciled the excited soldiers. That night the doctor's bungalow was ruined by fire. The culprit was untraced. After some days many huts of the 13th Regiment were burnt under mysterious circumstances.[6]

The wounds caused by absorption of Oudh were combined with the opportunity afforded by the outbreak at Meerut on May 10, 1857 and people, hoping to establish their won rule, supported the rebel cause, and the banner of revolt was raised in Lucknow on May 30, 1857.

The revolution spread rapidly to other towns of Oudh and the rebels succeeded in establishing their authority in many places one after another. Consequently, by the middle of June, the British regime in this province lay flat. In Lucknow the English did not leave the Residency building and faced the rebels till they were able to regain their lost power.

Hazrat Mahal, an influential lady was the chief figure in bringing about this insurrection. "She has excited all Oudh," said Russell, "to take up the interests of her son, and the chiefs have sworn to be faithful to him."[7] The boy's name was Brijis Quadir who was then eleven years old.

Hazrat Mahal became the regent queen and exercised all authority. She ruled the State diplomatically and proved a good leader and stateswoman. The Hindus and Muslims got high offices. She also honoured brave soldiers.[8]

Begum Hazrat Mahal was perhaps not fated to rule the State for a long time. In September 1857 the rebels were defeated in Delhi, and a discouraging ruinious news for her designs. Besides, Outram[9] and Havelock[10] from Kanpur had arrived to relieve the British garrison in the Residency of Lucknow. After a few encounters with the rebels, Outram was able to occupy Alam Bagh[11] on September 23, 1857, and finally reached the besieged Garrison on September 25.

The victory of the English in Kanpur was another setback to her plans. But nothing deterred her from her path. She kept up the spirit and held *Durbars.* She planned to commit suicide by taking poison instead of becoming a prisoner of the English.[12]

In the month of November, Sir Colin Campbell, Commander-in-Chief of the British Forces, along with a small reinforcement arrived at Lucknow. She gave a tough fight. Her soldiers became panicky and started running away. The rebels also became disrespectful to her. All this made her doubtful of the result of the struggle. The English Commander was able to escort the besieged garrison out of the Residency to Alam Bagh.

The rebels became reactive in Kanpur and thus compelled Campbell to retrace his steps. This move of the English again encouraged the Indian troops. The *Begum* used this opportunity and ordered for the occupation of Banaras and Allahabad. She also instructed *Nazims* and *Talukdars* to march on Azamgarh and Jaunpur (Districts of Uttar Pradesh). She convened a meeting of the chiefs on December 22, 1857, and criticised the leaders exhibiting no courage. She denounced them for their indifference and callousness. The *Begum* is reported to have complained, "Great things were promised from all powerful Delhi and my heart used to be gladdened by the communications I used to receive from that city but soon the king had been dispossessed and his army scattered. The English have bought over the *Sikhs* and *Rajahs,* and communications are cut off. The Nana has been vanquished, Lucknow is endangered—what is to be done ? The whole army is in Lucknow, but it is without courage. Why does it not attack Alam Bagh ? Is it waiting for the English to be reinforced and Lucknow to be surrounded ? How much longer am I to pay the sepoys for doing nothing ? Answer me now, and if you won't fight, I shall negotiate with the English to spare my life."[13]

She attempted to encourage the soldiers and appeared on the battlefield on February 25, 1858, mounted on an elephant.[14] Alam Bagh was vigorously invaded by a force sometimes led by Maulvi Ahmedula Shah[15] and sometimes by the Begum personally.[16]

Russell observed some : "Begum declares undying war against us; and in the circumstances of the annexation of the kingdom, the concealment of the suppression of the treaty, the apparent ingratitude to the family for money lent and aid given at most critical times, has many grounds for her indignant rhetoric."[17]

On March 2, 1858, the British started operations against Lucknow with thirty thousand soldiers under the command of Sir Colin Campbell and Jung Bahadur (Nepal). The British troops occupied one place after another till the rebels found their positions precarious and decided to evacuate. In the Central Court, Lucknow alone, 860 defenders fell a prey to this war.

Hazrat Mahal "never lost heart and moved alongwith her men with spirit that desarved better success."[18] She visited the battle-field motivating her troops. By March 18, 1858, all the strong points in Lucknow were in the possession of the English. But "a powerful force probably inspired by the Begum held Musabagh, a palace in Lucknow, till the 19th March 1858."[19]

Subsequently the Begum reinforced Maulvi Ahmedula Shah in his invasion on Shahjahanpur. On October 1, 1858, she issued instructions to the troops in a long letter, instructing them the line of attack. "This document," wrote the Chief Commissioner, "appears to be genuine and many of the movements ordered have been made and failed." She penned : "Imtizamood Dowlah is requested to concentrate a sufficient force including artillery for the defence of Pilibheet on the Bheera and Jugadpur roads, the leader to be Enayat Ali Khan..."[20] She not only issued instructions but also led the troops to the battlefield. Sarfras Begum writing to Akhtar Mahal, wife of Wajid Ali, who was at Calcutta made mention of Hazrat Mahal thus : "I did not know Hazrat Mahal was such a brave lady. Seated on an elephant she led her troops against the English without any fear. Alam Bagh was the scene of a pitched battle. Ahmedula Shah joined Hazrat Mahal and they fought with valour and courage but luck did not favour them."[21]

Another Begum, Sayda, wrote to Wajid Ali thus: "Hazrat Mahal showed such courage that the enemy was terrified. She turned out to be very daring. She has brought name to the Sultan Alam."[22]

Under adverse circumstances, the Begum had to escape to Nepal[23] with her followers and her son Birjis Qadir. The Nepalese authorities were reluctant to provide asylum to the rebels. The Nepal Government in a strongly worded letter on January 15, 1859, wrote that if she was to honour the treaty with the British Government, the rebels must be surrendered to that government. And therefore, "If you should remain or seek an asylum within my territory and frontier, the Gorkha troops will most certainly, in pursuance of the treaty agreed upon by both the high States, attack and make war on you... And be it known that Nepal State will neither assist nor show mercy to, nor permit to remain in its territories or within its frontiers, to those who have been so faithless and ungrateful as to do mischief and raise animosity and insurrection against their master..."[24]

But these threats, remained ineffective as the Begum denied to surrender to the English Government. The Nepalese authorities had to modify the decision and gave asylum on the condition not to communicate with the rebel leaders or with their forces or with the people of India.[25]

She experienced many difficulties in Nepal. Only women and boys under 12 were allowed to stay in her camp. The Begum complained thus: "The Gorkhas have reduced me to dust, they have joined the British, they have neither assisted my troops nor allowed also them to remain in the country, neither they have not allowed me to join them."[26] When the prime minister of Nepal proclaimed in the rebels' camps the Governor-General's terms and invited them to surrender, she refused, "They would rather die than surrender."[27]

English authorities offered her the conditions that "The Begum Hazrat Mahal will receive all the consideration which is due to her as a woman and member of a royal house. But political powers she shall never have, and she will do wisely to secure by prompt submission a generous treatment and an honourable position for the rest of her life"[28] and further that "The rebel leaders must submit themselves to the mercy and generosity of the Government unconditionally, their lives and honour being safe, if they have not taken part in the murder of the British subjects. This applies to all from Begum down to those of the lowest rank amongst them."[29]

The Begum rejected these terms as she could not imagine herself without political powers, there might have been a remote fear in her mind about revengeful treatment from the British as it was alleged in some quarters that she was a party to the murder of Europeans.[30] Instead of surrendering, she asked for armed assistance from the Nepalese authorities for conquering the British Province.[31]

After the mutiny was quelled, the Queen of England issued a proclamation to appease the people. She promised to respect the agreements entered into by the Company and the religious rites, etc. Begum Hazrat Mahal issued a counter proclamation challenging the truth and sincerity of the promises made by the English Queen in the proclamation. She warned the people not to believe in these promises "for it is the unvarying custom of the English never to forgive a fault, be it great or small."[32]

She condemned the article relating to agreement and contracts and asserted that they had nothing new. "The Company professed to treat the chief of Bharatpur as a son, and then took his territory; the chief of Lahore[33] was carried off to London and it has not fallen to his lot to return..."[34] The Begum dealt with each article in detail and unveiled the lies in it.

Her refusal to surrender to the British authorities denied her pension. Nepal Government, however, allowed her a *pension of Mohri* Rs. 400 a month. The Begum tried to come back to India in 1877 but orders were issued, whereby any request made by either Birjis Qadir and his mother, who was a very clever and designing woman, should not be allowed."[35] The Government of India clearly explained that "If they did enter the territories of the British Government they would on no consideration receive any assistance or allowance from Government and would be required to be under the surveillance of the magistrate of the district in which they might take up residence."[36]

Consequently, she could not come to India and hence had to reside in Nepal permanently. Thus, the Begum died for the great cause in exile, in 1879, in a land foreign to her.[37]

Rani Lakshmi Bai of Jhansi

While Hazrat Mahal was busy in exterminating the Englishmen from Oudh, Jhansi corresponded quickly to the rebel's cause. On June 5, 1857, there was an open rebellion at Jhansi.

Jhansi being a small Maratha State, had a strategically important geographical location. It could serve as a nerve centre for the Central Indian States and this prompted Dalhousie to hasten its annexation in 1854.

Jhansi was managed by Gangadhar Rao[38] till it became British territory. His wife, Rani Lakshmi Bai, was the daughter of Moropant Tambe who was in the service of Peshwa Chimmaji Appa on a monthly salary of rupees fifty. She was born on November 19, 1835, at Banares. Her name was Manikarnika but she became famous by the name she received after her marriage, Lakshmi Bai. Her mother Bhagirathi Bai died when she was a child and hence was brought up by her father. She was married at the age of 14 years to Gangadhar Rao, then 40 years of age.[39] An interesting detail of her has been written by John Lang who became her prime consultant after absorption of Jhansi.[40]

A son born to Gangadhar Rao and Rani Lakshmi Bai in 1851, died after three months. The former fell ill in 1853 and he adopted Anand Rao,[41] a five-year-old boy, who was named Damodar Gangadhar Rao, after adoption on December 19, 1853, in the presence of Major Ellis, the Assistant Political Agent and Major Martin, Commanding the Jhansi Contingent. Gangadhar Rao gave a letter to Ellis requesting to seek the necessary sanction of the Government of India for this adoption.[42]

Instead of approving to it, the doctrine of 'lapse' was enforced by Dalhousie in the case of Jhansi and the decision was conveyed in an official letter to Major Ellis, the Superintendent of Jhansi, dated March 7, 1854. The letter in part reads : "The State which was a tributory and dependent principality, held by grant from the British Government has reverted to that government."[43] When Ellis informed Lakshmi Bai, widow of the late Raja, described by Major D.A. Malcolm, the Political Agent, as a lady "who bears a very high character and is much respected by everyone at Jhansi,"[44] about the decision of the government, she said, *Meri Jhansi, Nehi Dungi*.[45]

New terms included a pension of rupees five thousand per month for her and a palace at Jhansi for her residence. She and her personal female attendants were not amenable to the British Court during their life time. Personal ornaments of the late *Maharaja* and the balance remaining in the public treasury, after closing accounts of the State, were referred to as her private property.[46] She repudiated these terms and expressed to Ellis. She also requested the Governor-General to allow her 31 days time to enable her to represent her case,[47] but the representation proved useless since the government was averse to revert the decision. She was no ordinary person and as such the irrevocable decision of the government did not help her to lead a life of submission and quietude. It aspired to fight for her rights to represent her case sooner.[48]

She addressed a *Khureẹtta* on December 21, 1854,[49] to the Court of Directors reminding them that by Hindu Law the right of adoption was absolute, fixed and indefeasible and this indefeasible right was not shifted to the East India Company nor was it lost or fortified by the ruler of Jhansi by any treaty or by conquest and it was not acquired by East India Company.[50] She felt that the adoption was not disputed as Damodar Rao was permitted to succeed to his father's property—it was the effect of that adoption which she presumed that the government disowned. Lakshmi Bai, therefore, questioned the justification and legality of the annexation of Jhansi. She, however, held that if it became necessary on grounds of expediency, the negotiations and agreement should have been entered and not "exercise of the powers without right of the great and strong against the weak and small."[51] She further informed the authorities that the absorption of Jhansi was a gross violation and negation of treaties of the Government of India and that the case of Jhansi has created unrest among the princes and chiefs of Upper India and they awaited the consequence of an application submitted by her interestingly because the decision given in case of Jhansi would help them to decide whether they were to have faith or distrust in the English rule.[52]

Finally, she asserted that "The people of Jhansi did not desire to be made the subject of the East India Company. On the contrary, without a single exception they testified their willingness and desire to remain the subject of your memorialist and her ward."[53]

Thus, the Rani not only demanded justice for her cause but she also expressed the sentiments of the people in general and the wavering faith of the chiefs in the British regime in particular, and, hence, cleared that the treatment given out to her, was being considered deeply.

Since the petition bore no tangible results, she sent a mission to England to represent her case costing her rupees sixty thousand. She tried her best to regain her lost position, but in vain. It was like a cry in the wilderness which went unheard and uncared for. Its effect on the mind is described by Forest thus : "Thus the Maratha Queen tall in stature, handsome in person, young, energetic, proud and unyielding from that moment indulged the stern passion of anger and revenge."[54]

Expressing her displeasure she had rejected the offer of a pension, but later she revised her judgement and accepted it. Her fury was further aroused when she was asked to pay the unliquidated debt of her ancestors amounting to *Nanashahi*, i.e., thirty-six thousand rupees. She protested that these were not her debts and were not contracted by her late husband and hence she was not liable for them. The Deputy Superintendent supported her in his recommendation[55] to the Lt. Governor, but in vain. She was asked to pay them from the private funds of the *Raja* made over to her, otherwise she was threatened with a deduction from her monthly pension. Another frustrating act of the British authorities was the refusal to advance money to observe the sacred thread ceremony of Damodar Rao, unless four sureties for the repayment of the observe amount were furnished. Such indifferent attitude of the government helped her to keep alive the issue of absorption and to look forward for a chance of redressal. She was "ready to take any opportunity of gratifying her revenge and being like many other Maratha women of rank, possessed of masculine spirit,[56] she was well-fitted to carry out her plans, and was ripe when the outbreak occurred in 1857."[57]

So far she had personal grievances to nurse; but before long, an opportunity was offered by the rulers which enabled her to make a common cause with the people of Jhansi who had continued to brood over the wounds and the disgrace of absorption. Kaye writes that "She hated the English with the deadliest hatred. And soon she began to cherish new-born grievances. Foremost among these were the killings of cattle by the English."[58]

Slaughter of cows was an unknown thing in the Brahmin State, but the British government was unaware of the religious sentiments of the people. They not only authorised killing of the cows but also established slaughter houses. The Rani and the people petitioned against it but it was fruitless. Hence an excuse was given to "increase the fear and religious passions which had been aroused among the sepoys by the question of greased cartridges and to scatter among them the seeds of disloyalty and contention."[59]

The government's verdict in favour of the two mistresses of the late Gangadhar Rao, allowing them to have the rent of village Sumberadah.[60]

In May, a widespread rumour spread in Jhansi and in other places that ground bones were mixed in the flour and that cow's and pig's fat had been used for manufacturing cartridges for the military use.

In the beginning of June 1857, a letter was received from the rebels in Delhi to say that "the whole army of the Bengal Presidency had mutinied and as the Regiment at Jhansi had not done so, men composing it were outcast and had lost their faith."[61]

This quickened the passage of revolt and Jhansi rebelled openly on June 5, 1857. The English had to take shelter in the city fort on June 6. On June 7, the Rani's adherents also joined the rebels. They released the prisoners, set fire to the "Kutchery" and murdered all officers. They also attacked the fort occupied by English. Fire was exchanged between the besiegers and the besieged till the night of June 6, when the forces withdrew and the Rani's men kept watch on the fort.[62]

The following morning, three persons, Messrs Scot, Purcells and Andrews, were sent from the English Camp disguished as Indian for help from the Rani but were murdered. Andrews was killed by Rani's servant at the palace door. The same night rebels got some guns and men[63] and the fort was reattacked on the morning of June 8, with greater strength and renewed energy. The English could not stay any longer and thus surrendered on condition that they would be allowed to leave Jhansi unmolested. But as soon as they came out, they were seized and taken to Jokham Bagh where all of them,[64] except Mrs. Multov, her two children and Mr. Crawford, who managed to run away, including ladies and children, were murdered.

In the evening the rebels made a proclamation : "The people are God's, the country is the King's (Pradesh) and the two religions govern."[65]

After the victory of the rebels, a dispute regarding the possession of Jhansi territory, between the Rani and Sadashiv Rao Narain Parowala, a relation of the late Raja. Lakshmi Bai got the territory after paying a large sum to the rebels and a proclamation was made : "The people are God's, the country is Padshah's and the Raj is Rani Lakshmi Bai's."[66] She, however, was to govern on behalf of her adopted son.

In the official *Narrative of the Events,* the facts regarding the actual complicity of the Rani in the reballion are recorded in the following manner : "Mr. Scott, Head Writer, the Deputy Commissioner's office, who lived near the lines and mixed much with natives and had much better information of what was going on, and placed his property in the keeping of a loyal native in the town of Jhansi. He persisted in avowing that he had good reasons to know that a mutiny was intended and that the Rani and the troops were one."[67] It is stated that about this time one Chatajee, an agent of an Indian Chief, informed Captain Gordon, Deputy Superintendent of Jhansi, that Bhole Nath, adherent of the Rani, conducted meetings with the Indian officers frequently visiting the Rani's palace and that treachery was intended.[68] Lakshmi Bai apparently apprehended danger and so sought permission to keep an armed guard for her protection as she said she was afraid of the enemy of the English.

Kaye, mentioning her share in the rebellion, writes that "with the Maratha instinct she was in danger from the enemies of the English and thus intimated that her interests were identical with our own while she was plotting our overthrow."[69]

Skene who was in charge of Jhansi district at that time, wrote on May 8, 1857 : "I do not think that there is any cause of alarm about this neighbourhood."[70] While the English were not aware of their enemies, she should have apprehended danger from them. She was familiar with the designs of the rebels and tried to please both the parties. By asking for an armed protection, on one hand, she showed the rebels that her interests were identical with them and that she had already started recruiting armed men, while on the other hand, she could tell the English authorities of having warned them of the peril if rebels' plot was ever discovered.

The Rani was popular and influential. She mentioned in her petition against the annexation that the people of Jhansi wanted her to be the ruler.[71] Sir Hugh Rose, who fought against her, mentioning the resistance put up by her soldiers writes : "The reasons was sufficiently clear, the people of Jhansi fought for the Queen and the independence of their country. Even after the city had fallen, her bounty and liberality rendered her an influential and dangerous adversary."[72] It is unbelievable that a person of her standing and influence should not have been trusted by the rebels while designing the overthrow of the British Government.

Rani's father, Moropant, one of the prime instigators of the mutiny in that part of the country, could not have probably kept her in the dark about the intending revolt. Her advice and help must have been sought by him.[73] The preceding detail, therefore, nullifies Majumdar's statement that "Rani Lakshmi Bai of Jhansi not only did not instigate the sepoy mutiny but had nothing to do with their design or programme."[74] As far as her role in the events that led to the massacre of Europeans, is concerned, Major Ellis, writing to the Secretary to the Government of India on June 26, 1857, i.e., about 18 days after the massacre, reported thus : "Sgt Kirchaff in the Canal Department who arrived here yesterday evening from Mohaba gives an account of conspiracy of Jhansi and Nowgong mutineers. Sadashiv Narain Rao Parolwala has been declared a rebel at Jhansi by order of the Agent of the Governor-General, Central India, but he has little or no influence there, and it cannot be doubted that the cold-blooded atrocities committed by our troops on the Europeans would not have been perpetrated had the Rani not encouraged them."[75]

Thornton, Joint Magistrate and Deputy Collector, in an official letter, informed Captain Bruce, Superintendent of Police at Kanpur on August 18, 1857,[76] that the mutineer intended to abandon Jhansi after they had seized the treasure. It was at the instance of "a Bundelkhand chieftainess, the Rani of Jhansi, wishing to regain power in the district, bribed them with large presents to take the fort and put all the Europeans to death before they finally departed for Delhi."[77]

The official report, recorded eight months following the actual occurrence, held the Rani liable for the murder of Britishers in Jhansi. It says : "Through the treachery of the Rani, the fortress of Jhansi whither the European residents had fled, on the native troops mutinying, fell into the possession of mutineers and a general massacre of all Europeans of every age and sex took place."[78]

Thomas Lowe, a medical officer with Sir Hugh Rose's troops while mentioning his entry in the palace at Jhansi, states : "In most of the rooms we found some relics or other of the unfortunate officers who perished here in the mutiny. These things showed that the Rani had not only participated in their murder but had positively shared in the plunder of their property."[79]

The worst allegation was brought against the Rani by Shahab-ud-Din, *Khansama* of Major Skein, who was at Jhansi and moved about the town carrying messages for, and from, his master. He was hauled up by the mutineers on several occasions but somehow he was let free. He states : "He saw *Karuk Bijlee* (Gun) was put in order by Rani's order to be used against the officers and that the town people, mutineer sepoys and Rani's servants were firing... One day before the murder of the officers, it was proclaimed in the town by the beat of the drum, that the country belonged to the King, the Rani had the rule and that the officers will the killed tomorrow." It was further stated by him that after the massacre of the Europeans "the Rani, jail *daroga* and *sawars* went to the *pultan* and orders to free the prisoners were given."[80]

Madar Baksh, another individual attached to Gordon, was engaged in helping the Europeans. In his statements he confessed of having taken a letter from his master to the Rani. In this letter Gordon had requested her to get them down from the fort and to send them to Duttia or Orchha. It was handed over to Moropant who in turn took it to her. She sent the same letter to the *Risaldar* through her lawyer Ajudhia Prashad. Madar Bakhsh later heard from "one of the Rani's *chobedars* who had been dismissed" that she sent another messenger named Zabita Khan to the Risaldar apparently with another message. After the return of Ajudhia Prashad, she sent a letter to the besieged Europeans, but the contents of this letter were unknown to him. He further stated to have heared that the Rani's sepoys took Europeans to the parade and killed them.[81]

But Bhagwan Brahmin, at that time at Jhansi says that Lal Bahadur *subedar* and Bakshish Ali, the jail *darogas,* brought the Europeans out of the fort after pledging safety to them. He states, "I did not hear that the Europeans were killed by the order of the Rani."[82]

Sheikh Hingan, *hookambardar* of Captain Gordon, seems to have carried some messages to the Rani from his master. He said that when Gordon heard that the Rani had supplied guns and sepoys to the mutineers, he wrote to her "to say it was her *Raj* and he and other gentlemen would go where she liked." He further stated that she sent a message through her servant to the besieged, bearing contents to this effect : "What can I do ? Sepoys have surrounded me, and say I have concealed the gentlemen and that I must get the fort evacuated, and assist them to save myself. I have sent guns and my followers; if you wish to save yourself, abandon the fort, no one will injure you." According to Sheikh Hingan, the mutineers promised that the Europeans would be able to leave Jhansi safely.[83]

A Bengali[84] attached to the Writer's Establishment of Jhansi Custom Collector's Office who was in Jhansi during these days and also was maltreated for his sympathy with the Europeans states : "The Rani placed guards at her gate and shut herself up in her palace. Captain Gordon sent a message to the Rani soliciting her assistance at this crisis, but this was refused as the mutineers threatened to put her to death and to set fire to her palace in case of her compliance with Captain Gordon's request. The Rani's guards then joined the mutineers." He further stated that three persons, Messrs Andrews, Purcell and Scott, disguised as Indians, approached the Rani for help; but the feint being discovered, they were taken to the palace of the Rani and she refused an interview with them. She sent them to the mutineers. She said : "She had no concern with the English swine." While on the fort he says that the Rani was threatened with immediate assassination provided she refused to side with the rebels. She accordingly permitted and supplied them with a reinforcement of 1,000 and two heavy guns she had ordered to be dug out of the earth.

As regards the killing of the Europeans, he observed that as soon as they came out of the fort, they were seized by the rebels and taken to Jokham Bagh and "then commenced the horrid massacre, the *daroga* of the jail first raising his sword and killing Captain Skein."[85]

Kaye, a renowned historian, writes : "I have been informed that none of the Rani's servants was present at the occasion of the massacre. It seems to have been mainly the work of our old followers. The irregular cavalry issued the bloody mandate and our *jail daroga* was foremost in the butchery."[86]

Mrs. Multov who was in the fort with the garrison and managed to escape with the assistance of an *ayah* recorded her impression thus : "Mr. Skein and Mr. Gordon went to the Rani and got about 50 to 60 guns and some powder and shots and balls and she sent about 50 of her own sepoys to the fort to assist us and at about 2 o'clock during the day they killed the gentleman who was with them and commenced burning the bungalow and speared Mr. Taylor who belonged to the cavalry, so he galloped his horse and came to the fort. As soon as the Rani heard of it, she got all her sepoys down from the fort. The Rani and her sepoys joined with the Regiment." She also mentioned that the European agreed to come out of the fort on a solemn promise from the rebels that their lives would be spared. This promise was countersigned by the Rani. But as soon as they came out of the fort, they were assassinated.

Mrs. Multov further stated : "I went out with *Ayah*, they did not take notice of me. She brought and left me in the Jokham Bagh in those Hindoo graves made like a house. I remained there for about a month. Dowlut Ram came from Saugor, and heard of me, he came to me that very evening. I sent Dowlut Ram twice to Saugor, he was caught twice on the road. Those letters came to Jhansi to the Rani and she was looking out for me and Dowlut Ram. So Dowlut hid himself, me and two children. It was the Rani's order, if any one catches us going out of town that she will give one hundred rupees as a present, in those days."[87] Secondly, she took her abode in Jokham Bagh, a Hindu cemetery. This place also witnessed the massacre of the English. She spent one month in a graveyard, a place not very secure, and could not be discovered by the rebels despite the announcement of the reward. But much reliance cannot be placed on her evidence.

Majumdar and Sen support the Rani's innocence by mentioning a letter written[88] by Martin, on August 20, 1889,[89] to Damodar Rao, the Rani's adopted son. Martin, mentioning the occurrence at Jhansi, writing, : "The poor thing took no part whatever in the massacre of the European residents of Jhansi in June 1857. On the contrary she supplied them with food for two days after they had gone into the fort—got 100 matchlock men from Kurrua and sent them to assist us."[90]

The Rani's letter written to the British authorities makes no mention to the help rendered by her to the Englishmen stationed at Jhansi. In fact she writes "that she could render no aid for want of guns and soldiers as she had only 50 to 100 people engaged in guarding her house."[91] Had she helped the British in their difficult hour, she would have never forgotten to mention it. Secondly, Martin's name appear nowhere in the official reports or enquiries nor does it occur in the statements made by servants in the service of the English officials at Jhansi. The official reports indicate that there were only two persons, i.e., Mr. Crawford and Mrs. Multov who fortunately escaped from Jhansi. Martin was not even with his compatriots in the fort as appears from his letter.

Sir Robert Hamilton who investigated these events mentioned the dispositions of Sepoy Aman Khan of 12 Native Infantry. He states that "his assertions are corroborated by and corroborate those made by others and as far as they go should say entitle up credit." Aman Khan took service with the Rani after the rebels left for Delhi. While under death sentence he reported that "the insurgents, previous to the mutiny, did not consult the Rani. He also stated that the mutineer sepoys placing their guns in position, threatened all the rest with immediate death if they refused to join them. Then all went to the palace of the Rani with loaded guns and demanded assistance and supplies. She was obliged to yield and to furnish guns, ammunition and supplies."[92]

Hamilton did not clearly accuse the Rani of complicity with the rebels, but he observed that Aman Khan was very reserved in any affair relating to his own regiment and always gave the bare answer. This assertion of Hamilton shows that Aman Khan might have kept back certain information and even this statement may not be the whole truth.

The Rani might have been obliged to help the rebels. But there was no question of obligation. If she was really faithful to the English, she should have left Jhansi and taken shelter with them, as was done by the Maharaja of Gwalior whose army had joined the rebels.

Secondly, she could have proved her loyalty by helping some of the Englishmen to escape. Two persons, i.e., Mrs. Multov and Mr. Crawfort were able to escape.

Thirdly, if the Rani was interested in retaining the goodwill of the British Government she did not have to pay a larger sum of money to the rebels to get back her lost territory.

Fourthly, there is an authentic detail available of the first day's event, i.e., June 5, 1857, relating to the revolt at Jhansi. Captain Gordon, Deputy Superintendent of Jhansi at that time, informed the higher authorities in a letter dated June 6, 1857, that problem had begun at Jhansi and that the magazine and all the treasure amounting to four and a half lakhs of rupees was seized by the rebels. In this letter Gordon made reference to the assistance given by the Rani of Jhansi or of the assistance expected from her. He states : "I have applied to Sumthur and Orchha for assistance. None can be expected from Duttia where the Raja has just died and a state of anarchy prevails."[93] Thus, from the very beginning, her behaviour as far as her faithfulness to the British Government was concerned, was suspected.

Lakshmi Bai moved in that period diplomatically. Her main problem was to regain her lost power and status. She, like a shrewd person, observed the things carefully. When she saw the British power dwindling and the sun rising on the rebels, she joined the insurgents openly.

None of these people were in a position to be associated with the Rani's designs and for that matter with the high officials, responsible for causing this insurrection. In the light of this conflicting evidence, it is not possible to arrive at a definite conclusion. However, it is not ruled out that the Rani might not have ordered the killing but she accepted the massacre of Europeans as a result of the revolt on the part of the sepoys.

Immediately after taking charge of Jhansi on June 9, 1857, she issued orders to the chiefs and officials of the State that she was seated on the throne and that they were to carry on business. Receipt of such a *perwanah* was reported by an Indian Magistrate of Mauranipur on June 10, 1857.[94] She also began recruiting men from Jhansi. Sepoy Aman Khan says that "after the mutineers left the station I entered the service of the Ranee on four rupees a month. None of the mutineers remained here—all the musks left by the mutineers and their uniforms that had been given to the poor people of the station were collected and given by the Rani to those who entered her service. In this manner 100 men, all from the people of the town, were raised by the Ranee. Besides these about 80 men from the Scindias' Contingent that were disarmed and disbanded at Asseer came in here and were employed by the Rani."[95]

This statement is further corroborated by Hingan, *hookambardar* of Captain Gordon thus : "The mutineers went away after three days and the Rani then raised two Companies of Sepoys and gave the command to three mutineers who had remained behind."[96]

On June 12, 1857,[97] the Rani wrote her first letter to the Commissioner informing him about the events in Jhansi and requesting for assistance. A second letter was written on June 14, 1857.[98] Some other letters followed later.[99]

It is apparent from the *parwanah* issued by the Rani on June 10, that she had selected the line of action and that her letters to the government were an eyewash. This correspondence exhibited diplomacy as she required time to build up her forces to face the formidable enemy and that she could safely do so by identifying her interests with the British.

She impressed upon the Commissioner, Saugar Division, with these letters the sincerity of her action and as such was authorised[100] by him to collect the revenue, to raise police and to do everything in her power to restore order.[101] But the Governor-General doubted her sincerity and accorded a conditional approval on the basis of the account supplied by Major Ellis : "Rani did lend assistance to the mutineers and rebels and she gave guns and men."[102]

Later she raised a body of fourteen thousand men and unearthed the guns, concealed by the former Raja and of which British authorities were unaware. She begun to cast cannons, and make ammunitions. She negotiated with the rebel Rajas of Banpur and Shahgarh. She also established a mint of her own. From the evidence of Deokeemunder Sahar, former orderly of the deceased Lt. Gordon of Jhansi, it seems that the Rani proclaimed in the town that her reign had commenced and that the British Rule was over.[103] She raised her own flag on the fort and assembled the *mahajans* to gift her their *nazranas*.[104]

The period, however, was fraught with affliation for the Rani, Sadashiv Rao, who failed to get Jhansi, posed himself to be a ruler at Kurrua (a town 30 miles West of Jhansi) on June 13, 1857. He issued a proclamation : "Maharaja Sadashiv Rao Narain has seated himself on the throne of Jhansi at Kurrua."[105] She sent her forces, Sadashiv Rao was defeated and was taken prisoner.

Another enemy was the Rani of Tehree. The latter's forces occupied Mauranipur on August 10, 1857. Lakshmi Bai suffered reverses in the beginning but in the war on October 23, with the Tehree's forces, she emerged victorious. She then sent a message demanding from the Rani of Tehree either the immediate surrender of Tehree and Orchha or retribution for the loss she had sustained.

Rani Lakshmi Bai wrote to Hamilton again on January 1, 1858,[106] informing him about the battle with Rani Tehree's troops, thereby expressing her loyalty to the British government. But it was reported on January 5, 1858, that the "Rani of Jhansi continued to rule over Jhansi, all disaffected and mutineers men that go to Jhansi are kept by the Rani. At this time she had 400 mutineers with her and the rest of the force was composed of relatives of the surrounding Thakoors. Although the news of the total defeat of the rebels at Kanpur and that of the advancing of the British Forces has been received by the Rani she seems to entertain no fears,"[107] showing the hollowness of her sincerity to the British Government. The letter was not acknowledged by Hamilton. This added to her determination to fight. Secondly, it served as a warning to her to be on guard. Combining in herself the attributes of a warrior and a stateswoman, she set about performing her duties rapidly.

Laskhmi Bai wrote to other *Rajas* and Chiefs "exerting them to save their faith and sacrifice everything for its sake."[108] She also wrote to Nana Sahib that "something must be done to cherish the State and afford it protection."[109] She was clearly in touch with Nana Sahib.[110] Very soon "she gained a great influence over the heart of her people. It was this influence, this force of character added to a splendid and inspiring courage that enabled her, some months later to offer to the English troops under Sir Hugh Rose, a resistance which made to a less able commander might even have been successful."[111]

There were several discouraging factors. The defeat of the Kanpur rebels was followed by the defeat of the Raja of Banpur. In a letter dated March 13, 1858, the Raja of Banpur wrote, "I, who appeased the English, inevitably fall and your force cannot face the English. I advise you to save your life as you can."[112] Later, on March 16, the Raja of Banpur with 2,500 horses and two guns took refuge in Jhansi. The Rani sent him supplies. Her officers told the military officers that if there should be a fight with the English they must strike, and whosoever had no mind to do this, let him at once resign his appointment.[113] By March 1853 she had 15,000 men in her service. She got all the large and small guns which escaped destruction at the time of absorption, repaired them and had eight new guns manufactured, thus making a total of twenty.[114]

The newswriter writing on March 17 stated : "that Rani's officers sent 'khureeta' to the officers commanding at Tel Bhat. The officers in rebellion against the English said to the Rani's officers that "we believing the Rani to be the enemy of the English, took service with her. We will not fight inside the city walls. Give us guns and we will fight outside the walls. And if it be your object by the 'khureeta' which you have sent to the English to make peace with them, pay up our arrears and dismiss us." The Rani's officers replied, "Rest assured you will be satisfied."[115]

Subsequently she ordered Rana Bouru Singh of Nirwar who had taken refuge in Jhansi to leave the town as she had no intention to fight the English. The report further adds : "It is believed that although the Rani publicly directed him to go... she in her heart wishes him to remain."[116]

On March 18 the messenger who took the letter to the Agent to the Governor-General returned with a message from him "Let the Rani come hither."[117] She then sent another letter. Her mind inclined both ways, to peace and to war, to war from fear of her rebel servants, and to peace from the advice of her other servants."[118] In fact she was confused at this critical period and ultimately she decided to face the enemy.

On March 20, she sent out all her men in the district to repair the town. The houses near the city wall were vacated, two small guns placed on the city walls and ammunition distributed. The next day, the city being besieged, the Rani and her advisors wrote a *khureeta* to the Agent stating their readiness to be obedient to the British Government. Before the *khureeta* was finished, the Rani and Gangadhar Bhaee Singh, one of the prominent rebel leaders in Jhansi, saw some sowars surrounding the town. Firing was ordered and[119] thus the historic fight began. Ball Charles writes, "The Rani had bravely determined to defend herself to the last, nor was there, at any time during the continuance of the siege, any symptom of weakness or vacillation on her part or that of her personal adherents."[120]

Sir Hugh Rose,[121] a seasoned soldier, held the command of the British forces. The siege began on March 22. The Rani's forces exhibited remarkable courage and returned shot for shot. Women worked in the batteries and carried ammunitions.[122]

Malleson writes, "It was sure that the Rani had infused some of her lofty spirit into her compatriots. Women and children were seen assisting in repair of the havoc made in the defence by the fire of besiegers and in carrying food and water to the soldiers on duty. It seemed a contest between the two races under the conditions unusually favourable to the besieged."[123]

Lakshmi Bai would approach the batteries to rouse the enthusiasm of her soldiers by her presence and her fiery words.[124]

On March 28, 1858, shells falling into the fort blew up five maunds of gunpowder and the building where it was stored and forty men were killed. The Rani was much distressed and distracted by this havoc caused by the enemy and took no meals till the evening. She took up her quarters in an underground house in the fort. On 29th, 30th and 31st March, much damage was done to the building, killing a hundred men.

On 31st March, twenty-two thousand men under Tantia Tope,[125] at the request of the Rani, marched against the British camp before Jhansi but he was defeated by Sir Hugh Rose. His defeat on the one hand shocked the Rani deeply and she had to face the enemy with her own resources, while on the other hand it encouraged and raised the morale of the soldier in Rose's camp. The fire was resumed again on 31st April 1858. "Her men hurled at the stormers all sorts of missiles, earthen pots filled with powder, logs of wood and whatever came handy. For a time it appeared like a sheet of fire out of which burst a storm of bullets, round shots and rockets destined for our annihilation. Every inch of ground was contested till the palace was reached. Jhansi was a slaughterhouse reeking under the eastern sky."[126]

The British soldiers were determined to punish the Rani whom they held responsible for the killings. She was well aware of the punishment, "Not one iota undaunted," writes Lowe, "prepared a commensurate resistance such as one indeed, as would have shed honour and fame upon the name of any princess, whose hands were unstained by the blood of the innocent and unoffending."[127]

When she realised her weak position, she cleverly escaped with her adopted son in darkness in the disguise of a man. She travelled a distance of twenty-one miles in the company of Afghans who escorted her. In the morning the flight was made known in the English camp and a pursuit was ordered. Captain Forbes and Lt. Dowker followed with 3rd Light Cavalry and 14 Light Dragon and a battle ensued between the two rival forces. Some forty men of the Rani's troops were killed. Lt. Dowker got severe injuries and had to give up the pursuit. The Rani escaped with four attendants. Lt. Dowker writes : "The Maratha Queen was as much at ease galloping a horse as in the *zenana* hearing her favourite minstrel and stern chase ensued."[128]

Lakshmi Bai with sixteen horsemen and one female attendant reached Bhandair.[129] On 5th April 1858, Lakshmi Bai and her attendant were put up at the Kutchery. She had been fasting for the last three days. Here as they were about the cook food, information came that the British troops were in their pursuit. She and her followers after taking milk started for Koonch[130] and joined Tantia Tope and other rebel leaders.

Jhansi fell but Kalpi[131] became the meeting place of all the rebels. Rao Saheb, the Nawab of Banda, Tantia Tope and the Rani of Jhansi, all together advanced to Koonch, a strategic town on the Jhansi Road, to fight the British. During the war the Rani disguised as a man and armed with a sword and a dagger, rode at the head of 50 *sawars* and 100 *matchlockmen*.

After a series of tough battles the rebels had to evacuate on 23rd May, 1858. Hugh Rose states : "While so many drawbacks weakened me, the enemy, physically speaking, was unusually strong. They were under three rebels leaders of considerable influence, Rao Sahib, a nephew of Nana Sahib, the Nawab of Banda and the Rani of Jhansi. The high descent of the Rani, her unbound liberality of her troops, and retainers and her fortitude which no reverses could shake rendered her an influential and dangerous adversary."[132]

Rani's capturing was planned. The Governor-General authorised Hamilton to offer reward of twenty thousand rupees.[133] The English General thought the work was over, but the Rani would not let him live peacefully as long as she lived. Gwalior became the next rebel centre. "The Rani, desperate and daring, then conceived the plan of marching to Scindia's capital and taking possession of that stronghold."[134]

"The Rani was a resolute and intrepid woman who infected her troops with her own fearlessness, hardihood and carried on the struggle against the English with a coolness and capacity that exhorted full and frank administration from our Generals. She it was, who in the darkest hour of her side's defeat made the astounding proposition that once more threatened the progress of our arms in India."[135]

This move surprised Britishers and the idea, observes Holmes, was "as original and as daring as that which prompted the memorable seizure of Arcot."[136] Gwalior fell to the rebels without a blow on June 4th and forces joined the rebels.

Friend of India of June 10th, 1858, stated : "Tantia Tope has been proclaimed Nana, Rao Sahib has acquired some other dignity and the Rani of Jhansi retains all her importance. Thus, the Marathas hope to recover their lost glory by eliciting an imposter for a *Peshwa* and by submitting to a woman stained with every crime."[137]

Rose retraced his steps on hearing the news and General Napier joined him. On June 16th, after a hard battle they defeated the rebels under Tantia Tope of Morar. Next morning General Smith also joined them. He invaded the city and met the force led by Rani at Kotah-ki-Sarai. The English troops were able to clear the place of the rebels. The Rani took interest in almost every phase of the battle. "It is characteristic of the Rani's thoroughness and capacity that she went out in person to supervise this important work. Disguised as a man she passed rapidly from post to post until the persistent and deadly fire of Smith's guns drove in her own artillery."[138]

Col. Sir R.C. Shakespeare, Agent to the Governor-General provides a reliable record of the death of the Rani which was told by Damodar Rao and the people. The rebels were in possession of Gwalior for eighteen days. The Rani, hearing of the British troops advancing, went to the roof where she was living and seeing the British troops she descended and mounted her horse to start, but European soldiers surrounded her and injured her left eyebrow and left hand and bullet pierced her right side. The guns of the fort having opened fire, the Rani returned. She fell from her horse as did a lady attendant, named Moondar, who had also been injured near her stomach.

After the return of English troops, some of the Rani's soldiers attended on her and gave her water to drink. But, she could not survive the bullet and thus passed away "the bravest and best military leader of the rebels."[139] Her corpse was taken to a garden under the fort. Damodar Rao performed funeral ceremonies and burned the body in a stack of grass.[140]

Her undaunted courage, determined fight and death in the battlefield will always motivate future generations. Malleson records : "Whatever her faults in British eyes may have been, her countrymen will ever remember that she was driven by ill-treatment into rebellion, she lived and died for her country."[141]

Rani of Ramgarh

The Rani of Ramgarh also participated in the outbreak of the 1857-58 war. Ramgarh is a small village in Dinderi Tehsil of

Mandala District in Madhya Pradesh. Raja Lachman Singh, the last ruler, expired in 1850. His only son Vikramjit was his heir. He had not ruled the state long when his mental unsoundness was discovered.

The British authorities, due to their expansion policy, took over the management of the estate and appointed their own *tehsildar.* A pension was fixed for the Raja and his family. The Rani protested this step but in vain.

The outbreak in Central India was a signal for the Rani to rise to the occasion and redress her grievances. Ramgarh became revolt centre in Mandala District in July 1857, and the Rani of Ramgarh its originator.[142]

She removed the *Tehsildar* and took over the administration. When the Commissioner at Jabalpur came to know, he ordered her on August 26th, to see the Deputy Collector of Mandala District. She neglected the order and started preparations to face the British.[143] She fortified Ramgarh by erecting barricades and increased her military strength. She also contacted the neighbouring chiefs and *zamindars* for seeking help from them.

On April 1, 1858, the British forces marched towards Ramgarh. She left the fort and led her troops to the battlefield. In an encounter with English troops in front of the town she suffered a heavy loss. Her small force was defeated and she fled from the town. She retained her courage and retired to the nearby jungles, from where she kept raiding the British camp. She expected help from the *Rewah* rebels who joined the English.[144] Her situation became precarious and her capture became certain. She never wished to be a prisoner of the British and hence borrowed a sword from her companion and plunged it into her own bosom. On her deathbed, she disclosed that she had stirred the people to rebellion.[145] This confession showed her honesty and conviction in the sanctity of her cause.

Rani Tace Bai

Tace Bai also followed her sisters in Central Asia and castigated her allegiance to the British authorities during the outbreak of 1857-58 war. But unlike Rani of Jhansi and Ramgarh she lacked courage. She was the daughter of Gopal Rao, a direct descendant of Gangadhar Govind, a former Raja of Jaloun. In 1842, the State had been merged with the British Government and Rani Tace Bai, a claimant to the State, was sanctioned a pension of twelve thousand rupees per annum.

After the mutiny of 1857-58, Gursari chief established himself as the undisputed master of Jaloun District with the exception of *parganas* Kachhewagarh and Duboh with headquarters at Jaloun. Tantia Tope heading the Scindia's forces who revolted on September 22nd after the fall of Delhi, reached this place on October 29, 1857. Gursari chief was unable to face Tantia Tope and agreed to surrender. However, another claimant, Tace Bai, put forward her claim. Tantia Tope supported her and put her son on the throne with the condition that she acknowledge the Nana and pay a sum of three lakh rupees. Thus she transferred her allegiance.

On April 12, 1858, when Tace Bai heard that Jhansi had fallen, instead of facing the English, packed up her luggage and left Jaloun for Ingumpur, advising her followers to go to a safe place.[146] She is reported to have rendered submission to the British.[147]

There was no charge against Tace Bai of mal-treatment of any Europeans or having been criminal of any atrocity. "There is no doubt that she joined the rebel party, set aside the authority of the British Government and cast off her allegiance."[148] As a consequence of her actions, the British authorities decided to deport Tace Bai, her son Govind Rao and her husband beyond the territorial dominions of Central India. Her pension of twelve thousand rupees was stopped. Her jewels worth thirty thousand rupees were sold and the money was credited to the Government treasury.[149] Tace Bai was deputed to Monghyr. The order of the Government of India was conveyed in a letter to the Secretary to the Government of Bengal considering the nature of surveillance to be used on her : "She is to be treated with consideration and respect, the surveillance over her is to be sufficiently strict to prevent all hope of escape to check all correspondence with her own country and obviate all chance of successful intrigue."[150] She remained a prisoner for twelve long years before she was released by the British.

Role of Other Women

There were other women in different parts of the country who supported the cause. Their role though not significant, their contribution to the cause of freedom was of considerable help. For example, the Thakurani of Budri contributed to the rebels funds, Rani Digambar Koer joined the rebels at Gorakhpur, and Rani of Tikari[151] (Gaya) added to the fortification of Tikari.

Former Rani of Jyetpore also used the opportunity afforded by this revolt. In defiance of the prohibition order issued by the Magistrate, she proceeded to Jyetpore with an armed force and established herself there. She was again addressed by the Magistrate and he informed her that without vacating Jyetpore quietly, she would not receive her pension of two thousand rupees. Various efforts were made to make her leave Jyetpore voluntarily. But she ignored those efforts. She was warned about the alternative of forcible ejection.[152] She was later expelled from Jyetpore.

Rani Jindan,[153] who was in Nepal during the troubles of 1857-58, used the opportunity and wrote letters in cypher to the Maharaja of Kashmir, which were intercepted and were supposed to be genuine.[154] In these letters, the Maharaja of Kashmir was exhorted to initiate an invasion on British territory when Jung Bahadur would simultaneously descend from Nepal and invaded Gorakhpur. Rani Jindan also informed the Maharaja of Kashmir of the arrival of Nana Sahib, Begum Hazrat Mahal, Banee Mahadeo and Hindustani sepoys, pleading with, and encouraging him to do everything possible.

Temple, then Comissioner of Lahore, discovered that Megh Singh and Kishan Singh, in Gurdaspur district, frequently visited the Maharani in Nepal and had lately used seditious words against the Government. These people were punished. Another person named Jowahar Singh, a relative of the Rani Kulwallee, widow of Maharaja Kharak Singh, was also discovered to have met the Maharani at Nepal. He was ordered to provide security by the British Government.[155] Rani Jindan was kept under strict surveillance and was forbidden to come to India or communicate with anybody in India or with her son in England.

Writing in 1862, Mr. Davies, Secretary to the Punjab Government, informed that the national feelings of the *Sikhs,* though repressed and extinguished, were likely to be excited by the return of the Rani to the Punjab.[156] She was, however, later allowed to write to her son in England. Her son, Maharaja Dalip Singh, was permitted to visit her in Nepal. He took her to England where she died in 1863.

Other women too attained martyrdom in the battlefield but their names still remain unknown. Gordon Alexandra observes : "Among the slain at Sikendra Bagh there were a few negresses. They fought like wild cats and it was not till after they were killed that their sex was even suspected."[157]

Forbes Mitchell mentions a woman shot at Sikendra Bagh. She was armed with a heavy old pattern pistol. Seated on a pipal tree, she killed six people.[158]

Russell also discovered a lady a few days later. She was dead but near her body was an enormous mine.[159]

In Delhi there was another lady who became famous under the name Maid of Delhi. She would go to the battlefield in a Sawar's uniform and was reported to have been worse than five soldiers in the battlefield. *Saddiq-Uli Akhbar* reported that she had been given a horse by the King.[160]

References

1. Holmes, T.R., *History of the Indian Mutiny,* London, 1898, p. 97.
2. Gough, General Sir H., *Old Memories,* Edinburg, 1897, p. 19.
3. J.C. Wilson's *Moradabad Narrative of Events* (Official), dated December 24, 1858.
4. *Ibid.*
5. W. and R. Chambers, *The History of Indian Revolt,* 1857-58, London, 1859, p. 88.
6. *Ibid.,* p. 89.
7. Russel, Sir. W.H., *My Diary in India in the Year 1858-59,* London, 1860, pp. 274-75.
8. Innes, Lieut-General J.J. Mcleod, *Lucknow and Oudh in Mutiny,* London, 1896, p. 117; *India Gazette,* Thursday, April 15, 1858, p. 355.
9. Outram succeeded Sleeman as Resident in Lucknow in 1854. He became Chief Commissioner of Oudh, and later was appointed to command Danpur and Kanpur Divisions.
10. Major-General Sir Henry Havelock had been in the Army for 42 years. He had earlier served in Afghanistan, Punjab and Persia. In the crisis of 1857 he was called upon to relieve Kanpur and Lucknow.
11. It is a garden in the suburb of Lucknow. Literally it means "The garden of the world". Within an enclosure of 500 yards, there is a building in the garden having a number of rooms.
12. Ball, Charles, *History of the Indian Mutiny,* Vol. I, London and New York, p. 246.
13. Commonwealth Relations Office, Vol. 163, pp. 443-45, quoted in *Civil Rebellion in the Indian Mutinies 1857-59,* Calcutta, 1957.
14. Malleson, G.B., *History of the Indian Mutiny, 1857-58,* Second edition, 1879, Vol. II, pp. 356-57.

15. Ahmedula Shah was a Muslim priest in Fyzabad. He preaced *Jehad* or religious war in various places. He was a famous rebel leader of Oudh and took a prominent part in this uprising. When British took over Lucknow, he fled to Shahjahanpur and kept on attacking the British forces till he died.
16. Forbes, Mitchell, *Reminiscences of the Great Mutiny, 1857-59,* London, 1910, p. 173.
17. Russell, Sir W.H., *op. cit.,* p. 246
18. Ball, Charles, *op. cit.,* p. 246.
19. *Ibid.*
20. *Foreign Political Secret, A Consultation,* No. 34-38 of November 26, 1858, (N.A.I.).
21. Mufti Intazamula Sahibi (edited), *Begumat Oudh ke Khatut* (Urdu), Delhi, p. 51.
22. *Ibid.,* p. 55.
23. There were a few Begums who along with their female attendants were taken prisoners by the British. Thus these women who once adorned the palace were reduced to pitiable plight. Russell who visited some of them, says: "We found them all in one large, low, dark and dirty room, without windows on the ground floor, and Bruce's entrance was the signal for shrill uplifting of voices and passionate exclamations from the ladies who were crouched down all around the wall." Russel, Sir W.H., *op. cit.,* p. 357.
24. *Foreign Political Consultation* No. 413L, July 15, 1859.
25. *Ibid.,* No. 183/4, August 19, 1859, (N.A.I.).
26. *Ibid.*
27. *Ibid.*
28. *Foreign Political Consultation* No. 413/C, July 15, 1859 (N.A.I.).
29. *Ibid.* No. 183/4, August 19, 1859 (N.A.I.).
30. The Chief Commissioner reporting about her compatibility in the murder of Europeans wrote, "There is evidence to show that the heads of Europeans killed in different combats were exhibited to her and in particular there is strong testimony to the fact that the head of Mr. Deverive, a telegraph employee murdered at Bunnee in the extension of his duty while the Commander-in-Chief was in Lucknow in November 1857, was sent on the Begum's private apartment, that she might feast her eyes on the sight and the bearer of the Trophy was rewarded with a dress of honour." *Foreign Political Consultation* No. 324, July 29, 1859.
31. *Foreign Political Consultation* No. 183/4, August 19, 1859, (N.A.I.).
32. *Foreign Political Consultation* No. 3022, December 31, 1858 (N.A.I.).
33. Maharaja Duleep Singh who was not able to come back to India.
34. *Foreign Political Consultation* No. 3022, December 31, 1858 (N.A.I.).
35. *Foreign Political Consultation* No. 360, October 1877.
36. *Ibid.*
37. *Foreign Political Consultation* No. 264, October 1879 (N.A.I.).
38. Jhansi had been virtually passed on to the British government during the misrule of Raja Raghunath Rao. It was handed over to Gangadhar Rao, brother of the late Raja in 1843.
39. *Sangharsh Kalin Netaon Ki Jiwanian* (Hindi) published under the auspices of History of the Freedom Movement Board, Uttar Pradesh, 1957, p. 148.

40. John Lang writes : "She was a woman of about the middle size—rather stout, but not too stout. Her face must have been very handsome when she was younger, and even now it had many charms—though according to my idea of beauty it was too round. The expression also was very good, and very intelligent. The eyes were particularly fine and the nose very delicately shaped. She was not very fair, though she was far from black. She had no ornaments, strange to say, upon her person except a pair of gold earrings. Her dress was plain white muslin, so fine in texture, that the outline of her figure was plainly discernible and a remarkable fine figure she had. What spoilt was her voice." Lang. J., *Wanderings in India and Other Sketches of Life in Hindustan,* pp. 93-94.
41. He was sixth in descent from the common ancestor Raghunath Rao, I.
42. Gangadhar Rao died in 1853.
43. *Foreign Political Consultation* No. 153-183, July 31, 1854 (N.A.I.).
44. *Ibid.*
45. Arnold, Edwin, *The Marquis of Dalhousie's Administration of British India,* Vol. II (London), 1865, p. 151.
46. *Foreign Political Consultation* No. 153-183, July 31, 1854 (N.A.I.).
47. *Foreign Political Consultation* No. 75 and K.W. March 2, 1 55, (N.A.I.).
48. Dr. Surendra Nath Sen in his book *Eighteen Fifty Seven,* p. 270, writes that there was no resistance made by the Rani. It is true that she did not take up arms against the decision of the government, but the Rani certainly did not hesitate to represent her case to the Governor-General and then to the Court of Directors.
49. *Foreign Political Consultation* No. 75, and K.W., March 2, 1855.
50. Major Evans Bell in his *The Empire in India Letters,* London, p. 210, expressed his opinion thus : "The hereditary rights of the Raja of Jhansi were guaranteed by the treaty of 1817 without reference or their titles or insignia and that treaty contained no clauses or expression restricting the ordinary operation of Hindu Law."
51. *Foreign Political Consultation* No. 75 and K.W., March 2, 1855 (N.A.I.).
52. *Ibid.*
53. *Ibid.*
54. Forest, G.W., *Selections from the Letters, Despatches and Other State Papers, 1857-58,* Vol. IV, pp. 2-3.
55. *Foreign Political Consultation* No. 26-31 and K.W., July 31, 1857 (N.A.I.).
56. Similar opinion has been expressed by Kaye : "Her resentment grew stronger and stronger. A woman of masculine energy and feminine vindictiveness, she eagerly awaited the rising of storm, well assured that her time would come." Kaye, J.W., *History of the Sepoy War,* London, 1876, Vol. III, p. 361.
57. *The Revolt in Central India, 1857-59,* Compiled in the Intelligence Branch, Division of Chief of Staff, Army Headquarters India, Shimla, 1908 (C.S.L.).
58. Kaye, J.W., *op. cit.,* Vol. III, p. 360.
59. Forest, G.W., *op. cit.,* Vol. IV, p. 3.
60. *Narrative of Events Mutiny in India, 1857-58,* Calcutta, 1881, Vol. I, p. 550.
61. This statement was made by Sepoy Aman Khan of 12 Native Infantry and was considered trustworthy by Sir R. Hamilton. *Foreign Political Supplementary Consultation* No. 283 of December 30, 1859.

62. *Narrative of Events Mutiny in India, 1857-59, op. cit.*, Vol. I, p. 550.
63. *The Revolt in Central India, 1857-59, op. cit.*, p. 20.
64. About 55 in number.
65. *Narrative of Events Mutiny in India, 1857-58, op. cit.*, Vol. I, p. 555.
66. *Ibid.*
67. Reference to this fact is also made by (Captain) P.G. Scott in his report thus : "Some days before it (Mutiny) occurred, Captain Dunlop commanding the Left Wing of the 12th Native Infantry and the station of Jhansi too, sent over to Major Kirkee letters from Major Skene, the Superintendent and Captain Gordon, Deputy Superintendent of Jhansi, informing him that they had learnt from separate sources that one Luckmen Rao, the servant of the Rani of Jhansi, was doing his best to induce the men of 12th to Mutiny. It was not known whether the Rani authorised these proceedings." Forest, G.W., *op. cit.*, Vol. IV, p. 1.
68. *The Revolt in Central India, 1857-59, op. cit.*, p. 16; *Narrative of Events Mutiny in India, op. cit.*, Vol. I, p. 550.
69. Kaye, Sir, J.W., *op. cit.*, Vol. III, p. 364.
70. *Narrative of Events Mutiny in India, op. cit.*, p. 550; Kaye, Sir, J.W., *op. cit.*, Vol. III, p. 364.
71. *Foreign Political Consultation* No. 75 and K.W., 2 March, 1855 (N.A.I.).
72. Martin, R.M., *Indian Empire (1858-61)*, Vol. II, p. 485, quoted in *Civil Rebellion in the Indian Mutinies, 1857-59*, Calcutta, p. 58.
73. *Foreign Political Supplement Proceedings* No. 280, December 30, 1859; Forest, G.W., *op. cit.* The fact that Rani's father was actively associated with the rebellion is also acknowledged by Sen, Surendra Nath, *op. cit.*, p. 274. He writes : "Rani's men had no reason to sympathise with the English in their difficulties and it may be assumed that Nana Sahib definitely identified himself with their enemies."
/4. Majumdar, R.C., *The Sepoy Mutiny and the Revolt of 1857*, Calcutta, 1957, p. 155.
75. Further Papers Relative to the Mutinies in the East Indies-Presented to both the Houses of Parliament by Command of Her Majesty, 1857, enclosure 166, p. 75.
76. Majumdar, R.C., *op. cit.*, pp. 144-45 examines various evidence available and comes to the conclusion that the Rani's guilt was more of her inference from the conduct of her servants and followers than based on any positive evidence. This finding is supported by him by quoting the first part of the report dated August 18, 1857 which reads : "It is the general impression that the sepoys were instigated by the Rani to attack the fort." But Majumdar does not take into account the second part of the report which categorically holds the Rani responsible for the rebellious acts.
77. W. and R. Chamoers, *op. cit.*, p. 88.
78. *Foreign Political Consultation* No. 355-362. April 30, 1858 (N.A.I.).
79. Lowe, Thomas, *Central India During the Rebellion of 1857-58*, London, p. 264.
80. *Foreign Political Consulation* No. 46/7, July 16, 1858 (N.A.I.).
81. *Foreign Political Supplement* (Madar Bakhsh), 287, December 30, 1859, (N.A.I.).
82. *Foreign Pilitical Supplement* No. 284, December 30, 1859.

83. *Foreign Political Supplement* No. 286, December 30, 1859.
84. His name is not given in the contemporary records.
85. Forest, G.W., *op. cit.,* Vol. IV, p. vii.
86. Kaye, W., *op. cit.,* Vol. VIII, p. 396.
87. *Foreign Political Consultation* No. 46/7, July 16, 1858.
88. Majumdar, R.C., *op. cit.,* p. 114.
89. Details of this letter are in Appedix B.
90. Parasnis, *Jhansi Sansthanchya Maharani Lakshmi Bai Sahen Hyanchen Charita,* p. 125, quoted in Sen, Surendra Nath, *op. cit.,* p. 279.
91. *Foreign Secret Consultations,* A, No. 304, dated July 31, 1857.
92. *Foreign Political Supplement* No. 280, December 30, 1859.
93. *Foreign Political Supplement Consultation* No. 280, December 30, 1859.
94. Malleson, G.B., *History of the Indian Mutiny, 1857-58,* London, 1858, Vol. I, p. 93; Forest G.W., *op. cit.,* Vol. III, p. 5.
95. Foreign Politicall Supplement No. 280, December 30, 1859.
96. *Foreign Political Supplement* No. 286, December 30, 1859, p. 465.
97. *Foreign Political Secret Consultation* No. 34, July 31, 1857 (N.A.I.).
98. *Ibid.*
99. Details of these letters are given in Appendix C.
100. Both Majumdar, R.C., *op. cit.,* p. 147 and Sen, Surendra Nath, *op. cit.,* p. 279 taking this proclamation into consideration have come to the conclusion that the Rani assumed the administration of her husband's principality at the direction of the constituted authority. The letter from the Commissioner authorising the Rani to look after the administration of Jhansi is dated July 2, 1857. But the Rani had long before this as is clear from the 'perwanah' issued by her on 10th June had taken over the administration of Jhansi independence of the British Government.
101. *Foreign Political Secret Consultation* No. 355, July 31, 1857. For details see Appendix D, Part II.
102. *Ibid.*
103. *Foreign Political Supplement* No. 288, December 30, 1859, p. 471 (N.A.I.).
104. *Ibid.*
105. *Narrative of Events, op. cit.,* p. 555.
106. *Foreign Political Supplement Consultation* No. 266, December 30, 1859 (N.A.I.).
107. *Foreign Political Supplement* No. 265, December 30, 1859, p. 405.
108. *Sangharash Kalin Netaon Ke Jiwanian* (Hindi), *op. cit.,* p. 162.
109. *Foreign Political Consultation* No. 61754 and K.W., December 30, 1859, Details in Appendix E. Majumdar, R.C., *op. cit.,* p. 147, writes : "Reference to the Rani's sending agents to the Nana in June must be a matter of interference or hearsay report . . . ." That it was not a matter of inference or hearsay is proved by this letter.
110. Nana Sahib Dhondu Pant was son of Mahadev Madho Narain and was born in 1824. He was one of the three adopted sons of Baji Rao, the last Peshwa. The Peshwa left his title and estate to Nana in 1839. He was one of the prominent leaders of the rebels. Nana assumed the government during the rebellion at Kanpur. Later when the British forces took over Kanpur, he made his way to Oudh and escaped to Nepal.

111. Malleson, G.B., *op. cit.,* Vol. I, p. 191.
112. *Foreign Political Supplement* No. 1764, December 30, 1859.
113. *Ibid.,* No. 1765, December 30, 1859.
114. *Foreign Political Consultation* No. 114-5, April 30, 1859.
115. *Foreign Political Supplement* No. 1765, December 30, 1859.
116. *Ibid.*
117. *Ibid.*
118. *Foreign Political Supplement* No. 1765, December 30, 1859.
119. *Foreign Political Proceeding* No. 127, May 28, 1858.
120. Ball, Charles, *op. cit.,* Vol. II, p. 290.
121. Hugh Rose joined the army in 1820. He took part in the Turco-Egyptian War and was later appointed Consul General there. He came to India in 1857 and assumed the command of the Poona Division. Later he was appointed Commander of the Central India Force and fought against Rani Jhansi and other rebel leaders.
122. *Foreign Political Consultation* No. 3572-3575, December 29, 1858.
123. Malleson, G.W., *op. cit.,* 1906 (Ninth edition), pp. 387-88.
124. Forest, G.W., *op. cit.,* Vol. 1V, p. 144.
125. Tantia Tope was born in 1814. His father was in the service of Peshwa Baji Rao II. Tantia was a prominent rebel leader and took part in almost all the stages of rebellion. Ultimately he was taken prisoner on April 7, 1859. He was court martialled and a death sentence was passed on him.
126. Forest, G.W., *op. cit.,* Vol. IV, p. 120-24.
127. Lowe, Thomas, *op. cit.* p. 226.
128. *Foreign Secret Consultation* No. 73 of May 28, 1858; Forest, G.W., *op. cit,* p. 126.
129. Bhandair is a town 21 miles from Jhansi.
130. A town 40 miles from Kalpi.
131. A town in Jaloun District, on the right bank of Jamuna.
132. Forest, G.W., *op. cit.,* Vol. IV, p. 81.
133. *Foreign Political Supplement* No. 1500 of December 30, 1859.
134. Lowe, T., *op. cit.,* p. 147.
135. *The Indian World,* Vol. VIII, July-December, 1900, p. 14.
136. Holmes, T.R., *op. cit.,* Quoted in Sen, Surendra Nath, 1857, p. 293.
137. *Friend of India,* Vol. I, June 10, 1858, p. 533.
138. *Indian World,* Vol. VIII, 1908, p. 14 Arnold Edwin, *op. cit.,* p. 152.
139. Forest, G.W., *op. cit.,* Vol. IV, p. 139.
140. *Foreign Politics—A proceeding,* No.395, April 1860.
141. Malleson, G.B., *op. cit.,* Vol. III, p. 221.
142. Rudman, F.R.R., *Central Provinces, District Gazetteer, Mandala District,* Vol. A, p. 255.
143. Government of Madhya Pradesh, *The History of the Freedom Movement,* (1956), p. 80.
144. *Ibid.,* pp. 80-81.
145. Rudman F.R.R., *op. cit.,* Vol. A., p. 255.
146. *Foreign Political Consultation,* No. 133, May 28, 1858.
147. *Foreign Political Consultation,* No. 139/47, August 13, 1858.
148. *Ibid.*
149. *Foreign Political Proceeding* No. 43, February, 1860.

150. *Foreign Political Consultation,* No. 8/12 and K.W., September 3, 1858.
151. Further papers relative to the Mutinies in the East Indies presented to both the Houses of Parliament, Vol. VII, p. 212 (N.L.C.).
152. *Foreign Political Secret Consultation* No. 138, December 18, 1857 (N.A.I.).
153. Rani Jindan was daughter of Munna Singh of village Chachar in Gujranwala district. She was the youngest wife of Maharaja Ranjit Singh and became by the recognition of her son Duleep Singh and Sher Singh the most influential personage in the Punjab. When the English gained power in Punjab, she was imprisoned. Rani Jindan, however, escaped and took asylum in Nepal.
154. *Foreign Political Secret Proceedings* No. 1052, February 12, 1859. For details of her letters, see Appendix F.
155. *Foreign Political Secret Proceeding,* Vol. II, 1862, p. 101 (N.A.I.).
156. *Ibid.*
157. Gordon, Alexander, Lt. Col. W., *Recollection of a Highland Subaltern During the Campaign,* London, 1898, p. 104.
158. Forbes, Mitchell, W., *op. cit.,* pp. 57-58.
159. Russel, Sir W.H., *op. cit.,* p. 357.
160. *Saddiq-Uli Akhbar,* Vol. 4, No. 3, July 20, 1857.

2

Social Reform

The subject of female emancipation of India during the colonial period (in a geographical sphere which today includes Pakistan and Bangladesh) was linked with both liberal and conservative currents of opinion and was the result not only of a challenge and resistance to imperialism but also of a movement to modify and strengthen traditional framework. Aggression by European powers in India dates back to the 16th and 17th centuries when Portuguese, Dutch, French and English trading posts had been set in the coastal regions. By 1763, British supremacy over the French was established and the British East India Company started to increase its influence. In 1784 under Pitt's India Act, the trading activities of the Company were separated from the national political administration and policies of victory and control were followed. By 1823 nearly all of India had been either directly merged by the British or was indirectly controlled by them through treaties with the princely states. The last aggressions were the victory of Sind in 1843 and the Punjab in 1849. In the interests of exploiting and controlling the country, the British army was strengthened, roads and railways were constructed, a civil service was established to administer the country and the infrastructure of the colonial economy was established. For the administration of these territories, the British had to create a local class of officials and therefore an English educational system was introduced. The first province to be the object of these policies was Bengal, where the Hindu (later Presidency) College was established in Calcutta. By the early decades of the century, an English-speaking Bengali petty-bourgeoisie had emerged, and it was sections of these groups that sponsored movements of reform, cultural revival and nationalist agitation in which the liberal and orthodox Bengalis played an important part.

The resistance to British imperialism was a long and constant struggle lasting nearly two hundred years. The British achieved their first major victory (under Robert Clive) at the renowned Battle of Plassey. Later the princes of Bengal and Oudh joined to challenge the British and the King of Mysore (Hyder Ali) also tried to oust the British but failed. In the late 18th and early 19th centuries, there were frequent battles led by the Mahrattas who opposed foreign rule. However the climax of the resistance was the 1857 Indian 'Mutiny'—the first war of independence—which started with a mutiny of Indian soldiers in the British troops, and spread to a large area of North India covering Meerut, Delhi, Cawnpore, Lucknow and Allahabad. With the suppressing of the resistance, the British adopted stern measures. Besides acts of revenge against local populations, the government passed an India Act in 1858 abolishing the East India Company and taking over all powers formerly vested in the Company.

The challenge of Imperialist domination and the imposition on India of a foreign culture, ideology and religion produced in its turn various movements of religious and social reform among Hindus and Muslims. These reformist movements such as the *Brahmo Samaj*—were planned to cleanse Hinduism of certain corrupt and decadent customs and to counter-act missionary propaganda by presenting the Hindu religion as one, compatible with progress and alteration. Social reform, too, became a famous issue among local intellectuals, like Raja Ram Mohan Roy, D.C. Karve, Syed Ahmad Khan, M.G. Ranade, the Tagore family, K.C. Sen, I.C. Vidyasagar, and Jotirao Phule who, motivated either by liberal thoughts of social change or with the hope of stopping drastic social change, were to launch expeditions to eliminate or correct some of the worst abuses prevailing in the society of the period.

The political response to imperialism started in the late 19th century with the development of Indian nationalism. The Congress in the early years was led by moderates, but later motivated by B.G. Tilak in Maharashtra and Aurobindo Ghosh in Bengal, became more effective.

Agitation for Social Reforms

The status of ladies in India had varied in different historical periods and in the different regions of the country. There were also several variations depending on class, religion and ethnicity. By the early 19th century, the glaring social vices affecting ladies were discussed by administrators, missionaries and the concerned members of the local bourgeoisie. While the Europeans stressed on the low status of Indian women as being an expression of the general backwardness of the country, the Indian reformers were eager to show that female status had been high in ancient India and that many warrior queens had made their mark on Indian history including Sultana Razia, who succeeded to the throne of her father, the King of Delhi (in the 13th century), who led her forces into war; Nur Jehan who exercised real power and led the army in war during the reign (in the early 17th century) of her husband, the Emperor Jehangir and Lakshmi Bai, the Rani of Jhansi, who during the war against the British in 1857, led her army on horseback in fierce wars against the invaders and died in combat.

Reform movements against 'social evils' affecting ladies started in British India in the early 19th century and have been usually attributed to external factors such as the impact of English education, missionary activities and liberal views from the West, as well as to internal expeditions such as the nationalist agitation against imperialism and the religio-cultural resistance by Indians to the challenge of Christianity and Western culture. The subjects handled by the reform movement—such as *sati,* widow remarriage, polygamy and women's property rights—were troubles of a certain strata of society, such practices being mainly confined to the higher castes and classes. They were matters raised by bourgeoisie, male social reformers from urban areas who planned to idealise female role as wife and mother in the context of patriarchy. Whether like the orthodox reformers they looked back to a Vedic golden age where ladies were believed to have possessed a high status, or whether they looked forward to a new fundamental based on liberal principles which negated the 'barbaric' heritage of the past—the male reformer's fundamental assumptions were that social reform and female education would revitalise and preserve the partriarchal family system, produce more companionate wives and better mothers and hence have a stabilising effect on society. The reformists felt that middle-class family structures were being threatened by the prevalent social vices. One of the common fears was stated to be that some high-caste widows who had been mal-treated and stopped from remarriage, had turned to prostitution. "Social rigidity, child marriage with its necessary consequences, child-widows, the social taint involved in widow remarriage, all combine to create in society a new class of women whom we are prone to call fallen".[1] This concern to stop the disintegration of family life, which was present both among the English educated and the non-Westernised intelligentsia, was a theme in the literature of North and South India. For as Mazumdar writes, "with increasing urbanisation, prostitution became more commercialised . . . . the large number of young high-caste widows, helpless victims of family neglect and even torture, was an obvious recruiting ground. This was a threat that could not be ignored by those who wanted to preserve the family and its economy from destruction. The debate on ill-treatment of widows, the denial of remarriage, child marriage and polygamy . . . . which raged in the newspapers and journals of the 19th century, bear ample testimony to this fear among reformers".[2]

The bourgeoisie in India, through the reform expedition were thus able, under the influence of liberalism or using slogans of cultural revival, to legally forbid the more extreme abuses affecting ladies. But the questions were taken up individually and fought out as single matter, with success measured by each legislative act that was passed. Since all the fields of social reform concerned the family, the impact of social reform may have been to increase conservatism and far from liberating ladies, to merely make conditions within the family structure less deplorable—especially for ladies of the bourgeoisie. For it is clear that while some Indians fought for social reform on the principle of liberal values, many conservatives experienced otherwise; for example, the renown Maharashtrian reformer M.G. Ranade (1841-1901), a lawyer, judge and legislative councillor in Bombay, expressed the idea that social reform was in the 'great Hindu tradition' of 'seeking out ancient principles in order to restate them'. Instead of destroying the structure, the reformer should "lop off the diseased overgrowth and excrescances and . . . . restore vitality and energy to the social organism".[3] In contrast was the leading Maharashtrian social radical, Jotirao Phule, who supported the rights of socially oppressed and started schools for females and 'untouchables'. Phule's *Satyshodhak Samaj* (1873), equality and equal education for both sexes and he pioneered the use of 'non-sexist phraseology', adding women to phrases like, 'all men are equal'.[4]

Even before the nationalist expedition had become politically active in India, the social reformers started movement on *sati* (the burning alive of Hindu widows on their husbands' funeral pyre) and the check on widow remarriage. These were two matters which could be safely handled since they were practices not existing in early times, were confined to the upper castes and classes, and if improved, would give India a good reputation of appearing to be 'civilised' without endangering the conservative family structures. Initially the British administration in India adopted a policy of non-interference, but its attitude changed when *Mrikyunjaya Vidyalankar* (the Chief Pandit of the Supreme Court) announced in 1817 that *sati* had no religious *shastric* authority and when other Bengali learners joined in the clamour for legislation agains *sati*. (Potts : 167 : 142-148). The pioneer in the movement against *sati* was Raja Ram Mohan Roy, a repuled Bengali, influenced by Western liberal thought and attempted to improve and revitalise Hinduism and for this objective had founded the *Brahmo Samaj*. He published articles against *sati,* translated into English. Criticising the female oppression, who Roy claimed were "treated worse than inferior animals", he penned, "what I lament is, that seeing women thus dependent and exposed to every misery, you feel for them no compassion, that might exempt them from being tied down and burnt to death".[5] His mobilisation of Hindu idea against the *Sati* system created the necessary public opinion, enabling the government, which was also being pressurised by missionaries on this subject, to make the practice a criminal offence.

Although there was provision in certain conditions in the ancient Hindu law for widows for remarriage, by the medieval period of Indian history, the higher castes had forbidden their remarriage. This issue emerged and expedition for a reform in the law was taken up in many parts of India and was led by reformers such as Iswar Chandra Vidyasagar (1820-1891)—a Bengali, who published a pamphlet "Marriage of Hindu Widows" and presented a petition to the government on the issue, and Debendranath Tagore, who made an organisation to campaign for widow remarriage and against other vices affecting women. The agitation with support from the press and the English officials, led to the Widow Remarriage Act but social custom could not be changed by legislation and it was only the very daring who violated tradition.

As in many Asian countries at this time, the reformers ideal was the monagamous family. Polygamy in India was practised by both Muslims and Indians of 'high' class or caste, the Muslims being permitted four wives but the *Kulin Brahmins,* for example, being allowed unlimited wives. The issue of polygamy was first raised by Hindu reformers who campaigned for its elimination and by Bengali playwrights and authors who ridiculed the practice and many petitions against it were presented to the government. The campaign was continued, especially by Vidyasagar who wrote tracts exposing its evils, but government policy at that time was against too much interference in traditional usages affecting family life.

The subject of child marriage was also one that was taken up by social reformers of the 19th century. Unlike *sati,* polygamy and the ban on widow remarriage, which influenced the upper segments of society, child marriage was much prevalent among Hindus, (but not practised by tribal groups). The practice was regarded as a religious and social obligation by 'higher' castes and a channel of protection of daughters (from men with economic power) by the 'lower' castes; in addition it was an economic protection, since male children commanded lower dowries[6]. The reformers best known for their agitation on this topic were Keshab Chandra Sen (born 1838) and Vidyasagar. As a religious reformer, Sen insisted that the usage of child marriage was a corruption of the scriptures, and penned, "the custom of premature marriage, as it prevails in this country is injurious to the moral, social and physical interests of the people and is one of the main obstacles in the way of their advancement"[7]. Vidyasagar said, that child marriage was linked to the problem of Indian widows—as many of the child brides were widowed at an early age. Some success was gained with the Marriage Act, fixing a lower age limit for marriage of fourteen for girls and eighteen for males. Further agitation and publications by reformers like Behramji Malbari who had used the press (including his own 'Indian Spectator') for the campaign against child marriage, led to the Age of Consent Bill of 1891, which raised the legal age of permission for sexual cohabitation from ten to twelve years for girls[8].

Another field of agitation was property rights for Hindu women. The prevailing unwritten usage was particularly tough on Hindu widows who had no claim on the husband's property except the right of maintenance, making them dependent on, and at the mercy of, their husband's relatives. In 1874, the Right to Property Act provided a widow a life interest in her husband's share of the property and a share equal to that of a son but did not provide a widow the right to own or dispose of this property and daughters continued to be excluded from rights of inheritance.

Female Education

Since the reform of 'social evils' was related to the question of the preservation and strengthening of fundamental family structures and the production of good wives and mothers, the question of female education frequently emerged—a policy favoured by both progressive and orthodox reformers. In India there had been many educated women in the upper classes, including famous women authors and poets, but no general education was available to women. Female education became an issue on which there was broader agreement than on other topics like widow remarriage, which had touched religious sensibilities. Many liberal reformers campaigned supporting female education, Vidyasagar being at the forefront of the campaign, establishing forty girls schools in Bengal. The Hindu philosopher while supporting female education, popularised the worship of the Goddess Kali by the concept of 'Supreme Mother'. He said, "I worshipped all women as representatives of the divine Mother. I realised the Mother of the Universe in every woman's form".[10] Ramakrishna's famous disciple, Vivekananda, a revolutionary on many topics, believed that a girl should not be educated in the modern sciences but taught to achieve fulfilment within the family.

In the 19th century, as in other countries, Indian reformers thought that social vices could best be abolished through education, and that education was mainly for the objective of producing good home makers and perpetuating conservative ideology. "Education would not turn the women away from their familial roles, but improve their efficiency as wives and mothers and *strengthen the hold of traditional values on society, since women were better carriers of these values*".[11] In addition, Christian missionaries were eager on using education for proselytisation and also for ensuring hopefully, that if the ladies became Christians, there would be no lapses back to the old beliefs by male converts. Female schools were begun by missionaries and the English residents in the leading cities, especially in Bengal, where the British had begun their first inroads in the mid-18th century. The first female school was founded by David Hare in Calcutta; Professor Patterson founded a female school in Bombay in 1848 and in 1851, J.E.D. Bethune began the Bethune girls' school in Calcutta, which subsequently became the first women's college. Many Indian reform groups like the *Arya Samaj and Brahmo Samaj* ran educational institutions for females and Indian ladies such as Pandita Ramabai, and Ramabai Ranade were involved in projects for female learning. The visit to India of Mary Carpenter, a renowned British social reformer—who made a report on women's education in India, resulted in the establishment of a teacher's training college in 1870.[12] By 1882 there were 2,700 educational institutes with 127, 000 pupils; the majority wre primary schools, but there were 82 secondary schools, 15 teachers' training institutes and one college.

Already the females had begun to write literary works in English (in rather Victorian style), one notable instance being a Bengali author Toru Dutt (1856-1878), who had travelled in Europe between 1869 and 1873 and published her first poetry book in 1876, entitled *A Sheaf Gleaned in French Fields*. By the 1880s Indian ladies also started to graduate from universities, the first being two students of Bethune school who completed their education at Calcutta University in 1883. By 1901 there were 256 women in colleges, the figure rising to 905 in 1921. In 1916, the Indian Women's University was begun in Bombay by D.K. Karve and the same year the Benares Hindu University was founded with an affiliated women's college. Although some women thus took admissions to schools and universities, even in the most educationally advanced states of India, the large majority of girls did not attend school.[13] Female education was mainly limited to the larger cities and towns and fulfilled the needs of the bourgeoisie and petty-bourgeoisie. The policies of promoting female education and the kind of education provided were not intended to promote female emancipation or freedom but to reinforce patriarchy and the class system. "The class bias of the reform movement was most pronounced in the field of education. The plea that education would only improve women's efficiency as wives and mothers left its indelible mark on the educational policy."[14]

Education enabled some ladies to get employment previously denied to them. The number of women in medical schools rose and a number of them were trained as teachers, nurses and midwives. In 1882, Cornelia Sorabjee, a *Parsi,* was the first Indian woman to graduate in law in Oxford. Another category of women pioneers were the Indian females who challenged convention by studying medicine, either in India or by visiting abroad to medical colleges in the West where ladies were accepted. The early lady doctors were Anandibai Joshi who in 1886 graduated from the Women's Medical College in Philadelphia and worked as a physician in the women's ward of the Kolhapur hospital; Kadambini Ganguli and who had studied in Britain and was the first woman graduate of Calcutta University and Bengal's first woman physician; Annie Jagannadhan who studied in the newly founded Edinburgh School of Medicine for women in 1888 and in 1892 became a house surgeon in a Bombay hospital and Rukmabai who aquired a medical degree from London University in 1895 and subsequently worked in the Women's Hospital in Rajkot. These women had to fight against the full weight of conservatism. To quote one instance "Rukmabai rebelled against Indian traditionalism, to study medicine. She deserted her husband who filed a suit against her. She was bitterly criticised and even sentenced to six months imprisonment if she did not agree to stay with him. A compromise was finally arrived whereby she had to pay a large amount of money to her husband. It was decreed in accordance with Hindu Law, that Rukmabai could never marry again."[15]

Female Agitation

Although the leading social reformers in the 19th century were men having objectives to reinforce family life, the ladies themselves started crossing the home boundaries and family limits envisaged for them by the reformers.

> "For the early pioneers of social and religious reform, women were at first objects of their emancipatory efforts, but in the course of the 19th and 20th centuries they became more and more subjects in the political and social sphere."[16]

There were various women activists and pioneers in the 19th and early 20th centuries, the majority of them related by birth or marriage to families in which the men had taken in religious or political reform movements.[17] The most notable among such pioneers was Pandita Ramabai (1858-1922), a famous Sanskrit scholar, whose brave and free life of activity in women's causes made her, perhaps, the foremost woman agitator of her time. Her life was not usual for a woman of that period. Her father, a Sanskrit scholar of Maharashtrian origin, taught his wife and daughter Sanskrit the believing that women had as much equal right to knowledge as men. The family led the life of nomadic scholars roaming over all parts of India, and Ramabai thereby obtained mobility and wide experience, became concerned with women's oppression and also achieved repute as a scholar, being examined and conferred the title of Pandita (scholar). For a woman to be conversant in theology in a society where religion is all pervasive, has always been a benefit in challenging social evils disguised as religious orthodoxy and Ramabai used her knowledge in the cause of women. She had two unique advantages, usually refused to women who are physically and intellectually confined, an understanding of social realities through nomadic travel and a command of Hindu ideology through the knowledge of the scriptures.

Using the argument that women had a high status in ancient India, Ramabai made an all-out invasion against the orthodox priests. Having been widowed (in 1882) with a new-born daughter, she had to fight for herself and face criticism for not accepting the traditional deportment of a widow. She started a life of travel and agitation, starting a series of *Mahila Samaj* (women's organisations) in Bombay state and campaigning for female education and medical training; she authored *Stri Dharma Neeti* (Woman's Religious Law), advocating female emancipation and attacking traditional usages harmful to females. In 1883, she travelled to Britain where she was in contact with the pioneer woman educationalist Dorothea Beale, principal of Cheltenham Ladies College and visited America and Canada in 1886, where she studied, delivered public lectures and came back to India in 1889 via Japan. She adopted Christianity, started a series of projects involving schools, orphanages, and widow homes and in 1889, was one of the few female delegates to the Indian National Congress. Her work not only motivated many other women but also influenced male reformers including M.G. Ranade and D.K. Karve.

The other field of activity that allowed women, to cross the confines of the home, was social bourgeoisie and the wives of male social reformers were active in social work among the poor and destitute. To quote only one instance among many, Ramabai Ranade (wife of M.G. Ranade) conducted free classes for women in sewing and first aid, visited hospitals and prisons and distributed food during disasters such as the 1913 famine.[18] The proliferation in the 19th century of social reform activity among different groups resulted in the formation under M.G. Ranade's guidance, of the Indian National Social Conference in 1887. The objectives of this organisation were to "strengthen the hands of the local associations and to furnish information to each association. . . . as to what is being done by others . . . . and to stimulate active interest by mutual sympathy and cooperation". Up to 1917 the Conference met separately but concurrently with the political organisation, the Indian National Congress, but after that date its activities were annexed into the general political agitation of the Congress.[19]

Muslim Women and Social Reform

While the early agitation for social reform was initiated from Hindu males and was concerned with the position and participation of the Hindu woman, the Muslims also began action regarding social reform in the late 19th century. Many of the topics agitating the Hindus did not apply to Muslim women since Muslim law permitted for widow remarriage, divorce and a portion of parental property. Concern was reflected by Muslim male social reformers on topics such as polygamy, *purdah* and female education. The most important Muslim reformer was Syed Ahmad Khan, (d. 1898) who championed Muslim higher education and in 1875, founded a Muslim university college at Aligarh and penned in his journal *Tahzib-ul-Akhalq* on all issues of social reform. Believing that the downfall of the Muslims was due to their reluctance to go in for Western education, he pioneered modern education for both men and women. He also opposed polygamy and expressed the view that since a man could not treat all his wives equally (as enjoined in the Koran), polygamy was not permissible under Islam. On this question Syed Ahmad Khan went against the strong flow of orthodox opinion, announcing that "Polygamy must be absolutely and definitely restricted . . . . monogamy should be the rule". He also challenged the orthodox view that Islam either favoured *purdah* (seclusion) for women or that it opposed women's education.[20] Other Muslim male reformers included Badruddin Tyabji, a Mumbai businessman who campaigned against the *purdah* system; Syed Imam, who financed a Muslim female school in Patna, believing that the country's progress was related to women's education and Hydari, a well-known writer, who expressed the prevailing views on the requirement for educating girls; "while the education of a boy helps him only, the education of a girl lifts the whole family to a higher stage of mental and moral life."[21]

Some efforts were made at female education by Muslim women themselves; Amina Tyabji, wife of Badruddin Tyabji, began a Muslim girls' school in 1895 and Begum Abdullah managed a similar school in Aligarh in 1906, founded by her husband, Sheikh Abdullah; this school subsequently became a women's college affiliated to the Aligarh Muslim University. Other Muslim women pioneers were members of Tyabji family. In various urban centres, Muslim women of renown families started local women's associations and in 1916, the Begum of Bhopal made the All-India Muslim Women's Conference. But such activities were not entirely approved of by the traditionalists who expressed their opposition to Muslim girls' schools and were furious by the resclution passed by the Muslim Women's Conference in 1917, that polygamy be eliminated.[22]

However, with the launching of the political struggles Muslim women started participating in the agitation. The Khilafat movement among Muslims in India (protesting against the dismemberment of the Monarchs) placed the female relatives of the leaders of the movement on the public platform; for instance, Mohamed Ali's mother Bi Amman, as well as his wife and Hasrat Mohani's wife, addressed women's meetings during this campaign, and when the brothers Mohamed and Shaykat Ali were imprisoned, Bi Amman came in public at the joint Muslim League and Congress Sessions of 1917. In subsequent, many Muslim women joined the *satyagraha* and non-cooperation movements. Thus, while participation in political activities was more conveniently tolerated, Muslim opinion was not ready for changes in laws regulating women's social status.

Women and Nationalist Agitation

In the political strifes against imperialism that Indian females (both Hindu and Muslim) started actively taking part in life outside the home and in this, they were supported by many nationalist political leaders. The expansion of female education and their admission to Universities had resulted in various English-educated, middle-class women by the late 19th century, and they made their presence in political activities. The Indian National Congress, permitted women to become members and at the sessions in Bombay in 1889, there were ten women participants from Bombay and Bengal. Bengal had come under British influences very early and became the vanguard of both Westernisation and political and reform expeditions related to national revival and nationalism. The women of the Bengali bourgeoisie also included the earliest pioneers of reform and political agitation; one of the best known was the author *Swarnakumari Devi* (1885-1932), Rabindranath Tagore's sister, who with her husband edited *Bharati,* a Bengali journal. In 1882, she began the Ladies Theosophical Society for women of all religions, during a time when there was an interest among Indian intellectuals in the Theosophical movement launched by Colonel Olcott and Helena Blavatsky. Swarnakumari, in 1886, also began a women's association *(Sakhi Samiti)* which was concerned with promoting handicrafts manufactured by women. In 1889, Swarnakumari was among the first women attending the sessions of the Indian National Congress. She was a famous novelist; her novels reflected the thinking of Bengali reformers, both men and women, educated in English, but maintained traditional values. In *'An Unfinished Song',* the heroine who is westernised, marries a doctor educated in England and is supportive of women's rights, but she holds on to certain orthodox values and "the traditional ideal of female religious devotism"[23]

In the 1890's, women constantly participated in Congress activities, among them women activists like Pandita Ramabai and female professionals such as Dr. Kadambini Ganguli. In the early 20th century, further active political female participation occurred with the increase in nationalism. Mass strifes for self-rule including the boycott of British articles took place during this age. There was also an increase of militant activity, bomb throwing and murders, especially in Punjab and Bengal; much violence took place after the partition of Bengal in 1905, and events such as the appointment of the 'extremist' leader B.G. Tilak in 1908, led to strikes by Bombay workers. Women joined the agitation, organised *swadeshi* meetings, boycotted foreign articles and donated money and ornaments to the nationalist movement. As a part of the campaign, a pamphlet 'A Vow for Bengali Women' was distributed, explaining the *swadeshi* movement to village ladies, calling upon them to take part in certain rituals which had a political importance and to boycott foreign articles. There were protest meetings all over Bengal and some of them consisted exclusively of women. The woman leader of this age was Swarnakumari's daughter, Sarala Devi who started physical exercise clubs, a *swadeshi* store for products made by ladies and organised the celebration of Bengali traditional festivals.[24]

During the years after 1915, there was an expansion of militant nationalism and a common programme of agitation between Congress and the Muslim League. Gandhi came back to India in 1915 and in 1919 launched a mass non-cooperation expedition against the British, resulting in wide repression of nationalists. During these years, several Indian and foreign women were at the forefront of the nationalist struggles.

The renowned Indian female leader was Sarojini Naidu, famed as a poetess and politician who after a Cambridge-education had involved into literary and political activity; she was a famous orator and was one of the chief figures of the Indian National Congress, becoming its President in 1925. Of the active foreign Theosophists, the foremost were Annie Besant, and Margaret Cousins, an Irish feminist who reached India in 1915. She took part in many of the social and political reform movements of the period.

The Congress leaders witnessed the advantages of mobilising ladies and in their lectures they always exhorted ladies to join the struggle. M.K. Gandhi was particularly aware of the power women could possess in a non-cooperation struggle which he visualised as a mass movement. Gandhi deplored all the present social evils which affected women, but he went further in asserting that he was "uncompromising in the matter of women's rights" and emphasized the importance of women's participation in political and social matters. "In order to play her full and destined role in world affairs, in the solution of conflicts by non-violent means, women must extend their hearts and interests beyond the narrow confines of their homes and family and embrace the whole of humanity."[25] Gandhi's ideas on women rights were, equality in some fields, opportunities for self-growth (whether married or unmarried) and the rejection of woman's role as a sex symbol. But there was no nation of economic equality. As Mies remarks "In Gandhi's idealised image of woman her economic activity, especially the aspect of her economic independence is not emphasized. As the most important activity he recommends to the women spinning and weaving, both of which he considers as religious acts and conforming to the "nature" of woman. On the economic independence of women he speaks evasively. The image of the modern independent career woman does not fit into Gandhi's conception of the ideal woman."[26]

Gandhi's ideal lady was the mythical Sita, the self-sacrificing monogamous wife of the *Ramayana,* who guarded her chastity and remained faithful to Rama despite many provocations. Sita was 'promoted' as the model for Indian ladies. "Gandhi was perhaps hardly conscious of the fact that his ideal of womanhood, which he considered to be a revival of the Hindu ideal, contained in fact many traits of the Puritan-Victorian ideal of woman, as it was preached by the English bourgeoisie". Moreover this image of woman had a "strategic function in the political movement."[27] Gandhi specially stressd the subject of non-violent struggle and asserted that women had great ability to bear suffering and could therefore play a key role in the movement. He claimed that the principle of 'non-violence' *(ashimsa)* and political non-violent resistance was fit for women as they were by nature non-violent. "I do believe", he wrote in 1938, "that woman is more fitted than man to make ahimsa. For the courage of self-sacrifice woman in any way superior to man."[28] It was advised that being used to forms of passive resistance in their routine lives, they could more effectively participate in socially-organised passive resistance and non-cooperation. Gandhi constantly projected a patriarchal notion of woman's role as complementary to man, embodying virtues of sacrifices and misery. In 1921 he stated, "To me the female sex is not the weaker sex. It is the nobler of the two; for it is even today the embodiment of sacrifice, silent suffering, humility, faith and knowledge."[29] Indian women themselves were to accept the Gandhian ideology and to champion *satyagraha* as a form of struggle particularly suitable for them. A woman's journal *(Stri Dharma)* authored in 1930 "Because the qualities which this new form of warfare is displaying are feminine rather than masculine, we may look on this life and death struggle of India to be free as the women's war."[30] Jawaharlal Nehru's views on the position of women were those of the enlightened reformers of the period. Having sympathised, while in Britain, with the cause of the suffragettes and been exposed to the liberal and socialist debates on the 'woman question', he took, (what was at that time) a 'progressive' stand on female issues. He particularly stressed the necessity for females to work outside the home to be economically independent, and not to consider marriage as a profession. "Freedom depends on economic conditions even more than political, and if a woman is not economically free and self-earning, she will have to depend on her husband or someone else and dependents are never free". Nehru motivated ladies to militant action. In 1931 he said "In a national war, there is no question of either sex or community. Whoever is born in this country ought to be a soldier."[31]

Despite the many declarations of good intention by male leaders, the majority of them still considered women's role as being basically housewives within a conservative family structure. Women activists themselves became subsumed in the political struggle, women being praised for being good *satyagrahis* (non-violent activists), but the real issues which concerned them as women, were being considered as secondary. The early agitation of the social reformers social vices affecting women in the family were supplanted by the nationalist topics which became predominant, bringing the neglect of agitation to fight women's unequal social and economic position. The few women's issues taken up, were those that interested the middle-class women's organisations, including the suffrage question. For instance, in 1917 a deputation of women met the Viceroy and presented demands for female franchise, and a deputation of four women visited Britain to lobby on this topic. In 1918, the demand was made for the granting of votes for women and the constitutional reforms of 1919 permitted the provincial legislatures to decide on the subject; Madras province was the first (1921) to permit women to vote; other provinces followed and in 1926, women were also provided the right to become legislative councillors, Dr. S. Muthulakshmi Reddi becoming the first lady legislative councillor in Madras in 1927.

In the mass expeditions of the 1920s and 1930s, women's participation was much apparent in certain acts such as the *khadi* campaigns (to wear homespun cloth), in the picketing of shops of foreign articles, in the Salt March of 1930, (when Gandhi inspired the people to break the government's monopoly of salt manufacture by marching to oceans and making salt themselves) as well as in the general political demonstrations and wide agitation which resulted with the call by Congress for civil violation. Kamaladevi Chattopadhyay was among the first to violate the salt law and recalled that "thousands of women strode down to the sea like proud warriors . . . they bore pitchers of clay, brass and cōpper . . . How had they broken their age-old shell of social seclusion and burst into this fierce light of open warfare ? What had . . . stirred them into militant rebels?" Woman all over India participated the struggle for independence, and many thousands were imprisoned. Of the 80,000 arrested during the salt *satyagraha,* 17,000 (21 per cent) were women. In 1931, the Congress delegates at the sessions in Karachi, congratulated the ladies "who rose in their thousands and assisted the nation in struggle for freedom."[32]

Women and Revolutionary Nationalism

Some Indian nationalist groups followed a more militant policy of revolutionary, violent action. These groups were active within India (especially in Bengal, Punjab and Maharashtra) as outside, where they could organise and canvass support. Various foreign women were linked with these revolutionaries and Communists among them Evelyn Roy, (wife of M.N. Roy) and Agnes Smedley (1892-1950), who worked with Indian revolutionaries in banishment in New York and Berlin. The known Indian woman in revolutionary circles in Europe was Bhikaji Cama (1861-1936), belonging to a wealthy *Parsi* family of Bombay. She deserted her husband at the age of twenty-seven and became active in nationalist politics, attending the Congress sessions in Bombay. She visited Europe in 1901 and became a revolutionary nationalist, championing the cause of Indian freedom in Europe and the USA, participating in 1907 in the Stuttgart Congress of the Second Communist International, on which occasion she lectured against British imperialism and hoisted the flag, which was to become the Indian national flag in 1947. She stayed in Paris, becoming the centre of Indian revolutionary activity in Europe, and was closely linked with the more radical and rebellion Indians, especially Krishnavarma and Vir Sarvakar whom the British consider as anarchists and terrorists. She was responsible for two revolutionary papers, *Vandemataram* and *Talwar* published in Geneva and smuggled to India. The British intelligence service was conscious to Cama's influence, reporting in 1913 that she was "one of the recognised leaders of the revolutionary movement in Paris", with contacts with other revolutionary groups in banishment in Paris Another active Parsi woman who had read in Paris was Perin D.S. Captain (1888-1958), the grand-daughter of a moderate nationalist, Dadabhai Naoroji. She and Bhikaiji Cama were delegates at a Congress on Egypt conducted in Brussels. It is hence not surprising that having failed to get Cama exiled from France, due to her contacts with Indian and foreign 'terrorists'; the British possessed her property in India and got the French to intern her during the First World War.[33]

In India too, there was terrorist, violent activity by women during the various times of agitation. For example, Saraladevi Chaudhurani who worked with the *Suhrid Samiti* (of Mymensingh), supported the male revolutionaries, and another, Har Devi, collected money for the revolutionaries in Lahore. In the late 'twenties another phase of violent action emerged in India. In Delhi, Roopvati Jain, aged seventeen was supervisor of a factory which manufactured chemicals for bombs. The Punjab revolutionary Bhagat Singh had various women collaborators including Sushila Devi, who was imprisoned several times, and Durga Devi who had shot a policeman in Mumbai. In Calcutta in 1928, a women students group *(Chhatri Sangha)* appointed and trained women revolutionaries, organised study circles and imparted lessons in cycling, driving and armed fighting; some of them stayed in a hostel in which bombs were made and delivered to revolutionaries. The members of this group included Kalpana Dutt, often putting on male attire, and was arrested and deported for life for her participation in the Chittagong Armoury raid, and Preeti Waddadar who suppressed a raid on a Railway Officers Club. This group also included two young girls Santi and Suniti who in 1931 shot dead the District Magistrate of Comilla and were sentenced to life imprisonment, Bina Das who shot the British Governor of Bengal at a college convocation in 1932 and was imprisoned, and Kamala Das Gupta, who carried bombs in Calcutta as courier. Many members of the *Chhatri Sangha* were motivated by the Indian Congress leader, Subhas Chandra Bose who was one of the main Congress Socialist leaders of the 1930s and made (in Germany and later in South East Asia) an Indian

National Army to combat the British. He made a special appeal to ladies to join the struggle and made a women's militia, called the Rani of Jhansi women's regiment led by Lakshmi *(Swaminadhan)* Sehgal, who was conferred the title of Captain.

Some of these patriotic ladies were ladies categorised as 'terrorists', were to join the Indian Communist Party (formed in 1921), one such example being the heroine of Chittagong Armoury raid Kalpana Dutt, who in subsequent years married P.C. Joshi, the Communist Party General Secretary from 1935 to 1948. According to the Communist Party, "these women martyrs had turned from normal nationalist politics to terrorism only because of their frustrations in the Congress non-cooperation movements; their conversion to communism, said the Party, represented a still higher stage of political 'maturity'."[34] P.C. Joshi, commenting on his wife's reminiscences of the Chittagong Armoury raid, penned, "To read her own story is to understand a living phase of our national movement, how in 1930s the vast majority of the terrorist detenus and prisoners became Communist", adding that terrorism was the infant and Communism was "the mature stage of their revolutionary lives."[35]

The Indian (including Pakistan and Bangaladesh case study of reform movements influencing female status and women's participation in political struggles in the 19th and early 20th centuries, gives sufficient material for a historical understanding of some of the typical problems faced by women's movements in the Third World. The most disclosing aspect has been the necessary convertism of what on the surface appealed like radical change. While highlighting and legally eliminating the worst excesses (like *sati*), stressing female education and inspiring women for *satyagraha,* the entire movement was proved an illusion of change while putting women within the structural limits of family and society. Revolutionary options or radical social changes affecting women's lives did not become a part of the demands of the nationalist movement at any of the long struggle for independence, and a revolutionary feminist awareness did not emerge within the movement for national liberation.

Women in the nationalist struggle used no occasion to raise matters that affected them as women. Rather than liberating themselves from traditional prohibitions and bondage as Mazumdar says, "the women's roles within the family as wives, daughters and mothers were restressed or extended to be in tune with the requirements of the family in a changing society". (Mazumdar '76 : 63). Thus, while Indian women were to take part in all stages of the movement for national independence, they did so in a way which was acceptable to, and dictated by, the male leaders and which matched the existing ideology on the status of women. As Mies has pointed out,

> "To draw women into the political struggle is a tactical necessity to any anti-colonial or national liberation struggle. But it depends on the strategic goals of such a movement whether the patriarchal family is protected as the basic social unit or not. The fact that the women themselves accepted their limited tactical function within the independence movement made them excellent instruments in the struggle. But they did not work out a strategy for their own liberation or struggle for their own interests. By subordinating these goals to the national cause they confronted to the traditional pativrata or sati ideal of the self-sacrificing woman."[36]

Nevertheless the instances of women's participation in a terrorist manner in political struggles as well as their involvement in strikes and working-class agitations and peasant rebellion (including the Telengana struggles in the early 1950's) show that Indian women, over a long period, have played an important role in both the anti-imperialist and the anti-capitalist protest movements. In contrast to the traditional protest, ideal of womanhood propagated in several ways even today, Indian women have another tradition of courageous activity in movements for social and political change.

Gandhi on Women

"Woman has been suppressed under custom and law for which man was responsible and in the shaping of which she had no hand. In a plan of life based on non-violence, woman has as much right to shape her own destiny as man has to shape his. But as every right in a non-violent society proceeds from the previous performance of a duty, it follows that rules of social conduct must be framed by mutual cooperation and consultation. They can never be imposed from outside. Men have not realized this truth in its fulness in their behaviour towards women. They have considered themselves to be lords and masters of women instead of considering them as their friends and co-workers. Women are in the position somewhat of the slave of old who did not know that he could or ever had to be free. And when freedom came, for the moment he felt helpless. Women have been taught to regard themselves as slaves of men. It is up to Congressmen to see that they enable them to realize their full status and play their part as equals of men.

This revolution is easy, if the mind is made up. Let Congressmen begin with their own homes. Wives should not be dolls and objects of indulgence, but should be treated as honoured comrades in common service. To this end those who have not received a liberal education should receive such instructions as is possible from their husbands. The same observation applies, with the necessary changes, to mothers and daughters.

It is hardly necessary to point out that I have given a one-sided picture of the helpless state of India's women. I am quite conscious of the fact that in the villages generally they hold their own with their men folk and in some respects even rule them. But to the impartial outsider, the legal and customary status of woman is bad enough throughout and demands radical alternation."[37]

"Legislation has been mostly the handiwork of men; and man has not always been fair and discriminating in performing that self-appointed task. The largest part of our effort, in promoting the regeneration of women, should be directed towards removing those blemishes which are represented in our *Shastras* as the necessary and ingrained characteristics of women. Who will attempt this and how ? In my humble opinion, in order to make the attempt we will have to produce women, pure, firm and self-controlled as

Sita, Damayanti and Draupadi. If we do produce them, such modern sisters will have the same authority as the *Shastras.* We will feel ashamed of the stray reflections on them in our *Smritis,* and will soon forget them. Such revolutions have occurred in Hinduism in the past, and will still take place in the future, leading to the stability of our faith."[38]

"Woman is the companion of man, gifted with equal mental capacities. She has the right to participate in every minute detail in the activities of man and she has an equal right of freedom and liberty with him. She is entitled to a supreme place in her own share of activity as man is in his. This ought to be the natural condition of things and not as a result only of learning to read and write. By sheer force of a vicious custom, even the most ignorant and worthless men have been enjoying a superiority over women which they do not deserve and ought not to have. Many of our movements stop halfway because of the conditions of our women. Much of our work done does not yield appropriate results; our lot is like that of the penny-wise and pound-foolish trader who does not employ enough capital in his business."[39]

Equality of Sexes

"I am uncompromising in the matter of women's rights. In my opinion she should labour under no legal disability not suffered by men. I should treat the daughters and sons on a footing of perfect equality."[40]

Marriage

"A large part of the miseries of today can be avoided, if we look at the relations between the sexes in a healthy and pure light, and regard ourselves as trustees for the moral welfare of the future generations."[41]

"Marriage is a natural thing in life, and to consider it derogatory in any sense is wrong . . . . The ideal is to look upon marriage as a sacrament, and therefore, to lead a life of self-restraint in the married state."[42]

The Purdah

"Chastity is not a hot-house growth. It cannot be protected by the surrounding wall of the purdah. It must grow from within, and to be worth anything it must be capable of withstanding every unsought temptation."[43]

"And why is there all this morbid anxiety about female purity? Have women any say in the matter of male purity? We hear nothing of women's anxiety about men's chastity. Why should men arrogate to themselves the right to regulate female purity? It cannot be superimposed from without. It is a matter of evolution from within and therefore of individual self-effort."[44]

The Dowry System

"The system has to go. Marriage must cease to be a matter of arrangement made by the parents for money. The system is intimately connected with caste. So long as the choice is restricted to a few hundred young men or young women of a particular caste, the system will persist no matter what is said against it. The girls or boys or their parents will have to break the bonds of caste if the evil is to be eradicated. All this means education of a character that will revolutionize the mentality of the youth of the nation."[45]

"Any young man who makes dowry a condition of marriage discredits his education and his country and dishonours womanhood. I wish that these movements would deal with questions of this character. Such associations often become self-adulation societies, instead of becoming, as they should be, bodies representing solid reform from within . . . . A strong public opinion should be created in condemnation of the degrading practice of dowry and young men who soil their fingers with such ill-gotten gold should be excommunicated from society. Parents of girls should cease to be dazed by English degrees and should not hesitate to travel outside their little castes and provinces to secure true, gallant young men for their daughters."[46]

Widow Re-marriage

"Voluntary widowhood consciously adopted by a woman who has felt the affection of a partner adds grace and dignity to life, sanctifies the home and uplifts religion itself. Widowhood imposed by religion or custom is an unbearable yoke and defiles the home by secret vice and degrades religion.

If we would be pure, if we would save Hinduism, we must rid ourselves of this poison of enforced widowhood.

The reform must begin by those who have girl widows taking courage in both their hands and seeing that the child widows in their charge are duly and well-married—not re-married. They were never really married."[47]

Divorce

"Marriage confirms the right of union between two partners to the exclusion of all the others when in their joint opinion they consider such union to be desirable, but it confers no right upon one partner to demand obedience of the other to one's wish for union. What should be done when one partner on moral or other grounds cannot conform to the wishes of the other is a separate question. Personally, if divorce was the only alternative, I should not hesitate to accept it, rather than interrupt my moral progress—assuming that I want to restrain myself on purely moral grounds."[48]

"For me, the married state is as much a state of discipline as any other. Life is duty, a probation. Married life is intended to promote mutual good, both here and hereafter. It is meant also to serve humanity. When one partner breaks the law of discipline, the right accrues to the other of breaking the bond. The breach here is moral and not physical. It precludes divorce. The wife or the husband separates but to serve the end for which they have united. Hinduism regards each as absolute equal of the other. No doubt a different practice has grown up, no one knows since when. But so have many other evils crept into it. This, however, I do know that Hinduism leaves the individual absolutely free to do what he or she likes for the sake of self-realization, for which and which alone he or she is born."[49]

Woman's Honour

"When a woman is assaulted she may not stop to think in terms of *himsa* or *ahimsa.* Her primary duty is self-protection. She is at liberty to employ every method or means that come to her mind in order to defend her honour. God has given her nails and teeth. She must use them with all her strength and, if need be, die in effort. The man or woman who has shed all fear of death will be able not only to protect himself and herself but others also through laying down his life."[50]

Prostitution

"Prostitution is as old as the world, but I wonder if it was ever a regular feature of town life as it is today. In any case the time must come when humanity will rise against the curse and make prostitution a thing of the past, as it has got rid of many evil customs, however time-honoured they might have been."[51]

Women's Education

"I have pointed out from time to time that there is no justification for men to deprive women or to deny them equal rights on the ground of their illiteracy; but education is essential for enabling women to uphold these natural rights, to improve them and to spread them; again, the true knowledge of self is unattainable by the millions who are without such education.

Man and woman are of equal rank but they are not identical. They are a peerless pair being supplementary to one another; each helps the other, so that without the one the existence of the othercannot be conceived, and therefore it follows as a necessary corollary from these facts that anything that will impair the status of either of them will involve the equal ruin of them both. In framing any scheme of women's education this cardinal truth must be constantly kept in mind. Man is supreme in the outward activities of a married pair and, therefore, it is in the fitness of things that he should have a greater knowledge thereof. On the other hand, home life is entirely the sphere of woman and, therefore, in domestic affairs, in the upbringing and education of children, women ought to have more knowledge. Not that knowledge should be divided into watertight compartments, or that some branches of knowledge should be closed to any one; but unless courses of instruction are based on a discriminating appreciation of these basic principles, the fullest life of man and woman cannot be developed."

Jawaharlal Nehru on Women

"Most of us menfolk were in prison. And then a remarkable thing happened. Our women came to the front and took charge of the struggle. Women had always been there of course, but now there was an avalanche of them, which took not only the British Government but their own menfolk by surprise. Here were these women, women of the upper or middle classes, leading sheltered lives in their homes, peasant women, working-class women, rich women, poor women, pouring out in their tens of thousands in defiance of government order and police *lathi.* It was not only that display of courage and daring, but what was even more surprising was the organisational power they showed.

Never can I forget the thrill that came to us in Naini Prison when news of this reached us, the enormous pride in the women of India that filled us. We would hardly talk about all this among ourselves for our hearts were full and our eyes were dim with tears."[52]

(From Jawaharlal Nehru, *The Discovery of India*).

"The lot of our womenfolk in prison was especially hard and painful to contemplate. They were mostly middle-class women, accustomed to a sheltered life, and suffering chiefly from the many repressions and customs produced by a society dominated to his own advantage by man. The call of freedom had always a double meaning for them, and the enthusiasm and energy with which they threw themselves into the struggle had no doubt their springs in the vague and hardly conscious, but nevertheless intense, desire to rid themselves of domestic slavery also. Excepting a very few, they were classed as ordinary prisoners and placed with the most degraded of companions, and often under horrid conditions. I was once lodged in a barrack next to a female enclosure, a wall separating us. In that enclosure there were, besides other convicts, some women political prisoners, including the one who had been my hostess and in whose house I had once stayed. A high wall separated us, but it did not prevent me from listening in horror to the language and curses which our friends had to put up with from the women convict warders.'[53]

Call to Rebel

"A great French idealist, Charles Fourier once said : "One could judge the degree of civilisation of a country by the social and political position of its women". And if we are to judge India today, we shall have to judge her by her women.

The future that we build up will also be judged by the position of Indian women. I must confess to you that I am intensely dissatisfied with a lot of the Indian women today. We hear a good deal about Sita and Savitri. They are revered names in India and rightly so. But I have a feeling that these echoes from the past are raised chiefly to hide our present deficiencies and to prevent us from attacking the root cause of women's degradation in India today.

I find from a reference to a report of this institution that it was started to give special instruction to women. It was laid down that while man was the bread-winner, woman's place was in the home and her ideal should be that of a devoted wife and nothing more. Her chief delight should be in skilfully rearing her children and serving her revered elders. May I say that I do not agree with this ideal of women's life or education? What does it signify? It means that woman has one profession and one only, that is the profession of marriage and it is our chief business to train her for this profession. Even in this profession her lot is to be of secondary importance. She is always to be of secondary importance. She is always to be the devoted help-mate, the follower and the obedient slave of her husband and others. I wonder if any of you here has read Ibsen's "Doll's House"; if so, you will perhaps appreciate the word "doll" when I use it in this connection.

The future of India cannot consist of dolls and playthings and if you made half the population of a country a mere plaything of the other half, an encumbrance on others, how will you ever make progress? Therefore I say that you must face the problem boldly and attack the roots of evils. We have *purdah* and child marriage and denial of rights to women in so many fields. Go to any country and you will see bright-faced boys and girls playing and growing strong in mind and body. Here children of the same age are kept in *purdah,* locked up in cages almost, and denied in a large measure all freedom. They are married just when they should be growing physically and intellectually and are thus stunted and made miserable for life.

If this Vidyapitha really stands for the progress of our women, it must attack these evil customs. But I should like to remind the women present here that no people, no group, no community, no country, has ever got rid of its disabilities by the generosity of the oppressor.

India will not be free until we are strong enough to force our will on England and the women of India will not attain their full rights by the mere generosity of the men of India. They will have to fight for them and force their will on the menfolk before they can succeed.

I hope therefore that this Vidyapitha will be instrumental in sending out, into the provinces and the country, women who are rebels against the unjust and tyrannical social customs of the day and who will fight all who oppose this progress; women who are as much soldiers of the country as the best men."[54]

Economic Bondage of Indian Women

Social reform legislation is fine and to be worked for and welcomed. But all the good legislation in the world will not render a man or woman an independent agent so long as he or she is economically dependent. It is this economic bondage, the root cause of the problems of the Indian woman and our energies must be directed. The joint family system of the Hindus, a relic of a feudal age, absolutely out of keeping with modern conditions, must go and so also many other customs and traditions. But the final solution lies only in a complete refashioning of our society.[55]

References

1. Suktankar quoted in Asthana '74:8.
2. Mazumdar '76 : 49.
3. Mazumdar : 76 : 43.
4. Omvedt : 75 : 46.
5. Krishna Basu : '78 : 41-2.
6. Mazumdar : '76 : 52.
7. Krisna Basu : '78 : 46-47.
8. Krishna Basu : '78 : 46-47 & 50.
9. Asthana : '74 : 27.
10. Everett : '79 : 55.
11. Mazumdar : '76 : 49-50 emphasis added.
12. Asthana : '74 : 135.
13. Asthana : '74 : 135-37.
14. Mazumdar : '76 : 53.
15. Asthana : '74 : 54-55.

16. Mies : '80, 117.
17. Everett : '79 : 45.
18. Asthana : '74 : 50-51.
19. Desai : '57 : 123-24.
20. Bhatty : '76 : 101 and 107.
21. Desai : '57 : 112.
22. Everett : '79 : 63.
23. Everett : '79 : 54.
24. Everett : '79 : 57.
25. Mazumdar : '76 : 56 and 59.
26. Mies : '80 : 126.
27. Mies : '80 : 127.
28. Gandhi quoted in Mies : '80 : 125.
29. Everett : '79 : 76.
30. Everett : '79 : 76.
31. Luthra : '76 : 5 and 3.
32. Aparna Basu : '76 : 24, 29-30.
33. Kulke : '74 : 210-11 and Nanavutty : '76 : 78-79 and 89)
34. Overstreet and Windmiller : '59 ; 235.
35. Overstreet and Windmiller : '59 : 235.
36. Mies : '80 : 121.
37. *Constructive Programme,* pp. 17-18.
38. *Speeches and Writings of Mahatma Gandhi,* p. 424.
39. *Speeches and Writings of Mahatma,* p. 425.
40. *Young India,* 17-10-'29.
41. *Young India,* 27-9-'28.
42. *Harijan,* 22-3-'42.
43. *Young India,* 3-2-'27.
44. *Young India,* 25-11-'26.
45. *Harijan,* 23.5.'36.
46. *Young India,* 21-6-'28.
47. *Young India,* 5-8-'26.
48. *Young India,* 8-10-'25
49. Young India, 21-10-'26.
50. *Harijan,* 1-3-'42.
51. *Young India,* 28-5-'25.
52. From Jawaharlal Nehru, *"The Discovery of India."*
53. From Jawaharlal Nehru, *An Autobiography.*
54. From a speech at the foundation-stone laying of the Mahila Vidyapitha, Allahabad, 31 March 1928.
55. From a review of Katherine Mayo's *'Slaves of the God'*, in *The Bombay Chronicle,* 25 April 1929.

3

Movement for Emancipation

The retirement of women through *Purdah,* the existence of child-marriage, and the custom of *Sati* had reduced women to a deplorable state in which education was no longer considered necessary. "The devices which were often justified as ways of protecting a woman, rapidly became the instruments of her degradation."

"A true reformer has not to write upon a clean slate, his work is more often to complete the half-written sentence. We cannot break with the past altogether for it is a rich inheritance and we have no reason to be ashamed of it. But while respecting the past we must ever seek to correct the practical growths that have encrusted it." From a wide view of the social reform movement in India, during the last 150 years, one important factor clearly emerges: the impact of foreign rule in India. The introduction of English education influenced powerfully the minds of educated Indians and sowed the seeds of logic and scientific approach to life. The principle of social equality, and the theory of providing equal opportunities to all classes of society to make their economic development influenced the thoughts and ideology of literate Indians. In the light of this fresh ideology, educated India started to examine the Hindu social framework, religion, custom and conventions. It is this enquiry that created the modern movement of social reform, which became a distinct entity with the work of Raja Ram Mohan Roy in 1825-33.

Abolition of Sati, 1829

The most notorious of the customs concerning women was *Sati* (the original term for a loyal wife). The self-immolation by widow on the funeral pyres of their husbands was common in Bengal. Over the centuries this particular exhibition of faithfulness had become accepted as a certain path to salvation, both for the widow and her deceased husband. Behind the questionable religious approval lie social and ethical factors. Indian males have traditionally found it hard to believe that any widow (as young as many of them were) could stay alone and remain pure and chaste. Besides, there clouded the very real problem of a "useless mouth" for the family to feed, in a society where single women had no status or occupation. May scholars deny existence of the *Sati* in Vedic times. Nehru asserted that early Sanskrit literature denounced the usage. Akbar the Great said of *Sati* : "It is a strange commentary on the magnanimity of men that they should seek their deliverance through the self-sacrifice of their wives."

The earliest European authorities in India were less scrupulous than the subsequent British to attempt outright suppression of this terrible practice. The Portuguese, the Jesuits under St. Francis Xavier, the Danes, the Dutch, the French and some British sought to inhibit the practice in their areas. By the turn of the nineteenth century, the presence of the Serampore missionaries in Bengal and their embarrassingly open reports to England had pricked the British conscience. In 1803, Williams Carey, the Baptist missionary at Serampore, had conducted a census of *Sati* cases within a radius of 30 miles from Calcutta and presented the figures before Governor-General Lord Wellesley, but the Government took no action. Meanwhile, William Carey and his colleagues delved deeply into Hindu classic and arrived the positive conclusion that Sati was mentioned but by no means commanded in the Hindu writs.

Ram Mohan Roy was the one man among Indians who brought about the suppression of *Sati* and made the forces move which led to the correction of plenty of these social evils. Although he must have seen many *Sati* cases, his opposition was crystallized in 1811, when he witnessed his own sister-in-law hushed onto his brother's funeral pyre, "a hysterical and unhappy sacrifice." His formal campaign commenced with a petition in 1818, announced that the use of force in throwing preys back on the fire, or even threats or sentimental coercion, composed "murders according to every *shastra* (religious law), as well as the common sense of all nations." He further stated that selfish economic inspiration, the will to avoid sharing a dead man's possession with his widow, often instigated complicity in the act.

His tract, and others that followed, inquired still deeper into psychological analysis of this practice. He argued, "It assumes the intellectual inferiority of women and their complete dependence on husband and family. It accuses women of a lack of resolution, when relatives apply undue persuasion or forcibly assist the victim to adhere to her voluntary resolve. It brands women as untrustworthy and implies that they are more subject than men to sexual passions." Roy upheld William Carey's contention that the scriptures did not consider such sacrifice as a religious duty; on the contrary, he announced, it required a pious and chaste life. So influential were his pamphlets, his individual pursuit, and his on-the-spot protests that a batch of distinguished Hindus in Calcutta submitted a petition to the government in 1819, echoing Roy's statements.

The Directors of the Company in London were distressed by the appeals from Carey, Roy and the Governor-General. In 1828, Lord William Bentinck became the Governor-General in India and a new era commenced. Lord Bentinck was looking for an opportunity to move against *Sati.* He considered *Sati* as grossly immoral and revolting to humanity, but he required evidence that *Sati* was not prescribed by Hindu scripture and that immediate abolition would not create bitter revolt. The first assurance he accepted from Carey and Roy; the second no one could guarantee.

The Minute on *Sati* (November 8, 1829) which prepared the road for legal action was a moving document, because it disclosed so clearly the inner wrestling of conscience. Lord Bentinck reported that four out of the five Hindu Judges had recommended immediate ban. Lord Bentinck wrote in the famous Minute on *Sati:*

> To consent to the consignment, year after year, of hundreds of innocent victims to a cruel and untimely end, when the power exists of preventing it, is a predicament which no conscience can contemplate without horror . . . But . . . to put to hazard, by a contrary course, the very safety of the British Empire in India . . . may be considered as a still greater evil . . .
>
> The first and primary object of my heart is the benefit of the Hindus. I know nothing so important to the improvement of their future condition, as the establishment of purer morality, whatever their belief, and a more just conception of the will of God. The first step to this better understanding

> will be disassociation of religious belief and practice from blood and murder . . . . when they shall have been convinced of the error of this first and most criminal of their customs, may it not be hoped that others which stand in the way of their improvement may likewise pass away, and that thus emancipated from those chains and shackles upon their minds and actions, they may no longer continue, as they have done, the slaves of every foreign conqueror, but that they may assume their just places among the great families of mankind.

The famous Resolution No. 17 issued by Lord Bentinck on December 4, 1829, created a new age for Indian women. The regulation not only prohibited *Sati* unconditionally, but also branded as companion in killing any collaborators who might help a widow in her self-immolation. The Constitution reaffirmed two basic positions involved in the long and constant controversy. First it declared that

> . . . the practice of Sati, or of burning or burying alive the widows of Hindus, is revolting to the feelings of human nature; it is nowhere enjoined by the religion of the Hindus as an imperative duty; on the contrary, a life of purity and retirement on the part of the widow is more especially and preferably inculcated....
>
> (Therefore) The Governor-General in Council, without intending to depart from one of the first and most important principles of the system of the Government of India, that all classes of the people be secure in the observance of their religious usages so long as that system can be adhered to without violation of the paramount dictates of justice and humanity, has deemed it right to establish (these rules prohibiting the practice of Sati).

Conservative Hindu remarshalled their debates and in England an English advocate demanded for repeal of Bentinck's Resolution, on the ground that it gratified only a few Christians and that suicide was no worse than officially favoured idolatry. To such fatuous arguments one might repeat the answer of Sir Charles Napier, when a Brahmin considered *Sati* as a national custom: "My nation also has a custom. When men burn women alive, we hang them.... Let us all act according to national custom."

Raja Ram Mohan Roy's contribution was great, for he strengthened the hand of the Governor-General in India and worked almost alone to block the requested repeal in England. But the encouragement and active support of the missionaries, especially William Carey is also unforgettable. Thus, a partnership across differences of race and caste, terminated the hysterical practice of *Sati* and set the way for the emancipation of Indian females.

TABLE 1
Statistics for the Years 1815-1828 Showed the Following Figures for Satis in Bengal

Year	*No. of Satis*	*Year*	*No. of Satis*
1815	378	1822	583
1816	442	1823	575
1817	707	1824	572
1818	839	1825	639
1819	650	1826	518
1820	598	1827	517
1821	654	1828	463

Enquiries were made to find out which regions were the worst affected and statistics were collected. In Bengal the British were in a favourable position to collect reliable data.

Source: P. Thomas, *Indian Women Through the Ages* (New York: Asia Publishing House, 1964), p. 293.

Widow Remarriage Act, 1856

When *Sati* was abolished by law in 1829, the widow persecution became an avowed social custom among certain castes and communities. The death of her husband was regarded as proof of her crime and to help her expiate it, in many Indian states there developed a curious proceeding of routine persecution. Since, as a rule, she lived in the house of her deceased husband, her life was made all the more miserable. The mother-in-law could only consider her as the virtual murderer of her son who would not have expired, as per the then prevailing interpretation of the law of KARMA, had his wife been virtuous. Hence the widow was prohibited to appear happy or wear bright clothes or jewellery. The had to drudge day and night and was the prey of all sorts of insolence by other domestic women. The tragedy became more poignant when the widow was a child, as very often happened.

A natural result of the abolition of *Sati* was the recognition of the right of the widow to remarry. But the British were reluctant to take the initiative. "The suffering of the living was less spectacular than the agony of the burning widow," and the British Government desired to treat the issue of widow remarriage as a purely social affair to be decided by Hindus themselves. Luckily, enlightened Hindu public opinion had made enough leeway to make legislation in this direction possible.

Of the many Indians who advocated the cause of the widow during this age, the most significant was Ishwar Chandra Vidyasagar who, like Raja Ram Mohan Roy, came from Bengal. The main hurdle against widow remarriage, according to the orthodox viewpoint, was its disapproval by the Hindu law-givers. In 1855, Vidyasagar, principal of the Sanskrit College, Calcutta; published a document entitled *Remarriage of Hindu Widows* quoting various stanzas from Hindu scriptures sanctioning widow remarriage and requested for legislation in its support.

The learned Hindu pundits condemned the pamphlet and its writer. They maintained that the permission for widow remarriage was meant for the bygone golden period having men good and women virtuous, but not for the present age with its evil men and unchaste women. They pressurised Vidyasagar to desist, but failed: He presented a petition to the British Government demanding legislation on this issue.

The British, after much consideration, decided to legislate in support of widow remarriage. In November 1855, the Honourable J.P. Grant, member of the Legislative Council, produced a Bill "to remove all legal obstacles to the marriage of Hindu widows." There were forty petitions signed by 60,000 people opposing the proposed legislation, and twenty-five petitions bearing 5,000 signatures in its favour. Despite this overwhelming opposition, the measure was adopted and passed into law on July 25, 1856. The constitution of the Act thus explained:

> Whereas it is known that by the law as administered in the civil courts established in the territories under the Government of the East India Company, Hindu widows with certain exceptions are held to be, by reason of their having been once married, incapable of contracting a valid second marriage, and the offspring of such widows by any second marriage are held to be illegitimate and incapable of inheriting property, and whereas many Hindus believe that this imputed legal incapacity, although it is in accordance with established custom, is not in accordance with the dictates of their own

conscience, and whereas it is just to relieve all such Hindus from this legal incapacity of which they complain, and the removal of all legal obstacles to the marriage of Hindu widows, will tend to the promotion of good morals and to the public welfare . . . For obvious causes, while legislation for *Sati* was influential, the Hindu Widow Remarriage Act remained a dead document for a long time. *Sati* could be prevented by police, but policemen could not arrange the remarriage of the Hindu widows. The law said to the widow "You may marry," but the caste said "You shall not;" and caste won for a long time. Though some organizations such as the *Brahmo Samaj* and *Arya Samaj* actively favoured widow remarriage, and a Widow Remarriage Society was even framed to function as a marriage bureau for widows, so deep-rooted was the prejudice at that time that even the most vociferous lawyers of the reform often evaded the subject when it touched their homes. A famous exception was the son of Vidyasagar who married a widow.

In the census of 1881, the number of Hindu widow stood at 2.1 million and reformers started to despair. The futility of sheer legislation to promote widow remarriage was blank to every reformer. In August 1884, Mr. Malabari, a leading citizen of Bombay, sent a note to the Government illustrating the failure of the Widow Remarriage Act of 1856. He emphasised the opposition of the orthodox Hindus and the general disabilities of ladies, which stopped widows from utilising the law, and the need for doing something positive on the issue. Mr. Malabari had dedicated his life to the rise of Indian women, but he was a follower of Zoroastrian religion and, as such, was not regarded competent to prescribe legislation for the Hindus. So the British Government decided to defer action "until sufficient proof is forthcoming that legislation has been asked for by a section of the Hindu community itself."

It is now over a century since the Act was passed, but widow remarriages are hardly celebrated among orthodox Hindus. Though routine persecutions and humiliations have been deserted widow remarriage is still considered among the Hindus as sullying the memory of the deceased man. "Further, the feeling that the widow is second-hand goods is so strong in India that even old widowers are reluctant to marry widows, when virgins are readily available." How little development legislation had been able to achieve in the matter of widow remarriage, can best be seen from the following table for widows under twenty-five years of age in the census of 1931, the first taken after the promulgation of the ban of child marriage by the Act of 1929:

TABLE 2
Widows Under Twenty Five Years of Age

Age Group	*No. of Widows*	*Age Group*	*No. of Widow*
0-1	1,515	5-10	105,449
1-2	1,785	10-15	183,998
2-3	3,485	15-20	514,394
3-4	9,076	20-25	846,959
4-5	15,018		

Source: P. Thomas, *Indian Women Through the Ages* (New York: Asia Publishing House, 1964), p. 301.

Widowhood was living death, and the strictures imposed upon her made her virtually passive. These severe bans were not by society only,but even some orthodox religious communities imposed strictures on them. Following is a pronouncement of the *'Bhakti Society'* on the action of widows : (From the *Shiksha Patri* (Epistle of Precepts) of Swami Nayarana, See Chapter II.)

> Widow shall serve the Lord Krishna with minds intent on Him as their only husband, and they shall live under the control of their father or other male members of their family, and never in independence. They shall never touch at any time any men except nearest relations, and when young they shall never without necessity engage in conversation with youngmen. If any infant male child touches them no blame attaches to them any more than from contact with a dumb animal, nor if they are compelled from necessity to talk with or touch an old man. They shall never receive instructions of any kind from any men except their nearest relations, and they shall often mortify their flesh by vows and fasts. They shall never give away to others the money required for their own support and they may give away only that which is in excess. They shall eat only one meal a day and shall sleep on the ground. They shall never look at animals engaged in the sexual act. Widows shall never dress like married women, nor like a female ascetic, nor like a mendicant nor in any unbecoming attire . . .

They shall never join in the frolics practiced at the Holi festival, nor shall they put on ornaments or finely woven clothes composed of cotton or metal threads.

The future of a man marrying a widow is marked with great fears; he is expelled from his society and besides, other people coming in contact with him, would be expelled too. This is exhibited in the following document in which a high caste Hindu is expelled for marrying a widow.

A proclamation of Caste Excommunication by the Kapole Banyas Against Madhowdas Rugnathdas for his marriage to a widow, issued May 14, 1871 in Bombay.

1. That as the custom of widow remarriage is not in our caste, and as such remarriage is contrary to the prevailing practice of our caste, and is opposed to what we conscientiously believe to be the law enjoined by our religious *Shastras,* the said Madhowdas Rugnathdas having married the said widow, Dhunkorebai, they have rendered themselves ineligible for such social intercourse as that of eating and drinking with the caste, and of giving and receiving in marriage. Therefore, no member of the caste shall hold such intercourse with them.
2. That if any member of the Kapole caste will eat or drink with the said Madhowdas Rugnathdas or Bai Dhunkore, or hold such intercourse with them as that of giving and receiving in marriage, such member renders himself equally ineligible for holding such intercourse with the caste, and no such intercourse shall be held with him.
3. That if it be proved hereafter that any member or members of our caste had aided, or taken part in, the remarriage of Madhowdas Rugnathdas with Dhunkorebai, the caste shall not hold with such member or members any such intercourse as it stated above. (Story of a Widow Remarriage, p. 54.)

The Age of Consent, 1891

One of the main causes for child-marriage, championed by subsequent law-givers of the Hindus, was that the fertile age of a woman should not be permitted to be wasted.

In post-vedic literature and in the earlier codes, pre-puberty marriage is not insisted and modern scholars are divided in their viewpoint about the antiquity of child-marriage in India. According to the law-giver Marichi, "a father who gives in marriage a girl of eight goes to heaven, the giver of a girl of nine, Vaikunta; one who gives his daughter in marriage before he attains the age of ten attains the heaven of Brahma. But the father of a girl married after puberty goes to hell." While the ceiling on marriageable age was thus set, the no minimum was mentioned, and even infants were married. At first these injunctions were followed only by the Brahmins, but gradually other castes followed them. The two reformers Beramji Malabari and Mahadev Govind Ranade of Bombay sought to achieve legislation against child-marriages, and succeeded in raising the age of consent from 10 years to 12 in 1891, the last reform in India effected by influencing English viewpoint either by officials in India or public protest in England. The British government became very conservative and reluctant to move in social issues after the passing of the Age of Consent in 1891 because over this subject even the reformers had different opinions. Many reformers like Bal Gangadhar Tilak insisted that "no alien government had the right to interfere with the customs of the people, however worthy the cause."

While the sheer formality of a marriage ceremony could not be opposed to by a government forsworn to non-intervention in the religious observances of their subjects, the torture of child-wives by sadists could reasonably come within the boundary of criminal law. Also about 1891, the attention of the Government and the people was directed to various cases in Bengal where girls of tender age either died or were mutilated, and then it was proposed to raise the age of consent within marriage from ten to twelve. This proposal was widely objected to throughout India, but both the Government and enlightened public viewpoint took a determined stand and the Bill was passed. Sir Andrew Scoble, the sponsor of the Bill, met the objections raised on the ground of religious neutrality by announcing that it was the right and duty of the state to intervene for saving of any class of subjects where a proved necessity emerged.

Child-marriage did not end immediately after the Act was passed as it took more time for the general public to witness the evils of this custom; yet a solid beginning had been made. The literate higher classes disliked the marriage of girls till about the age of fifteen or sixteen but the child-marriages were still much prevalent in the villages.

The Sarda Act (Prohibition of Child-Marriage Act), 1929

A legislative measure of far-reaching significance in the matter of the emancipation of Indian females was the passing of the Act banning child-marriage in 1929. Since Rao Bahadur Harbilas Sarda sponsored the Bill, it is popularly called the 'Sarda Act'. The Act, passed by the central legislative assembly in September 1929, became law on April 1, 1930. It represented a legislative effort to deal with the problem of child-marriage. The main provision of the Act was that "marriage of a male under 18 or a female under 14 years of age constituted a penal crime punishable with fine and imprisonment." Hindu emotion accept the prohibition, which was strengthened by the support provided to the Act by women all over the country. But Moselm agitation adopted a strange virulent form. "It is a well-known fact that, particularly among Moslems, the immediate result of the knowledge that an Act was about to be passed prohibiting child-marriage, was the celebration, before it was given effect, of a very large number of child-marriages which would otherwise have been performed later."

Protests came from other areas also parents apprehended that they would have their daughters longer on their hands and would be unable to get them married. There was chance of their getting into problem. They would have to be kept out of mischief, and learning as a means of securing this increased expenditure. Others felt scared that the postponement of marriage would increase their difficulties in finding matches for their daughters.

Deeply-rooted practices of old standing are not merely by legislation. Social reformers, women's organization and political leaders like Gandhi had to labour to eradicate this practice. As a consequence of this Act, there was a decided in increase the percentage of girls attending school. The Sarda Act was passed just one hundred years after the practice of *Sati* had been decreed illegal, and thus marks an epoch in the liberation of Indian women. But the passing of the Act did not in itself achieve that goal : along with it must go much strenuous attempt for education and enlightenment.

Female education made a great stride in 1929. There was a marvelous increase of forty per cent in the number of girls attending high schools in Bengal. Certainly one factor in this increase was the Sarda Act itself.

Rise of Indian Nationalism

Nationalism is a complex term, involving all those factors past, present, and future which provide solidarity to a batch of people residing on a compact territory. It implies "a community of ideas, ideals and beliefs which is consummated by two conditions which must be present, viz., location or common territory and government of common loyalties to a political ideal and organization." Even the concept of nationalism indicates a psychological experience which emphasises the loyalty of the individual to the nation state. The particular background against which the Indian National Movements arose, was essentially a result of the British rule in India. These forces were mainly responsible for arousing in the Indian people the emotions of nationalism, ultimately producing the emergence of many reform movements in fast succession during the nineteenth century. These movements were, "the first national breaches in the fortress of medievalism and the declaration, in social reform-language, that the modern Indian nation was born and was growing." The first effect of the modern western culture practised a rejuvenating influence on the Indian community, for it unleashed those flows of logical and liberal thought which ultimately led to her remarkable renaissance of the modern ages.

Call for independence brought women out of the four walls of their homes. Freedom movement brought a change in the lives of many a woman and early decades of twentieth century saw change in status of Indian woman what otherwise would have taken centuries to achieve.

Women were seen rubbing shoulders with men in an attempt to overthrow the British rule. They were willing to go to jail, donated all they had, picketed here and there. It was a freedom struggling going on but it was also a celebration time for Indian womanhood. This movementt hastened the process of woman liberation.

4

Active Role in Freedom Movement

"The women of India should have as much share in winning *Swaraj* as men. Probably in this peaceful struggle woman can outdistance man by many a mile. We know that a woman is any day superior to man in her religious devotion. Silent and dignified suffering is the badge of her sex. And now that the government have dragged the woman into the line of fire, I hope that the women all over India will take up the challenge and organize themselves,"[1] Mahatma Gandhi appealed in to the Indian women to enter the struggle for India's freedom. "If nonviolence is the law of our being, the future is with woman."[2] "If Indian women arose, he said, "no one could prevent the country's march to independence." Only with the advent of the Gandhian age, females really played any important role in nationalist politics. Women had already started playing a role before 1919.

From the very inception of the Indian National Congress, its membership was welcome to women. At its first session Allan Octavian Hume asked political reformers "of all shades of opinion" never to forget that "unless the elevation of the female element of the nation proceeds *pari passu* (with an equal pace) with their work, all their labour for the political enfranchisement of the country will prove vain."[3] Ten women attended the fourth session of the Congress at Bombay in 1889. Like the males, females participated from Calcutta and Bombay including Swarnakumari Devi, sister of Rabindranath Tagore. She had abandoned *purdah* and together with her husband, edited the Bengali journal, *Bharati,* having thus achieved the name of being the first Indian woman editor. Swarnakumari began "Sakhi Samiti" (Ladies Association) to infuse among Indian women an active and enlightened interest in country's welfare.[4] From

Bengal, also came Kadambini Ganguli, a graduate of Kolkata University and the first woman doctor from Bengal. Other women included Pandit Ramabai, Mrs. Shevantibai Trimbak, Mrs. Shantabai Nikambe, Mrs. Kashibai Kanitkar and Miss Manekjee Cursetjee, and they developed into famous educationists and social reformers. There were Hindu, Brahmo, Parsi and Christian ladies representatives. Pandit Ramabai represented the Arya Mahila Samaj, Poona. Swarnakumari Devi were selected to represent the Bengal Ladies Association. Swarnakumari Devi and Kadambini Ganguli attended the Congress session as delegates in 1890. The latter had the honour of being the first woman to speak from the Congress platform when she proposed a vote of thanks to the President, Pherozeshah Mehta. Saraladevi Chaudhurani, daughter of Swarnakumari, who had to play an active role in the nationalist movement in the coming years, composed a song inspiring the people of different provinces of the country to join the freedom struggle and trained a group of over fifty girls to sing it in chorus at the Congress Session in 1901. The proceedings of the 1902 session of the Congress at Ahmedabad started with the singing of the National Anthem by Lady Vidyagauri Nilkanth and her sister Sharda Mehta.[5] I mention this with particular pride.

II

Partition of Bengal

The partition of Bengal, fostered a new spirit of patriotism. In September 1905, Rabindranath Tagore declared his strategy for observing "rakhi-bandhan" on the "partition day," 16 October, and women participated in this. Another rite observed on the "partition day" was *arandhan,* suggested by Romendrasundar Trivedi, asking women not to useful for cooking that day. Protest meetings were convened by women and about five hundred of them witnessed the laying of the foundation-stone of the Federation Hall at Calcutta on 16 October 1905. On the same day, Romendrasundar Trivedi's *Benga-Lakshmir Brata-Katha* was recited before a widely attended meeting of ladies in Janikandi in Murshidabad district. Women organized *Swadeshi* fairs and Saraladevi Chaudhurani opened "Lakshmir Bhandar" selling only indigenous articles, gave up use of foreign cloth and smashed their foreign bangles. Bipin Chandra Pal addressed ladies meetings during his tour of Eastern Bengal in February 1907, and the women of Tangail gave a grand feast to Surendranath Banerjee on his visit to Mymensingh later that year. A ladies meeting was convened August 1907 at the house of the famous physician and a *Swadeshi* enthusiast, Dr. Nilratan Sircar, to respect Bhupendranath Dutta's mother and various women in Barisal offered their savings to the "Swadesh Bandhab Samiti."[6]

Women helped in distributing revolutionary pamphlets and literature and in maintaining connections between different revolutionary leaders. Sister Nivedita was a great source of motivation to many young men and women. Mrs. Ramsay McDonald, who accompanied her husband in his tour of India, visualised that the *Swadeshi* movement could not have succeeded without the female assistance some of whom "do not know how to read or write, but in spite of this the *Swadeshi* movement is spreading very much in the places where one would hardly think there would be an opportunity for its growth."[7] But still the female participation was limited. There were no women leaders.[8] Girls were not included in the *samitis* or volunteer movement and the existing ideology of the period was still too conservative to permit women to participate on equal basis with men. Sarojini Naidu was the first Indian lady to make politics her full-time profession. Born in a scholarly family, daughter of a scientist, legend in the refinements of Hyderabad culture, educated at Cambridge, a poetess and literary legend, she was drawn into the vortex of politics. Gopal Krishna Gokhale was her political "guru" till his death in 1915 and he encouraged her to join the Congress. At the 1906 Congress session Sarojini's oratory coupled with her young looks, charmed the audience. In December 1915 at the Bombay session, as a delegate from the Union Provinces, she favoured a resolution on self-government. As a member of the Home Rule League, she led a deputation of women to England, members of it were Annie Besant, Mrs. Herabai Ardeshir Tata and Miss Mithan Ardeshir Tata. The delegation waited upon the Secretary of State, Edwin Montagu, and presented a memorandum proposing for female voting rights.

But a few women here and there was an exception. Actually the women were still not active enough in Indian politics during the first two decades of this century.

Gandhi provided a new direction, courage and motivation to the freedom movement and drew into it females in large numbers. In South Africa, his *Satyagraha* "army" included woman Justice Searle of the Cape Town Supreme Court, had delivered the judgement, announcing only those marriages legal, celebrated according to Christian rights and registered by the Registrar of Marriage, a challenge to Indian women and under the leadership of Gandhi they joined the *Satyagraha* struggle. Gandhiji first sent a party of sixteen, including Kasturba, from Phoneix Settlement in Natal to the Transvaal. After a few days a batch of eleven ladies from Tolstoy Farm in the Transvaal crossed into Natal with no permits and were arrested. The coal miners marching to Charlestown consisted of 127 women. Most of these women, were arrested and ill-treated in prison. One of them, a sixteen-year-old girl, Valliamah Moonsamy Moodaliar came out of prison with a fatal temperature and died soon afterwards.[9]

With his experience of South Africa behind him, Gandhi was conscious of the female potentialities as passive resisters. As he experimented with his weapon of *Satyagraha* in India, he felt that women could take part in it together with men. During the textile mill-workers' strike in Ahmedabad, his chief lieutenant was Ansuyabehn, the sister of the textile magnate, Ambalal Sarabhai. Women were drawn to Gandhi by his magnetic personality, his distinctive naturalness and transparent sincerity. Addressing public meetings in various parts of the country, he appealed to women to donate their ornaments for the national cause and help him to arrange collections for the *Tilak Swaraj* Fund. He compared British rule to *Ravana-rajya* and stated that as Sita did not cooperate with Ravana, so the Indian people must not cooperate with this *Rakshasi-Sarkar.*[10] He told the Indian women that he expected great things from them and that he had unshakable faith in their capability to sacrifice and bear suffering. Sushila Nayar recalls a meeting convened at Rohtak where the hall was full of women in *lehangas* and rustic clothes and Gandhi and his out-stretched hands received money and jewellery for the *Tilak Fund.*

In September 1920, the non-cooperation resolution was presented before the Congress session at Calcutta and ratified at Nagpur in December. In the first non-cooperation movement, women in the several parts of the country joined the processions and propagated use of *khadi* and *charkha.* Some of them deserted government schools and colleges. Renuka Ray recalls that she heard Gandhi's lecture in Calcutta in 1920 and the lecture made great impression on her. The girls of Diocesan College, of which she was a student, approached a women's meeting where the Mahatma asked them to sacrifice their jewellery. Renuka Ray gave away hers, followed by a large number of women. Many of these girls, including herself left their studies and joined the non-cooperation movement.[11] Vijaya Lakshmi Pandit narrates the first impression of Gandhi on her, when he visited Allahabad and stayed at Anand Bhawan. "I sat on the ground with my cousin and the little figure began to speak. He was quite incongruous. . . . He spoke very bad Hindi and yet the interesting thing was that none of these things seemed to matter after the first few minutes. He was saying something which was gripping everybody. He was compelling people to look at him, so listen to him . . . . And he ended by appealing to women to give him something." Since her cousin possessed only two rupees, she felt ashamed to give such a meagre amount. Mrs. Pandit took out her gold bangles and put them in the *khadi* cap of the volunteer—an Allahabad University Student—who was going round receiving donations. She regretted that she did not give away more.[12]

Basanti Devi accompanied her husband, Deshbandhu Chittaranjan Das, in his tours of Bengal and urged women to boycott foreign articles. Her sister-in-law, Urmilla Devi and niece Suniti Devi and she herself were arrested on 7 December 1921 on the allegation of "obstructing the gentlemen of Calcutta" by selling *khadi,* but they were freed after a few hours. Under the leadership of the women of C.R. Das's family, women volunteers roamed about the streets of Calcutta selling *khadi.* Basanti Devi presided over the Bengal Provincial Conference at Chittagong in April 1922. In the same year Kasturba Gandhi presided over the Gujarat Provincial Conference and urged women to take to spinning and wearing *khadi.* In Lahore in December 1922, Kasturba presided over a meeting where the President of the Reception Committee was Lala Lajpat Rai's wife, Radha Devi. In Allahabad, Rameshwari Nehru began a *"Kumari Sabha"* to encourage girls to talk and debate and participate in public discussions. Mrs. Pandit was an eloquent speaker at these meetings and Jawaharlal used to provide her the points for her lectures.[13] Women like Hemaprabha Majumdar, received *lathi* blows and revealed so much strength that C.R. Das called her "the only man outside jail." The women of Contai district Midnapur assisted Birendra Nath Sasmal's movement there. Bee Ammam, mother of Mohammad Ali and Shaukat Ali, discarded her veil, and addressed meetings all over India, championing the use of *khadi* and Hindu-Muslim unity. Mrs. Abdul Quadir, another Muslim lady, played an active role at Lucknow. Yet, women's participation in the first non-cooperation movement was not on a large scale and was mainly limited to those, whose husbands, fathers, brothers or sons had already joined the struggle and were in prison.

In the Borsad *Satyagraha* of 1923-24, women participated in large numbers. In fact Gandhi remarked that he had never seen such large gatherings of women. Thousands of women attended meetings. In Borsad nearly five thousand, in Auklao four thousand, in Kaithar five thousand and in Alaras almost every woman in the village attended meetings of Gandhi. Women exhibited greater strength than men when police confiscated their cows, buffaloes and other property.

In the Bardoli *Satyagraha* of 1928, women were not visible first, but from April onwards they outnumbered men in political assemblies and convened their own separate meetings also. Sardar Patel's experience was that in steadfastness of purpose, answered simplicity and purity, they were better than men. Women singing patriotic songs thronged his meetings. The peasants of Bardoli were compelled to abandon their land; their buffaloes and cows were confiscated; their domestic articles were auctioned. But they still didn't pay taxes. The women supported their men completely. Manibehn Patel, Mithubehn Petit and Bhaktibehn Desai set their tents and huts on the land announced to be sold by the government.[14] Bardoli set a new example as this was the first time that simple, unsophisticated rural women participated in the freedom movement, though they belonged to the well-off sections, who possessed the land they cultivated.[15]

The year 1930 began with the promise of independence and in March, Gandhi opened the new phase of *satyagraha* by declaring that he would break the salt law. His design was to walk from his *Ashram* at Sabarmati to Dandi, a small village on the sea-coast about 241 miles away, and to manufacture salt on the beach there, thus violating the government monopoly of salt making. Gandhi included no woman in the group of 79 marchers which left Sabarmati on 12 March 1930. This disappointed women. When the women of his *ashram* advised him to take at least four or five of them along with him, he replied that there would be time sufficient for that. Englishmen would not touch women, just as Hindus would not murder cows. It might be regarded cowardice to put women with them in this march. Feminine reaction to this check on women breaking the salt law was bitter. Dadabhai Naoroji's grand-daughter, Khurshedbehn, wrote an angry letter to Gandhi asking him the reason of his preventing women from joining him.[16] Mridula Sarabhai, then a student of Gujarat *Vidyapith,* jumped into the movement despite Principal Kaka Kalelkar's orders not to do so.[17] Both these bold young women were arrested at Ahmedabad. Women refused to accept any boundaries to what they could and could not do; this division of sexes in a non-violent campaign sounded to them unnatural and contrary to the awakened consciousness of modern Indian womanhood. They felt that no marches, no imprisonments, no demonstrations should be conducted without them.

Though no women accompanied Gandhi on the historic parade to Dandi, women were everywhere on the way to greet him and to hear his words. At the village of Abhrama on 10 April 1930, in a gathering of five thousand, two thousand were women; at Matwad, on 11 April, one-fourth of the audience was women; at Dandi on 13 April, more than 500 women received him.[18] Some women were, definitely, attracted not by Gandhi's politics, but believed that he was an embodiment of "Ranchodrai", i.e., Shri Krishna, hence they appeared in their thousands to see him." In his lecture all a long the route from Ahmedabad to Dandi, Gandhi urged women to refuse to carry *chatties* of toddy, and picked alcohol and toddy shops and stores selling foreign cloth. He asked them to wear *khadi* and to ply the *charkha.* He assigned them tasks such as picketing which sounded to many of them rather secondary. He attached great significance to these activities. He said : "Drink and drugs sap the moral well-being of those who are given to the habit. Foreign cloth undermines the economic foundations of the nation and throws millions out of employment. The distress in each case is felt in the home and therefore by women."[19]

In Mumbai, Kamaladevi Chattopadhyay and Avantikabai Gokhale were among the first women to break the salt law. Kamaladevi recalls that on 6 April 1930, "thousands of women strode down to the sea like proud warriors. But instead of weapons, they bore pitchers of clay, brass and copper; and, instead of uniforms, wore the simple cotton *saris* of village India. One watched them fascinated and awestruck. How old had they broken their age-old shell of social seclusion and burst into this fierce light of open warfare? What had stirred their ancient quietude and turned them into militant roles? Undoubtedly the women turned this struggle into a beautiful epic."[20] When the police raided the Bombay Congress House where salt pans had been manufactured, they found their way obstructed by Mrs. Perin Captain, Mrs. Jamnabehn Ratanabehn and five other female volunteers. Kamaladevi Chattopadhyay also stood by the Police Superintendent who humbly asked her to move away. She refused.[21]

Kamaladevi, Hansa Mehta, Jaishri Raiji, Manibehn and others arranged a parade on August 1, on the death anniversary of Tilak. Since the processions were prohibited in Bombay's Fort Area, the police would not let them proceed, they sat through the entire night in the open in rain. Hansa Mehta and others made the *Desh Sevika Sangh* which played a significant role in organising picketing in Bombay. It was so effective that government announced it illegal.[22] Through the summer of 1930, "day by day, the streets of Bombay would come alive in the early morning with songs of freedom sung by troupes of patriots rousing the people to action . . . . Women could be found all over the city, sitting outside the liquor shops and foreign cloth shops, plying their little 'spinning wheels' (called *taklis*), silently warning every Indian that he must not buy from that shop. Sometimes, the stool on which these women sat through the heat of the day, were provided by the shopkeepers whose trade they were destroying. Many of the women had never taken any part in public life before. Some came straight out of *purdah;* at the end of the day, they would have no idea how to go home, and must patiently wait till a husband or a son came to take them away.'[23] Horace Alexander described the situation thus :

The salt *satyagraha* in Madras was directed by T. Prakasam who was arrested soon and so was Nageswara Rao Pantulu. Durgabai was nominated his successor by T. Prakasam, thus becoming the second dictator of the salt *Satyagraha* in Madras. She held the campaign for over a month and ran the Udyavanam camp sending out 80 to 90 volunteers every day. She was arrested and sentenced to one years' imprisonment which she spent in the central prison for women in Vellore.[24]

George Slocombe of the *Daily Herald* penned in his despatch on the Wadala salt raid : ". . . One of the raiders carried out her mission with quiet dignity, very impressive to behold. It was a woman who emerged from the crowd, climbed through the barbed wire and approached the salt mound, as if it were an altar, and filled her sari with salt as part of some unknown ritual."[25] Besides breaking the salt law, ladies also sold salt packets and auctioned them to collect funds.

In Gujarat, where female participation was perhaps the largest, special classes were conducted in the Sabarmati Ashram to train women *satyagrahis.* Mridula Sarabhai here led the way. She was arrested and sent to Belgaum prison. The *Rashtriya Stree Sabha* carried on a wide propaganda for use of *Swadeshi*. Kasturba, Saraladevi Sarabhai, Mridula Sarabhai, Indumati Sheth, Mithubehn Petit, Nandubehn Kanuga, Khurshedbehn Naoroji were among the leaders in Ahmedabad.[26] Most of them were either from the families of millowners-Sarabhais, Kasturbhai Lalbhai, Ranchodlal Chotalal or from the Sabarmati Ashram. Mithubehn Petit who led in picketing liquor shop, was the grand-daughter of Sir Dinshaw Petit and had joined Gandhi from the 1920s. Khurshedbehn was Dadabhai Naoroji's grand-daughter and a full-time worker. But thousands of women-students, teachers and average housewives joined the *prabhat-pheries,* processions and picketed shops. Women marched in the streets carrying *kirpans* in their hands.[27] They were not educated or sophisticated. Gangabehn Vaidya became widow at sixteen. She had studied about Gandhi's struggle in South Africa, met him in Bombay and he suggested her to learn spinning at Manibhawan. Subsequently she became an inmate of Sabarmati Ashram. On 21 January 1931 she led a procession of 1,200 women in Borsad. The procession was *lathi*-charged, Gangabehn was beaten up and bled profousely, but she did not leave the tricolour she was carrying. She was in and out of prison till 1934, when she settled in Bochasan performing constructive work in the rural arears.[28]

At Calcutta, a Ladies Picketing Board was formed and several women's organisations such as the *Nari Satyagraha* Committee, *Rashtriya Mahila Sangh, Nikhil Jatiya Nari Sangh* broke the salt law and sent groups of women for picketing and courting arrest.

In Delhi, various women were arrested and some hundreds visited the courts to persuade the lawyers to withdraw from the courts. Granddaughter of Swami Shradhanand, Satyavati led women to picket shops and persuade the rich ladies who came to bathe in the Jamuna to abandon foreign clothes. Her role in awakening women in Delhi was undoubtedly marvellous.

The women of the Nehru family has spontaneously replied to the Mahatma's call to join the civil disobedience movement. Vijaya Lakshmi, Krishna, Swarup Rani and the sick Kamala were in the front line of leadership in Allahabad, arranging processions, addressing meetings and picketing foreign cloth and alcohol shops. Once when the police *lathi*-charged a procession, frail Swarup Rani received a blow on her head and fainted.[29]

A procession of five thousand women inaugurated the civil disobedience movement in the Punjab. *Prabhat-pheries,* meetings and picketing became almost an order of the day. Lala Lajpat Rai's daughter, Parvati Devi and Lado Rani Zutshi, the wife of a cousin of Jawaharlal Nehru, were distinguished among the leaders in Lahore. Mrs. Zutshi's daughter, Manmohini Sahgal recalls how Jawaharlal visited Lahore and met her mother and other women leaders. He was very furious and said : "Everywhere else the movement has started but you are still debating. What is the matter?" When the women indicated that the Punjab was not near the sea, Jawaharlal said : "Don't be silly. You may not be near the sea, but you have a big river, the Ravi, and breaking the salt law is only a symbol."[30] Its climax was a great meeting at Baradari, on the edge of the Ravi. On 10 April 1930, a mammoth meeting of the citizens of Lahore was convened in the Municipal Gardens outside Mori Gate under the auspices of the city Congress Committee to describe to the people the programme of civil disobedience which was to start in Lahore the following day. At least 40,000 people attended meeting including a thousand women. A group of ladies including the wife and daughter of Lajpat Rai, put the *tilak* mark on the foreheads of Dr. Satyapal and Dr. Mohammed Alam and garlanded them amidst repeated cries of *jais.*[31]

The *satyagraha* campaign against the salt law was inaugurated at Jalandhar on 17 April 1930 by *Raizada* Hans Raj in the presence of a gathering of 20,000 persons. A procession containing 400 women and 20,000 men marched to the Gandhi *Mandap.* Women performed the *Tilak Ceremony.* Then the volunteers made salt.[32]

In July 1930, when Lord Irwin was to preside over the Central Assembly, it was decided that there would be picketing by a gang of lady volunteers on the first day and twenty-seven women from Lahore, Ambala and Simla were selected for this objective. Just before the beginning of the session, these women went in groups of twos and threes, and stood outside the Central Legislative Assembly Hall. They carried black flags concealed under the folds of their *saris.* As soon as the Viceroy came and got down from his car, they took out the black flags concealed and shouted "Irwin, Go Back." Then they retired marching in a procession, singing national songs. Back Lahore, Manmohini Sehgal then president of the Students' Union organised picketing at college gates and organised students' strikes. She was arrested accompanied her friends. In the Lahore prison at this time were Mrs. Zutshi, Smt. Rajpati Kaul, Parvati Devi, Smt. Asaf Ali and Satyavati from Delhi.[33]

The women of Bihar also came courageously in front. Shrimati Mira Devi, daughter of Shri S.B. Bhattacharya, a professor of St. Columbus college at Hazaribagh, was arrested. Mrs. Hasan Imam presided over various meetings of students at Patna and a large people attended meeting at Barh. Accompanied by her daughter Mrs. Sami, Mrs. C.C. Das and some other women, were among a procession of women at Patna on 15 July to commence an intensive campaign of boycott of British articles. During the week ending 25 July 1930, Patna witnessed two demonstrations participated by nearly 3,000 women. Mrs. Hasan Imam, Mrs. Sami, Mrs. C.C. Das, Miss Gauri Das and Smt. Vindhya Vasini Devi were summoned to court Section 30 of the Police Act and Section 143 of the Indian Penal Code. Mrs. Imam was fined Rs. 200 and the others Rs. 100 each. She formed a committee of women at Muzaffarpur to campaign about spinning. Mirabehn toured Bihar, carrying on a successful propaganda for the use of *charkha.* Women leaders were also pioneering non-payment of *chowkidari tax.*[34]

Among scores of Karnataka women who participated in the struggle for freedom were Kamaladevi Chattopadhyay, Umabai Kundapur, Krishnabai Panjikar and Ballari Siddama. Gowramma and her co-workers offered *satyagraha* in front of the house of the Patel of Akonji, north Kanara. The police dragged them about, beat them with canes and routed them in filthy language. Women provided food and shelter to Congressmen carrying on their work incognito and often acted as messengers carrying confidential information from one camp to another; and when the call for *satyagraha* came, proved fervent *satyagrahis.*[35]

Same was repeated everywhere in India; women marching in processions, singing patriotic songs, picketing alcohol and foreign cloth shops. Over 80,000 persons were arrested during the salt *satyagraha* of whom more than 17,000 were women.[36] "We felt proud of our people and especially of our womenfolk all over the country" penned Jawaharlal Nehru in Naini jail, "I had a special feeling of satisfaction because of the activities of my mother, wife and sisters, as well as girl, cousins and friends; and though I was separated from them and was in prison, we grew nearer to each other."[37] The Karachi Congress in March 1931 specially congratulated Indians "who rose in their thousands and assisted the nation in the struggle for freedom."[38]

Women in the Indian states did not stand remote. In the Viramgam *satyagraha* in May 1930, seven hundred women were *lathi* charged.[39] In the Rajkot *satyagraha* of 1938-39[40] and the movement in Limbdi at the same time, ladies were active.[41] In Rajkot, Kasturba was imprisoned accompanied by Manibehn Patel and Mridula Sarabhai. Kamaladevi arranged agitation in Ram Durg state in Karnataka in the thirties.[42]

In the Individual Civil Disobedience movement, inaugurated by Gandhi in October 1940, ladies courted arrest. One of the first to do so was Sucheta Kripalani who was incharge of the ladies department of the A.I.C.C. since 1939.

Gandhi was arrested on 9 August 1942. The "Quit India" movement had practically no leader since all senior members of the Congress had been jailed. The news of these arrests spread, spontaneous *hartals* happened all over the country. Women marched in processions, meetings and demonstrations and arranging strikes. In Assam, Kanaklata Barua, a teenager girl, led a procession of five hundred and was murdered in the police firing. In Medinipur district in West Bengal, women played a remarkable part and fell to police excesses. In Bombay, one of the most dramatic series was the role of Usha Mehta who operated an underground radio station. Dr. Rammanohar Lohia was the leader of this group. The "Congress Radio" news broadcast at 7.30 in the evenings from August to 13 November 1942, was prepared by Usha Mehta till she, together with her colleagues, was arrested. Usha was put in a solitary cell for two months and cross-examined daily for hours together. She was awarded four years' rigorous imprisonment and shifted to Yeravda jail, where she was one of 250 women political prisoners.[43]

Aruna Asaf Ali was one of the most significant women personalities underground, evading arrest. She published bulletins and edited, with Lohia, the *Inquilab*. A reward of five thousand rupees was announced for her capture. Yusuf Meherally was to write subsequently that if "the heroine of 1857 was the *Rani of Jhansi,* that of the 1942 revolution was undoubtedly Aruna Asaf Ali."[44]

Women's Freedom Struggle

While thousands of women who joined the freedom struggle replied to Gandhi's call, could not accept his creed of nonviolence. During the *Swadeshi* agitation in Bengal in 1905, some women assisted the revolutionary leaders. Saraladevi Chaudhurani, maintained close links the revolutionary leaders. Saraladevi Chaudhurani, maintained close links with the *Suhrid Samiti* of Mymensingh and also toured widely in the Punjab and opened *Arya Samaj* branches for ladies. Here also many women sympathised with revolutionaries. Har Devi, wife of Roshan Lal, a renowned lawyer of Lahore, collected funds for assisting the anarchists.

Revolutionary organisations sprang up in 1930s. They were particularly active in Bengal, Dacca, Comilla and Chittagong being the strong focuses. Young college girls joined these confidential societies. Kalpana Joshi nee Dutt and Preeti Waddadar were related to the Chittagong Armoury raid. Preeti led a raid on the Pahartali Railway Officers' Club, as a consequence of which, one European lady was shot. Preeti took potassium cyanide and committed suicide. Kalpana, often dressed as a male was very active in this field. She was arrested in relation to the Chittagong armoury supplementary trials and was sentenced to life transportation.[45]

Santi and Suniti, two girls in their teens, shot dead Stevens, District Magistrate of Comilla in December 1931. They were arrested and put to life sentences.[46] Bina Das, daughter of Beni Madhav Das, who had taught Subhas Bose, of Ravenshaw College, Cuttack was a student of Diocesan College, Calcutta. On 6 February 1932 when Sir Stanley Jackson, the Governor was delivering the convocation speech, Bina got up from her seat, took a few steps and shot him. A bullet whipped past the Governor's ear. Bina was caught but she constantly fired till her ammunition was finished. She recalls her experience that she was creating a crack in the solid structure of the British rule by opening fire on the Governor—a symbol of its authority and power. "The Governor of Bengal represents a system which kept enslaved three hundred millions of my countrymen and experienced country-women,"[47] she stated. She was tried and put to nine years' rigorous imprisonment.

"The *Chhatri Sangha* (Women Students Association) began at Calcutta in 1928 consisting of about one hundred members, was a significant training and recruiting ground for future revolutionaries. Girls from *Brahmo* Girls' School, Victoria School, Bethune College, Diocesan College and Scottish Church College joined the *Chhatri Sangha.* They arranged study circles, took lessons in *lathi* and sword play, learnt cycling, motor driving and one of them even learnt to fly an aeroplane. They became volunteers in the Calcutta Congress of 1928 with Subhas Bose as their G.O.C., Kalpana, Preeti, Bina, her sister Kalyani, Santi, Suniti—were all members of the *Chhatri Sangha.* Some of them had to desert their homes and for them a hostel—*Punya*

Ashram—was begun in Calcutta by Bina and Kalyani's mother. Bombs were collected in this hostel searched various times by the police. Kamala Das Gupta, another revolutionary, recalls how she carried bombs in small leather or tin suitcases to be put in the hostel or despatched to different people.[48]

In Delhi, Smt. Roop Vati Jain at 17, was looking after a bomb factory under Chandra Shekhar Azad. This factory at Qutab Road, run as "Himalayan Toilets" produced picric acid, nitro glycerine, gun-cotton and other materials for bombs. Mrs. Jain was expert in washing picric acid which left yellow, easily dictable spots on the skin. Sushila Devi, another revolutionary worker, cut her finger and applied mark of blood as *tilak* on the forehead of the revolutionaries, Bhagat Singh and Batukeshwar Dutt on 9 April 1929. Because of her link with Bhagat Singh to whom she sent letters, *rakhi* and food, she was arrested and jailed. She was announced an absconder in the Delhi and Lahore conspiracy cases and imprisoned many times. Durga Devi joined the freedom struggle at 16. Bhagat Singh's wife, and along with one-year-old son travelled with her to Calcutta to attend the A.I.C.C. session. She shot a police sergeant at Hamilton Road, Bombay. She was elected president of the Delhi Provincial Congress Committee in 1938.[49]

All these young girls were strong idealists and highly emotional and impulsive. They hated the British intensely and contact with revolutionaries and their literature ignited their imagination and "a world of heroism and romance" was revealed before their eyes.[50] Their design was to attack on Europeans as widely as possible. They believed in individual acts of heroism, "maximum sacrifice by a minimum number," not in building up of a mass expedition.

In January 1942, an Indian Independence League was formed in Kuala Lumpur and Indian women in Southeast Asia worked for the cause of India's independence. In March 1943, a women's section of the League was started and Indian women in Malaya, Thailand and Burma became volunteers. In July of that year Subhas Bose addressed a meeting and his call to women to share the onus of the war for independence infused a new spirit into the movement. A women's regiment, Rani of Jhansi Regiment, was made with Lakshmi Sehgal nee Swaminadhan as the Captain who was Minister of Social Welfare and Medicine in the *Azad Hind* Government.

In the first entry of his *Indian Diary,* November 1917, Edwin Montagu wrote : "I received a letter from Jaipur in the vernacular and a request for an interview from the women of India".[51] Montagu was mentioning a letter signed by four members of the Senate of the Indian Women's University. A group of fourteen Women's Indian Association. The Franchise Committee, presided over by Lord Southborough, received various petitions from educated women stressing the grant of vote to women on the same property qualifications as for men, or to at least lady gradutes. Annie Besant, Sarojini Naidu, Herabhai Tata and Milthan Tata, members of a deputation which provided evidence before the joint parliamentary committee on the Government of Indian Bills also took up this subject. In 1918, the Indian National Congress unanimously passed a resolution favouring voting rights for ladies. When the Franchise Committee went to Mumbai, a petition signed by eight hundred women was presented to it. Similar requests were made by the Women Graduates' Union of Bombay as well as all the branches of the Indian Women's Association, the women's branch of the Home Rule League and other women's associations. Women presented as witnesses before the committee did not recommend extension of franchise to ladies on the ground that in the existing social conditions in India, it was early to do so.[52] The Government of India Act of 1919 left the responsibility of deciding the question of female franchise to be settled by the provinces. The provincial legislatures, one after another, started enfranchising women on the same grounds as men. Madras was the first province to remove the disqualification, and also had the reputation of having the first Indian woman legislator, Dr. S. Muthulakshmi Reddi, chosen Deputy Speaker of the Madras Legislative Council. Though a nominated member, she resigned her portfolio protesting against Gandhi's arrest in 1930. Kamaladevi Chattopadhyay, the first women to risk contesting an election, when she stood as an independent candidate from South Kanara in 1926. Though her election campaign was arranged by Margaret Cousins and many of friends, she lost by a margin of 515 votes.[53] By 1926 women enjoyed franchise on the same grounds as men in all provinces so far as elections to the provincial legislatures were concerned. The Government of India Act of 1935 extended the franchise to more than six million women, a great improvement on the figure of 315,000 under the Act of 1919.[54] Thus, women voters increased by no less than twenty-one times. Even then only 2½ per cent of major women had got the right to vote.[55]

In the 1937 elections, 8 women were elected from "general" constituencies and 42 from the "reserved" ones. Six ladies became ministers when the provincial cabinets were formed. Vijaya Lakshmi Pandit became Minister for Local Self-Government in U.P.; and later Ansuyabai Kale, and J.T. Sipahimalani became Deputy Speakers in Madhya Pradesh and Sind respectivley; and Hansa Mehta, Begum Shah Nawaz and Sarojini Naidu, attended the Round Table Conference during 1930-32.

In the Constituent Assembly when it met in December 1946, there were 14 women members. Ammu Swaminathan, Ḍakshayani Velayudhan and Durgabai from Madras; Hansa Mehta from Bombay; Malti Chowdhury from Orissa, Sucheta Kripalani, Vijaya Lakshmi Pandit, Purnima Banerjee, Kamala Chaudhri and Begum Aizaz Rasul from U.P.; Sarojini Naidu from Bihar; Begum Jahanara Shah Nawaz from the Punjab and Lila Roy and Begum Ikramullah from Bengal.[56]

In February 1946 disturbances occurred in Calcutta to protest against the sentence given to Captain Abdul Rashid of the Indian National Army. The police fired on three occasions in different parts of the city. On 12 February, a mile-long procession constituting a lakh of people, in which women also joined, marched through Dalhousie Square area in protest against Captain Rashid's sentence. In the same month, the Bombay naval ratings struck. Thousands of railway employees, textile workers and students marched in processions and struck. In Bombay, there were frequent clashes between the police and military on the one hand and defiant crowds on the other. Kamal Donde, a member of the Communist Party, died of a bullet injury, and Kusum Ranadive received a bullet injury when the army fired near Elphinstone Bridge. Students' and workers' strikes took place in Calcutta and Madras to sympathise with the demands of Royal Indian Navy personnel and to protest against the repressive policy of the government participated by women.[57]

Most ladies joined the freedom movement because like the men, they were motivated by patriotism and desired the end of British rule from their motherland. A significant factor was family influence. Women from families such as those of Motilal Nehru, C.R. Das, Jamnalal Bajaj or Lajpat Rai naturally wished to share the privations and miseries of their men. Where the environment at home was nationalistic, women also imbibed it. Bina Das's father was a teacher and a friend of Subhas Bose.[58] Kamala Das Gupta recalls how her father was associated with the *swadeshi* movement in Bengal.[59] Sucheta Kripalani's family had been wearing and using *Swadeshi* since the 1920s.[60]

Books also played some role into motivate ladies. Mrs. Besant's autobiography impressed Kamaladevi;[61] novels such as Saratchandra Chatterji's *Pather Dabi* motivated some of the Bengali revolutionaries.[62] But personalities were more significant. Dhiresh Mazumdar, a student leader, had a great influence over the young girls, who joined extremist groups in Calcutta as did Surya Sen in Chittagong. Subhas Bose in Bengal, Vallabhbhai Patel in Gujarat, Rammanohar Lohia, Jawaharlal Nehru and, above all, Gandhi were effective in drawing women into the political arena. According to Sucheta Kripalani, Gandhi's personality motivated confidence not only in women, but in their guardians—husbands, fathers, brothers who did not prevent their women-folk from coming out of their sheltered homes to march in the streets. If Gandhi's leadership had been absent, such a large number of women might not have emerged.[63] Gandhi's letters to Manibehn Patel, Prabhavati Devi, Gangabehn and others disclose how he understood their courage, hopes and ambitions.[64] He prescribed before each of them different objectives and encouraged them to face challenges. He asserted that women were true *satyagrahis* without whom he could do nothing. He provided them important objectives. He assigned them specific tasks and his programme had a special appeal for them. His way of struggle was such that women could conveniently participate. In a non-violent struggle, the qualities required could be fulfilled by women-tolerance, ability to suffer. strength. Gandhi believed women as one of the most oppressed clear of Indian society and had developed a capacity for bearing suffering, which, if properly employed, could result in their deliverance. The biographies and autobiographies of women in the nationalist movement, disclose the tremendous influence of Gandhi on them.

The general atmosphere also favoured womens' participation in the struggle. Hansa Mehta recalls that she took to politics in 1930 because the environment in those days was such that one could hardly avoid the infection.[65] Usha Mehta recalls the patriotic songs and slogans she heard from the street and how they motivated her. In Yeravda prison she asked her fellow prisoners the reason of their regard for a local leader and above all for Mahatma Gandhi. These women belonged to different sections of society and all parts of Maharashtra; some being Gandhians, some socialists and a few communists.[66] Kamaladevi Chattopadhyay discovered women from all classes in jail including plantation workers.[67] According to Manmohini Sahgal, most of the women joined them in Lahore were from the middle or lower-middle class. No Harijan women were there but only a few Muslims. Not all were college-educated but most were literate in Hindi.[68]

Earlier, political awakening among women as among men in India was limited to the cities, and largely to those with middle-class background, namely, the professional, business and literate classes. The widening of the scope of the nationalist movement brought into its ranks participation by industrial employees and certain peasant sections, *patidar* peasant women of Ras,[69] Borsad,[70] Bardoli,[71] Karadi and Matwad were active in the *satyagraha* movement in these areas. Midnapur was politically very conscious and village ladies actively participated in the freedom movement. In the 1930s, simple, unsophisticated women marched in processions alongwith those of the Nehru family at Allahabad or the Sarabhais at Ahmedabad. Some Muslim women discarded their *purdah* and joined the struggle, and a few *Parsi* women also joined the struggle under the leadership of Gandhi. Many more ladies participated in the salt-*satyagraha* and the civil disobedience movement than in the non-cooperation movement. In 1942, only a few bold women like Aruna Asaf Ali, Sucheta Kripalani and Usha Mehta carried on "underground" activities.

Women organized themselves into groups and wanted to join processions, face police firing and go to jail. They broke the salt law, picketed shops selling alcohol and foreign manufactured fabric. Women joined terrorist groups and assisted in editing and distributing banned newspapers and making bombs. Young girls in their teens and women with children went to jails where conditions were uncomfortable. Many jails were dark, dingy places with damp air, musty smell and bats hanging from the ceilings. The meal for ordinary prisoners was inedible. Policemen sometimes poked fun or jeered at lady prisoners. No bathrooms existed in the cells, and women prisoners got embarrassed for being sent to toilets accompanied by male "guards". These young girls passed the best years of their youth in jail. They were confined in aloof cells and often cross-examined for hours to make them provide complete information about their colleagues. Banalata Das Gupta, a young revolutionary, was made to sit on a stool for three days hungry so that she would disclose the names of those who had supplied her with revolvers.

There were broadly three stages in the movement for the female emancipation in India. In the first stage, beginning in the early nineteenth century with Raja Rammohun Roy, efforts were made to change the religious base of certain social practices and conventions and to apply logical and humanitarian criteria to problems like *sati,* widow remarriage and child marriage. In the second stage from the mid-nineteenth century onwards, women's education was greatly emphasized. The entry of women into the political arena marked the third phase. From this point onwards the women's emancipation movement was not the dream of a few social reformers, but part of a much larger political crusade. As women participated in political activity, many of the taboos and prohibitions imposed on them, were either lifted or ignored. Political upheavals bring about social change, and it is suspicious if a century of preaching and social work would have brought about the same change in the status of Indian women as achieved in two decades of political struggle in India. By their participation in political expedition, Indian women assisted their own movement for liberation. In India, feminism and nationalism were closely associated. As the national movement acquired momentum, the dream of independence became the only concern for people. The cause was Indian; the goal being India's independence. The women's movement in India had none of the man-woman antagonism attribute of women's movements in the West. In India, women were accepted as political companions and provided equal opportunities for participation in the freedom struggle and they have a proud record.

References

1. *Young India,* 15 December 1921.
2. *Young India,* 10 April 1930.
3. J. Murdoch (comp.) *Twelve Years of Indian Progress, Extracted From the Indian National Congress; the resolutions of its Thirteen Sessions* (Madras, 1898), p. 36.
4. Usha Chakraborty, *Condition of Bengali Women around the Second Half of the Nineteenth Century* (Calcutta, 1963), pp. 127-28.
5. B.B. Mazumdar, and B.P. Mazumdar, *Congress and Congressmen in the Pre-Gandhian Era, 1885-1917* (Calcutta, 1967), p. 128.
6. Sumit Sarkar, *The Swadeshi Movement in Bengal* (New Delhi, 1973), pp. 287-88.
7. Jogeshchandra Bagal, *Jattiya Andolane Banga Nari* (Visva-Bharati, Bhadra, 1361 B. Sen), pp. 15-16.
8. Interview with Smt. Vijaya Lakshmi Pandit, NMML.
9. M.K. Gandhi, *Satyagraha in South Africa,* (2nd ed., Ahmedabad, 1950), pp. 281, 282-85.
10. *Navajivan,* 28 November 1920.
11. Transcript of interview with Smt. Renuka Ray, NMML.
12. Smt. Vijaya Lakshmi Pandit, *op. cit.*
13. *Ibid.*
14. Manibehn V. Patel, *Borsad Satyagraha* (Gujarati) (Ahmedabad, 1972), p. 101.
15. Mahadev Desai, *The Story of Bardoli, being a History of the Bardoli Satyagraha of 1928 and its sequel* (Ahmedabad, 1957), p. 118.
16. Usha Bhatt, "Role of Women in the Freedom Struggle in Ahmedabad," unpublished Ph.D. thesis, Gujarat University (Gujarati).
17. Susmita Medh (ed.), *Jyoti Vikas Yatra* (Ahmedabad, 1971), p. 290.
18. *Source Material for a History of the Freedom Movement in India, Mahatama Gandhi,* Vol. III, Pt. III, 1929-31. Collected from Maharashtra State and Government of India Records (Bombay, 1969), p. 31.
19. *Young India,* 10 April 1930.
20. Tara Ali Baig (ed.), *Women of India* (New Delhi, Publications Division, 1958), p. 19.
21. N.N. Mitra (ed.), *The Indian Annual Register,* Vol. 1, Jan-June 1930, p. 36.
22. Transcript of interview with Smt. Hansa Mehta, NMML.
23. Horace Alexander, *Gandhi Through Western Eyes* (Bombay, 1969), p. 64.
24. Transcript of interview with Smt. Durgabai Deshmukh, NMML.
25. *The Indian Annual Register,* Vol. 1, Jan.-June 1930, p. 119.
26. Usha Bhatt, *op. cit.*
27. Interview with Smt. Vinodini Neelkanth, NMML.
28. Kaka Kalelkar (ed.), *Bapuna Patro, Gangabehnne,* No. 6 (Ahmedabad, Navjivan Press, 1960) (Gujarati).
29. Smt. Vijaya Lakshmi Pandit, *op. cit.*
30. Transcript of interview with Smt. Manmohan Sahgal, NMML.
31. *The Tribune,* 12 April 1930.
32. *Ibid.*, 19 April 1930.
33. Smt. Manmohini Sahgal, *op. cit.*

34. K.K. Datta, *History of the Freedom Movement in Bihar, 1928-41,* Vol. II (Patna, 1957), pp. 114-16.
35. G.S. Halappa, *History of Freedom Movement in Karnataka* (Bangalore, 1964), Vol. 11, pp. 440-41.
36. P.J. Thomas, *Indian Women Through the Ages* (Bombay, 1964), p. 331.
37. Jawaharlal Nehru, *An Autobiography* (Loodon, 1941), p. 224.
38. *Indian National Congress Resolutions, 1930-34* (Allahabad, n.d.), p. 62.
39. Kantilal M. Shah, *Viramgam Satyagraha* (Ahmedabad, 1974) (Gujarati).
40. Ramnarayan N. Pathak, *Rajkot Satyagraha* (Ahmedabad, 1974) (Gujarati).
41. Bapalal Doshi, *Limbdi ni Ladbat* (Ahmedabad, 1974) (Gujarati).
42. Interview with Smt. Kamaladevi Chattopadhyay, NMML.
43. Transcript of interview with Usha Mehta, NMML.
44. *The Tribune,* 18 February 1946.
45. Kalpana Dutt, *Reminiscences* (Bombay, 1945).
46. Interviews with Santi Ghose and Suniti Chowdhury, NMML.
47. Interview with Smt. Bina Das, NMML.
48. Transcript of interview with Smt. Kamala Das Gupta, NMML.
49. *The Hindustan Times,* 15 August 1972.
50. Smt. Kamla Das Gupta, *op. cit.*
51. Edwin Montagu, *An Indian Diary* (London, 1930), p. 5.
52. *Report of the Franchise Committee* (1918), pp. 4-5.
53. *One who knows* (Dr. (Mrs.) S. Muthulakshmi Reddi) *Mrs. Margaret Cousins and her work in India* (Madras, 1956), p. 63.
54. A.B. Keith, *A Constitutional History of India, 1600-1935* (Allahabad, 1961), p. 359.
55. *Report of the Indian Franchise Committee (1932),* Vol. 1, p. 166.
56. *The Indian Annual Register,* Vol. II, July-Dec. 1946, pp. 317-25.
57. *Ibid.,* Vol. I, Jan.-June 1946, pp. 308-10.
58. Smt. Bina Das, *op. cit.*
59. Smt. Kamala Das Gupta, *op. cit.*
60. Transcript of interview with Smt. Sucheta Kripalani, NMML.
61. Smt. Kamaladevi Chattopadhyay, *op. cit.*
62. Smt. Kamala Das Gupta, *op. cit.*
63. Smt. Sucheta Kripalani, *op. cit.*
64. Kaka Kalelkar (ed.) *Bapuna Patro, Bhenone* (Gujarati). Translation into English by Kaka Kalelkar, *Bapu's Letters to Ashram Sisters,* I (Ahmedabad, 1952).
65. Smt. Hansa Mehta, *op. cit.*
66. Smt. Usha Mehta, *op. cit.*
67. Smt. Kamaladevi Chattopadhyay, *op. cit.*
68. Smt. Manmohini Sahgal, *op. cit.*
69. Chandrakant Patel, *Swatantra Andolanma Raas* (Ahmedabad, 1975), (Gujarati).
70. Shivabhai G. Patel, *Borsad Satyagraha* (Ahmedabad, 1975), (Gujarati). Munibehn Patel, *Borsad Satyagraha, op. cit.*
71. Mahadev Desai, *The Story of Bardoli, op. cit.*

5

Foreign Women in Independence Movement

Besides hundreds and thousands of Indian Women who devoted their lives for the sake of their country, there were a large number of noble and courageous foreign ladies who witnessed in India—its religion, its philosophy and its culture as a whole, hope for the redemption of the universe. They felt that in India's spiritual death universe shall find its grave.

These noble women who were sick of the material west, found in India and in its civilization, peace for their depressed souls. These women can be classified under following three heads :

1. Those who cared for India and assisted her from their own lands; (some of them coming occasionally to India);
2. Those who were deeply influenced by the great Indian celebrities like Swami Vivekananda, Aurobindo Ghosh, Mahatma Gandhi, and visited India to serve its cause under those great men; and
3. Besides there was another group under the great lady Dr. Annie Besant who served the cause of India as they wished.

The first group includes those gentle ladies-wives of viceroys in India who departed to their country with a soft corner for India and on occasions attempted to clarify many misunderstandings among their countrymen for a better understanding of the Indian problems. They were Lady Rippon, Lady Minto, Lady Pentland, Lady Willingdon, Lady Irwin, and Lady Mountbatten.

Lady Emily Luyton and her husband suffered in the hands of Indian bureaucracy for their support for Indian cause. Members of the groups of English women Associations included Mrs. Hume Stanford, Miss Bornice, Mrs. Gracelankesher, Mrs. Anne

Hodgkinson, Mrs. Gorbett Ashley who arranged meetings for Indian women for propagating the cause of Indian liberation, and created a sympathetic opinion in the minds of people in England.

Agatha Harision and Lady Pethic Lawrence also adopted a sympathetic attitude towards India. The great novelist, Pearl S. Buck tried her best to awaken interest in India in remote lands.

Sister Nivedita

'Here Reposes Sister Nivedita who Gave her All to India'

—*Epitaph on Her Samadhi*

Sister Nivedita passed away at Darjeeling on 13 October 1911. Ras Bihari Bose, while paying a tribute to her, stated if we were aware of a budding national life, it was in no small dimension due to the lessons of Sister Nivedita.

She was one among the host of foreign ladies who were influenced by Swami Vivekananda, and his philosophy of Hinduism. Born in Ireland, on 28 October 1867, she came to India in January, 1898, in search of truth, and was received by Swami Vivekananda. She was to work for the liberation of Indian women. She was deeply impressed by the ideas and ideals of Indian women. She once commented that India was above all, the land of great ladies. She however, felt that Indian women required to nurture among themselves a wider and broader definition of the nation, above the concepts of home and family, to take part along with men in building a free and strong India.

Death of Swami Vivekananda, created turmoil in Indian politics. She released herself from the obligations of the Order. She spoke and penned against the British policy in India. She criticised Lord Curzon for the Universities Act of 1904 and partition of Bengal 1905. She was aware of disastrous situation of Indian economy and held British imperialism liable for it. She attended the Banares Congress in 1905 and favoured the Swadeshi Movement. She assisted Nationalist groups like the Dawn Society and the Anusilan Samity. She was a member of the Central Council of Action formed by Aurobindo Ghosh and undertook the editorship of the *Karmayogin* when he left for Pondicherry.

She propagated for the cause of India throughout America and Europe. Swami Vivekananda depicted her as a real Lioness, Rabindra Nath Tagore as Lok-Mata and Aurobindo Ghosh as Agni-sikha.

The Mother

Mira Alphonse, the Mother, was born in Paris in 1878. She had exhibited depth of vision and fragrance of expression even in her early childhood. She visited India in 1914 and met Shri Aurobindo. She was linked with the work of Shri Aurobindo when he commenced a philosophical monthly, *Arya* on August 15, 1914, to demonstrate his vision of man and his divine destiny.

She took charge of *Ashram* in Pondicherry in 1926. She motivated Aurovelle, the international town near Pondicherry, to serve as a meeting centre for the disciples of Shri Aurobindo.

Her promise was, "Lord, we are upon earth to accomplish the work of transformation".

Paying her tribute to the late Mother at a women's assembly in Kanpur, the Prime Minister, Mrs. Indira Gandhi, described her as a dynamic woman, who came from France and accepted the Indian culture. She played a significant role in inspiring women like Mrs. Besant and Mrs. Sen Gupta. The Mother had also contributed to enrich India's ancient heritage and culture, she said.

Mira Behn

Mira Behn, or Mira as she was most often called, appeared from the blue to the Indian movement as an expression of life's awareness to its own drawbacks. She was the western world's acknowledgement of crime and of the wish to atone. This was not at all in her own consciousness, but in that which put her forth. Gandhi never evoked her. He only told her to come if she desired. She came as a daughter not only of the western mentality but, specifically, of that section which had manufactured and governed the British Empire of India. Her father had been the naval commander-in-chief there.

This is how Madeleine *Slade* born and bred in England in affluent atmosphere of a proud aristocracy, came to serve the cause of Indian independence by identifying herself absolutely with the life and work of Gandhi, who pledged to Rollan that he will leave no stone unturned, to assist her to become a bridge between East and West.

She was the daughter of a British Admiral and was born in 1892. She deserted the luminous life and toiled and hardened her hands and feet to serve. She accompanied Gandhi to England in 1931. In 1934, she undertook a journey to America and Britain and succeeded in acquiring sympathy for Indian cause. She was sent to jail in 1932-33 and 1942-44 for the cause of Indian freedom.

Margaret Cousins

Mrs. Margaret Cousins approached India to learn but remained here to serve. They were well-equipped with the experience and practical prudence of the west. They were Irish in origin; *suffragette* in sympathy and former participants in the Irish Home Rule agitation. They were pushed to India by her spiritual and cultural heritage.

Mrs. Margarete Cousins in her book *Indian Womenhood* Today gives a revealing comment :

'Being Irish, in India neither as a Christian missionary nor a British Government servant, nor for any political propaganda and having already studied and gained much from Indian philosophies—Vedic, Buddhist, and Islamic, it was easy for me to evaluate strong and weak points in present day contemporary Indian civilization, and within my first year of landing on Indian soil I was dedicated to the service of India *via* service to that half of India—its womanhood which seemed to me the most direct instrument for leverage of the whole people. If the problems of womanhood could be solved it would most fundamentally and successfully be done in accord with the centuries old spiritual attitude of the Indian Race—soul towards womanhood and all its implies, influences, and controls.

Establishment of Women of India Association on 8th May 1917 was great landmark in the Indian History. Undoubtedly the history of women welfare association in India can be traced from the mid 19th century but the renaissance that Women Association of India created among the Indian women, was a remarkable achievement. This association and she was very ably assisted by Mrs. Cousins.

In 1928, women Association of India decided to establish regular links with women groups in England, for informing them of the aspiration of India and its women.

It was, therefore, under the motivation and suppression of these foreign women that many Indian women not only helped the cause of national freedom in India but also conducted a very constructive and fruitful propaganda to present the Indian difficulties before the British public and the members of the House of Commons, through their sister concerns in Britain.

The new voice of women constituted a part of the new voice of mother India where the demands for national independence and development soon rang out as clarion calls.

Mrs. Laxmi Menon in a seminar on the position of women in South Asia in 1952, New Delhi, paid a worthy tribute to the work of these women. She stated, "The awakening came from the sympathy and understanding of veteran champions of women's political rights in Britain. To day it is impossible to conceive the movement apart from the great contribution made by Mrs. Besant and Mrs. Cousins. If the former, born revolutionary and champion of all wars against injustice, inspired the movement, the latter who had already played a remarkable role in the feminist movement both in England and Ireland strove with amazing persistence to realise that inspiration in actual practice. To them both Indian women owe a deep debt of gratitude."

Dr. Annie Besant

Dr. Besant was born in London on 1 October, 1847. She accompanied by Charles Braudlaugh, did more than anyone had done in a hundred years to reject the barriers of bigotry and prejudice, who achieved the greatest conquests of their age for the independence speech and liberty of the press which Britain enjoys today.

She was a votary of truth and her entire life was a series of evolution. She approached India in 1893, influenced by its great religion and philosophy. But the condition in India was deplorable. She found that Indians had almost lost their moorings and were not proud of their own culture. She attempted to awaken them to their lost heritage by dedicating herself for the cause of religion, devotion and education of India. And she was careful that Indian revival must be through Indian traditions and customs and not on the European concepts. As early as 1898 and later in 1902, she emphasised upon Indians to wear Indian dress, use and develop Indian manufactures. She further motivated Indians to develop Indian language for a national one.

For this and many other of her speeches she was condemned as most mischievous and untrustworthy by the Indian bureaucracy. She carried out her work for the awakening of India till about 1913. But the next year was a turning point in her life when she joined active Indian politics. She demanded Home Rule for India and suffered internment from June to September 1917. By then she had attempted and achieved unification of the Congress and Hindus and Muslims in 1916. She had done tremendous work to formulate favourable viewpoint about the Indian question in outer universe. The August declaration of 1917 is attributed to her attempts.

She suitably became the president of Indian National Congress in 1917. Tilak announced that we were nearer our objectives due to her sincere efforts. Gokhale regarded her a true a daughter of Mother India.

Gandhi's arrival receded her to the background but she carried out her advocacy for the Indian independence. The commonwealth of India bill was one of her subsequent achievements. She expired at Adyar, Madras on 20 September 1933. Flags of fifty-four countries were exhibited in cremation ground. Floral tributes were paid to her services by the prominent Indian leaders. Subash regarded her a doughty fighter for Indian independence. Jawaharlal Nehru stated that in India her memory would endure specially for her participation in our freedom struggle in the critical days of the great battle and afterwards.

Whenever we talk of women's emancipation in India, no matter where the talk is initiated, the person whose contribution in this regard is unforgettable is herself a foreign women, Yes! Ms. Annie Besant. In her concern towards India and her outlook towards Indians, she was more original Indian than an indigeneous person. She started the movement of women's emancipation in an organised manner with the help of then existing women's organisation and also gave direction to their battle for ballot. Present text is divided in three sections, I, II and III puts forth her vision about position of women. Section III of the chapter carries substance of her first lecture delivered on the political status of women.

I

Indian women were provided more educational opportunities. Women organisations were established and women participation in political activities was recognised. Legislative measures against *sati,* ill-treatment of widows, ban on widow remarriage, polygamy and child marriage, etc. were introduced.

Significantly, Annie Besant understood the political and biological and psychological difference between men and women. While never advocating any rivalry between both the sexes she upheld the dignity and status of women both in the eastern and western cultures. She wanted them to be partners in thinking and struggling together in harmony.

She endeavoured for improving the status of Indian women in accordance with the Indian ethos, of course, in conformity with the modern changed conditions.

In search for understanding her views, the chapter examined mainly her writings and speeches on the above subject.

In India, beginning of British rule did not merely mean a new political rule, but it also had deep-rooted implications on the economy and the ideology of Indian people. Particularly after industrial revolution in England, the rulers changed India into a colony which produced raw material for Britain.

The country passed through complex economic and political changes and had a far reaching influence on the entire social structure. During the period there were two major movements which affected the status of women. These were the Social Reform Movements of the nineteenth century and the Nationalist Movement of the twentieth century. Both these movements raised the issue of equal status of women. The social reform movements have been regarded as a key to the intellectual processes that went into the making of modern India. The problems which attracted the attention of nineteenth century social reformers were *sati,* the ill-treatment of widows, the ban on widow marriage, polygamy, child marriage, refusal of property rights and education to women. Social reformers felt that these social evils should be eradicated by raising consciousness to this effect and making people sensitive to the injustice done on women. They thought that by giving women the access to education and by enacting progressive legislation, social change should be introduced.

Raja Ram Mohun Roy, Ishwar Chandra Vidyasagar, M.G. Ranade, Mahatma Phuley and others from all parts of the country raised their voice against some of the unjust and evil practices while social reformers like Dayanand Saraswati, Swami Vivekananada and Annie Besant believed in evolution of the status of women from the Indian cultural situation.

Alongwith this, another very powerful force which helped change the position and attitude towards women was the Nationalist

Movement particularly during the Gandhian era. Though in the liberal and militant phase of the freedom movement, Indian women were slowly entering the political field. A more significant mobilisation, anyway, took place after 1920.

In the Non-cooperation Movement of 1921 and the Civil Disobedience Movement of 1930 new techniques of movement like picketing and boycotting of foreign goods and liquor shops and non-cooperation in various governmental activities were being rectified. Role of Indian women in History was witnessed radical changes. Vedanta declared the presence of one and same self in all beings. Subsequently, hard rules and practices turned women into just manufacturing machines. Fact remains that all nations attained greatness by paying proper respect to women. Vivekananda said that :

> "The principal reason why our race has so degenerated is that we had no respect for these living image of *shakti.* Manu says, 'where women are respected, there the gods delight, and where they are not, there all work and efforts come to naught'. There is no hope of rise for that family or country where they live in sadness".

II

Prior to coming to India Annie Besant was a fighter for the women's causes, a free-thinker and socialist reformer, an anti-imperialist, an educationist and a birth control agitator. She had written about the stories of women poisoned in lead works, exhausted in nailworks, driven to prostitution by the starvation, made old and haggard by ceaseless work. She gave her first lecture in 1874 on the political status of women. Following quote represent her views on the subject.

> "All women to grow freely, to develop as nature bids them, and they will find room for home cares in their minds, and the warmest nestling place in their bosom will be the haven of the little child. But if you check, and fret, and carp at them, you will not succeed in souring them and in making them hard and bitter."

In her own words, way to progress and prosperity lay in:

> "Liberty for every human being, equality before the law for all in public and in private, fraternity of men and women in peaceful leadership. These are the promise of the dawning day. Co-partners in every righteous project, co-soldiers in every just cause, men and women in the time to come shall labour, think and struggle side by side. The man shall bring his greater strength and more sustained determination, the women her quicker judgement and purer heart till man shall grow tenderer, and woman stronger, man more pure, and woman more brave and free. Till at last, generations hence, the race shall develop into a strength and beauty at present unimagined, and men and women shall walk this fair earth hand in hand, diverse, yet truly one, set each to each as perfect music unto noble words."

Madam Annie Besant also agreed with Manu that "God created Women to be mothers, and to be fathers, Men". She also agreed with Manu that women was "the Devi" the light of the Home". Annie Besant believed that the strength and weakness of all social movements in Indian was due to the status of women in her household. An article of 1923 expresses interest in the welfare of the Indian women.

"The seclusion of Indian women, over a large part of India for some centuries, has narrowed their views and their sympathises and the prevalence of the English Education of boys while, until lately, girls were outside it, has deprived their opinion of weight in public matters, while in social customs, affecting home life, they have remained supreme. Religious by heredity and training her religion is more devotional than intellectual in most cases, more ceremonial than philosophical: she is a passionate devotee, but in modern times, rarely a sage. For centuries she has not taken active part in public life, save when born in royal families, as she want to do in earlier days. But she is intensely practical, and what she learns she puts into practice. Very swiftly is she awakening now, and reclaiming her ancient power, and movements for Social Reform such as the abolition of child marriage, the education of girls, the checking of infant mortality—these will never sweep the country until Indian women take hold of them."

She was of the opinion that the need was great and pressing, for the strength of the Nation, the robustness of men, the control of the nervous diseases to which educated men were peculiarly liable, with the premature old age which had the long lives so frequent a century ago. These evils were she thought, largely the result of premature motherhood, of ill-nourished childhood of unhealthy conditions surrounding expectant mothers, the passing away of customs necessarily hygienic, carried on under religious sanctions, unreplaced by similar care, based on scientific authority.

> "When women work in the factory, when they are crowded into large towns and dwell in congested *chawls,* they are flung into conditions unknown to the traditional village life, are left without help in adapting themselves to the new ways, and the infants die like flies, death-doomed are yet they are born."

Madam Besant quantified a new facts: in 1918, in British India, there were 8,430,560 births—a birth rate of 35 per 1000. In that same year the true number of infant deaths was 2,252,034—a death rate of 267 per 1,000. In the Central Provinces and Bihar the birth rate was highest, 13 per 1,000: the death rate among infants was also the maximum: the ghastly number of 399 per 1,000 was reached.

"Under these circumstances one wonders how many more die without record, and we know how many of those who survive grow feeble, ailing, and gradually wither away".

An important cause for this she felt was child marriage. In Calcutta alone the Bengal census recorded 18,256 child-wives, of whom 14,749 were between 10 and 12 years of age. There were 2,696 child-widow under 15. Malnutrition prior to and after birth was another and even greater cause among the poor: in the free schools for panchama children in Madras, a medical examination revealed that 78 per cent of the little pupils were suffering from malnutrition. This was, in fact, the danger which treatened the life of the nation, for it meant low vitality and weak grip of life. If epidemics swept away millions, it was because such tens of millions were perpetually under feed starving fathers generate, and starving mothers gave birth to infants who were starved before they were born.

Thus, to conclude, following are the questions for women's emancipation.

1. Spiritual and religious education
2. Pre-natal Medical care
3. Proper Nourishment
4. Special education in child care.
5. Respect for women
6. Removal of social and political disabilities
7. Cooperation in progress of home, society, nation and the world.

III

An Extract of First Speech on Annie Besant on Political Status of Women

The "rights of man" do not rest on a higher authority. They are not privileges held at the favour of a superior; they have their root in the nature of man; they are his by "divine"—that is to say, by *natural*—right. Kings, presidents, governments, draw their authority from the will of the people, the people draw their authority from themselves.

It is perfectly true that the want of representation in Parliament is not, *in itself,* a grave injury. In itself, I say, it is of secondary importance; its gravity consists in what it involves. You do not value money for its own sake—those little yellow counters are not intrinsically beautiful, nor are they in themselves worth toil and trouble and danger; but you value them for what they represent; and thus we value a vote, as a means to an end. In a free country a vote means power. When a man is a voter he counts as one in an election—his opinion influences the return. When the working classes wished to alter laws that pressed hardly on them, they agitated for Parliamentary Reform. "What folly! what waste of time! what throwing away of strength and energy! how unpractical! Why agitate for an extension of the franchise, when so many social burdens require to be lightened?" Why? Because they knew that when they won the franchise they could trust to themselves to remedy these social anomalies—when they had votes they could make these questions the test of the fitness or unfitness of a candidate for Parliament. Non-voters, they could only *ask* for reform; voters, they could *command* it. And this is the answer of women to those who urge on them that they should turn their attention to practical matters, and leave off this agitation about the franchise.

Tie up a man's hands, and then sneer that he has no aptitude for writing; or chain his feet, and show his natural incapacity for walking. John Stuart Mill has remarked: "The ladies of reigning families are the only women who are allowed the same range of interest and freedom of development as men, and it is precisely in their case that there is not found to be any inferiority. Exactly where and in proportion as woman's capacity for government has been tried, in that proportion have they been found adequate." In France, at the present day, the women rule business matters more than do the men, and the business capacity of French women is a matter of notoriety.

Those who stand up to champion an oppressed class do not look for gratitude from those for whom they labour. It is the bitterest curse of oppression that it crushes out in the breast of the oppressed the very wish to be free. A man once spent long years in the Bastille; shut up in his youth, old age found him still in his dungeon. The people assailed the prison, and among others this prisoner was set free; but the sunshine was agony to the eyes long accustomed to the darkness, and the fresh stir of life was as thunder to the ears accustomed to the silence of the dungeon; the prisoner pleaded to be kept a prisoner still. Was his action a proof that freedom is not fair? The slaves, after generations of bondage, were willing to remain slaves where their masters were kind and good. Is this a proof that liberty is not the birthright of a man?

What we demand is the right to choose our own representatives, so that our voice may have its share in making the laws which we are bound to obey. We share the duty of supporting the State, and we claim the right of helping to guide it. Taxation and representation run side by side, and if you will not allow us to be represented, you have no right to tax us.

In 1861, fifteen years ago, there were three and a half millions of women in England working for their livelihood; two and a half millions of these were unmarried, and were, therefore, unrepresented. Is there no pathos in these figures? Two and a half millions struggling to live honestly, but mute to tell of their wants or their wrongs. Mute, I say, for not one in a thousand has the power of the pen. And this is not the worst. Oh! friends, below these, pressed down there by the terrible struggle for existence, there is a lower depth yet, tenanted by thousands of whom it is not here my province to speak, thousands from whom a bitter wail goes up to which man's ears are deaf. Surely women need representation; surely there are grievances and wrongs of women which can only be done away with by those whom women sent to Parliament as their representatives.

Allow women to grow freely, to develop as nature bids them, and they will find room for home cares in their minds, and the warmest nestling place in their bosom will be the haven of the little child. But if you check, and fret, and carp at them, you will not succeed in keeping them back, but you will succeed in souring them and in making them hard and bitter.

Liberty for every human being, equality before the law for all in public and in private, fraternity of men and women in peaceful friendship, these are the promise of the dawning day. Co-workers in every noble labour, co-partners in every righteous project, co-soldiers in every just cause, men and women in the time to come shall labour, think and struggle side by side. The man shall bring his greater strength and more sustained determination, the woman her quicker judgment and purer heart, till man shall grow tenderer, and woman stronger, man more pure, and woman more brave and free. Till at last, generations hence, the race shall develop into a strength and beauty at present unimagined, and men and women shall walk this fair earth hand in hand, diverse, yet truly one, set each to each "As perfect music unto noble words."

To conclude, no single parameter is indicative of women's status and thus no single endeavour can improve their status in society as well as politics on health front, she need proper nutrition and special medical care. On social front, she need treatment equal to men and finally in politics, mere equality before law will do not suffice. There is a strong need to seriously implement the legal provisions meant for them.

> The moral training which should make men and women understand that growing knowledge and power is duty, is one of the most vital lessons for these modern days.
>
> —*Annie Besant*

6

Non-Cooperation Movement

> To call women the weaker sex is a libel; it is men's injustice to women. If by strength is meant moral power, then woman is immeasurably man's superior. Has she not greater intuition, is she not more self-sacrificing.... has she not greater powers of endurance, has she not greater courage? Without her man could not be. If non-violence is the law of our being, the future is with woman. I have nursed this thought now for years.
>
> —*Mahatma Gandhi*[1]

After closely witnessing the political condition and events in the country for nearly three years in the beginning, Gandhi equipped the freedom fighters with new arms of passive resistance, popularly known as *Satyagraha* (passive resistance, movement), a strategy he had earlier employed in South Africa.

Political Conditions

The years following the First Word War are most promising in the annals of the freedom movement for, during this period an organised and country-wide effort to overthrow the British rule was started by boycotting the government on necessary things and by launching *Satyagraha*. It was perhaps due to this technique that the freedom struggle which was more or less a monopoly of the intellectuals found a fertile land amongst the national masses and invited interest of the rich and the poor, the old and the young, the literate and the illiterate, industrialists and labourers, merchants and customers, lawyers and doctors, teachers and social workers, and above all, of ladies who now came in front to join the Satyagraha Army.

Lately, ladies had been taking increasing interest in socio-political issues; fillip to this was provided by the partition of

Bengal, the treatment of Indians in South Africa, the Home Rule League of Annie Besant, the First World War and by the Women's Indian Association which appeared in existence in 1917. This organisation became the pivot around which women assembled to discuss and demand their rights. A decade later an all-India orgnisation, the All India Women's Conference, was founded and its political target was self-government. The members stressed the need for responsible government which could satisfy the aspiration of the people.

The question of suffrage for women placed a common platform. The silence observed by the Montagu-Chelmsford Scheme on this issue, spite the representation made to the Secretary of State, accentuated the common sentiments. Later the Southborough Committee was requited to collect reforms and on the question of franchise. This committee journeyed to India. When it visited Bombay a requisition signed by eight hundred ladies of the Presidency was submitted to it.[2] besides similar requisitions were sent by the Women Graduates Union Bombay, all the Branches of the Women's India Association which figured about forty, the women's branch of the Home Rule League, the Bharat Stree Mandal and by the member of the All India Women's Deputation which had earlier met the Secretary of State on this issue.

Indian ladies also emerged personally as witnesses before the Southborough Committee to express their opinion. The Southborough Committee opposed the extending of franchise to women on the basis that the prevalent social condition in the country did not warrant franchise for ladies. Margaret Cousins, on behalf of the Association, said "Is this handful of men better able to judge these condition than were the thousands of Indian delegates of the Bombay and Delhi Congresses?[3] They urged the removal of disqualification in all the term of reforms.[4] Resolution were passed in various parts of the country this decision.[5] Mrs. Besant and Mrs. Naidu, present in England as members of the deputation to provide evidence before the Joint Parliamentary Committee, took up the case for ladies franchise. Mrs. Hirabai Tata[6] and Mrs. Mithi Bai Tata[7] were sent to England by the Women's Committee to display strong feelings of Indian women on this subject. The Joint Select Committee, however, put the responsibility of deciding the question of franchise on women to be handled by the future Legislative Councils of India for each province.

Madras was the first province to discard the disqualification of sex for the legislative franchise on April 1, 1921 and other provinces followed in its wake.[8] Thus, the women of India had started to understand their rights and responsibilities. They were aware of the assistance given to the British for successful closing of the war. Some of them had assisted in collecting battle funds while others in sewing clothes and do performing other odd jobs. Many had lost their brothers, fathers or husbands as soldiers who fought for the Allies.

India had assisted the British Government with men, money and materials throughout the war. It was, therefore, natural for looking for reward in the way of political development of the country. But a vehement demand on the part of the leaders of the people was ignored it led to the enactment of the Rowlett Bills which aimed at suppressing the existing modicum of liberties. Following the armistice it was expected that there would be some solace but the condition didn't change. For example, the transport facilities were disorganised, the cost of living was still high in 1919 "and the few cotton rungs which the poorest ryot wears became almost unpurchasable."[9]

Immediately after the publication of the presented Rowlett Bill in January 1919, a meeting was conducted by the Indian National Congress in the Gandhi *Ashram* (Ahmedabad), wherein a resolution[10] was passed to violate this Act, if passed.

One of the Bills was, however, passed facing opposition and it offered the Government powers in an emergency to judge cases without trial. The passing of the Bill came as a jolt to the nation as a whole. Gandhiji, therefore, declared his intention of launching a *Satyagraha* movement on 30 March 1919. It was postponed to 6 April, but unluckily the news did not reach in time to many places with the consequence that 30 March was observed as a day of *hartal* and inauguration of the disobedience movement. In the beginning the movement was non-violent, but gradually it became violent due to provocation by the police, and also, probably, because people were not trained enough to participate in such a mass movement non-violently. The happenings moved fast and the condition in the Punjab, as compared to other provinces, was critical. Fermentation existed in the districts of Lahore, Gurdaspur and Amritsar. People appeared in mobs and the rowdy elements destroyed the railway carriages, telegraph wires and the government buildings, the post offices and a few places were burnt as well. The Government retaliated sternly. Martial Law was proclaimed; the Punjab watched a reign of fear which dragged on till 11 June 1919.[11]

This movement culminated in the firing which took place in Jallianwala Bagh at Amritsar. In this city a peaceful assembly of twenty thousand people was shot on 13 April 1919 under the orders of General Dyer. According to the Hunter Enquiry Committee Report, four hundred people were shot dead and twelve hundred wounded. Over and above this, people were insulted in a variety of ways. The ladies had to suffer as well and there were examples of ruining the modesty of women. In some villages women were called out from their houses and harassed. Their and aces women were forcibly unveiled and fielty language was used against them.[12] The country demanded redress of the Punjab atrocities and the All India Congress Committee accepted these demands and asked for a neutral enquiry. Ultimately, compelled by the circumstances the Government appointed an Enquiry Committee with Sir Hunter as Chairman. The Indian National Congress also recruited another committee for the same.

The next year witnessed the Report of the Hunter Enqiry Committee. The recommendations and findings of this Committee were unsatisfactory. The Government's decision was "that Dyer's" action was commanded by a stern though wrong sense of duty.[13] Following the government decision, Dyer was censured and was deprived of his command. The action was approved by the House of Commons but there was furore in the House of Lords over Dyer's punishment. Besides, he was even hailed as protagonist by certain section of the people and a propaganda in his favour was launched which included the sponsoring of a fund for him. He was also offered twenty-three thousand pounds and a sword by the English ladies in India.[14]

This action strengthened nationalism in India. Added to this was the unsettled position of Turkey, the 'Khilafat'[15] movement which greatly roused the feelings of the Muslims of India.

Turkey was regarded the greatest Muslim power by the Muslims of this country. The Sultan of this Empire was 'Khalifa' of Islam and as such temporal head. During the war Muslims assured by the Prime Minister of the England that the Turks would be preserved. A deputation of the Muslim Khilafat Conference also visited England to present their viewpoint as regards Turkey and the *Khilafat.* The Government paid no heed to these requests and the draft treaty called the Treaty of Severes published on May 14, 1920,[16] put aside all the promises made during the war and this dissatisfied the Muslims further.

Gandhiji felt this as an opportunity to bring the two communities together. He, therefore, warned the Government that if justice was not done to the Muslims he would restart Satyagraha.[17] A special session of the Congress conducted in September 1920 in a resolution approved the resumption of policy of "progressive non-violence, non-cooperation until the said wrongs were righted and *Swaraj* established."[18] To achieve this goal a nation-wide programme of boycotting titles and honour, elections and legislatures, schools and colleges, courts and tribunals was started. The people were advised not to join military service. The Government 'durbars', official and semi-official functions were boycotted. The sale and use of alcohol and foreign fabric was prevented through quietful picketing.

Mahatma Gandhi believed in power of women. Writing in 1921 he said : "I expect great things from you, I expect the women to do their full share in the struggle. Let government capture everyone of our soldier I don't mind. Our work is so very easy that even our women can carry it out without difficulty."[19] The *Satyagraha* movement inaugurated by Gandhiji was such that women could not sit and witness the war between the Government and the people and so a quick reply was made to the call of Mahatma Gandhi, women came forward. They marched in processions, propagated the use of Khadi, and even courted arrests. Though the number of ladies arrested was very small, yet a beginning was marked and an example set that, if required women would face the most difficult situations.

Bengal had been in the vanguard of the freedom struggle and women of this province wasted no time and came out in the field. They organised *Mahila Karma Samaj* or the Ladies Orgnisation Board of the Bengal Provincial Congress Committee,[20] to continue campaign and constructive work amongst the ladies of Bengal. The organisation possessed its own office and facilities for the stay of all time workers also. Branches of this organisation were spread all over Calcutta. A batch of twenty-five or thirty women workers were provided number of houses to continue their work. The women members of the organisation addressed meetings as well. In one such meeting organised by Smt. Inder Prabha Majumdar and Smt. Radu Bibi, in response to the appeal made by these ladies many women left their jewellery, broke their foreign bangles and pledged not to wear these again.[21] In a single meeting at Gauhati (Now Guwahati) (Assam) sixty women volunteers were enlisted. They went about on foot carrying the message to the people to discard selling or wearing foreign cloth.[22]

Smt. Basanti Devi and Urmila Devi, wife and sister, of Deshbandhu Das, were the leaders of the women's movement in Bengal. They wandered about the streets of Calcutta selling Khaddar and campaigning against the use of foreign fabric and the habit of liquor. They were arrested while selling handloom cloth.[23] The others who were arrested with them were Smt. Anukul Mitter, Smt. Surya Shome, Smt. Umashi Devi, Smt. Satya Devi, a few boys and eight *Sikh* ladies. They were, however, freed in the evening.[24] But their arrest excited the people of Bengal and further strengthened the movement. Afterwards when Smt. Urmila Devi was interviewed in Ahmedabad and asked why they had courted arrest, she asserted, "We felt that although Bengal was sympathetic, it was only a sort of passive sympathy. To make it most dynamic we thought Bengal must be appealed to in a special manner of involving, of course, a special measure of sacrifice and so, our arrest produced the desired effect."[25] She urged the ladies to join the ranks of volunteers. She stated that women would be called upon to hold responsibilities while men were being jailed.

Mrs. Basanti Devi also presided over the Bengal Provincial Congress Session in 1922 at Chittagong. She stated, "Freedom will come as a matter of course to the extent we are able to do penance by our sacrifice, by our sorrows and sufferings, by our patience and by the strength of our character."[26]

In Bombay, women also protested meetings against His Royal Highness, the Prince of Wales' visit and the municipal address which was to be offered to him on behalf of the citizens of Bombay. After the meeting, they marched in a procession to a temple and offered prayers for the achievement of Swaraj.

Kasturba Gandhi, having her first lesson in Satyagraha in South Africa, occupied her place here as well. She presided over meetings and also toured several States campaigning for the success of the movement. Presiding over the Gujarat Provincial Conference she condemned untouchability and preached Swadeshi. She requested the women to for the adopt spinning and weaving of *Khadi.* "If we want to earn Swaraj," she said, "we shall have to fill the bowl of Goddess of Freedom."[27] When it was conveyed to her that her son Devadas Gandhi had been arrested, she said: "Only two sons of mine have gone to jail, but twenty thousand sons of mother Hind are in jail; how can I bemoan my lot! Young sons of mother Hind, carry on the work of Khaddar with such zeal that you may either regain your brothers or join them in jail."[28]

In the Punjab the first ladies' meetings was convenced on the 6th and 7th of December in 1922, presided over by Kasturba Gandhi. Randha Devi, wife of Lala Lajpat Rai, was the Chairman of the Reception Committee. In her address (this was read on her behalf by Smt. Parvati Devi) she announced that the goal of the conference was to warn to the idlers while the leaders were undergoing imprisonment.[29] She motivated her country women to support the *Swaraj* movement with enthusiasm and courage, characteristic of Punjabi ladies.

Parvati Devi

Parvati Devi,[30] an ardent worker of the Congress, was arrested in Meerut for the so-called inflaming lectures. She was taken to Agra Jail in jail-uniform. No one was permitted to be on the platform. As a mark of respect ladies marched in a procession on December 16, 1922.[31] She was convicted and was sentenced to two years imprisonment, the highest sentence so far awarded to any women.

Bai Amman (Abadi Bano Begum)

Bai Amman was one of the significant personages at this time. She belonged to an aristocratic Muslim family but discarded veil when her sons[32] were deprived of their freedom. She addressed meetings all over India. She was invited to join the deputation for women's franchise. But she denied on the basis that she would rather inspire her own countrymen than visit an Englishmen conveying a petition.

Addressing a meeting at Lahore, she said the Indians have committed two blunders during the last 150 years; they sided with the British which captured their own King and secondly, they assisted the English during the outbreak of 1857. Without these mistakes there was no chance of these "merchants" being supreme in India and shakling Indians in the fetters of serfdom. "Would they," she continued, "commit another folly and put their aged mother to shame?" "Be man," she added, "and carry out the determination you have formed."[33]

In an open letter Bai Amman thanked the people for their kind emotions towards her and her sons. She expected that the Muslim women would rise to the occasion and assist the national cause by putting every pice, and handful of grain that could be provided as duty to India. She penned, "We had been sacrificing ourselves for our fathers and husbands and sons, but so long as this spirit of Indian womanhood is not lost, I, for one, feel that nothing really is lost."[34]

She advised the establishment of *Panchayats* throughout India. She ardently, championed the use of *Khaddar* and the Hindu-Muslim unity.[35] She served of the cause of the Khilafat, Swaraj and Hindu Muslim Unity. In this connection she visited Rawalpindi, Gujranwala and Kasur.[36] In a meeting at Simla in September 1922, she made a special appeal to ladies to take up Khaddar. She was eager to visit the Frontier Province, but orders were issued for bidding her entry into that region.[37]

In another meeting in the Punjab she said that some people houses or jewellary to their children after their death, but she opined that nothing was as good as freedom and asked women to leave Swaraj after their death for the children. *Swaraj* she said, could not be achieved by asking, but was sure to arrive if people had valour and women a heart to sacrifice for the cause.[38]

Bai Amman addressed another ladies, conference at Bombay where six thousand people gathered. A resolution requesting the women to enrol as members, was passed at the gathering. At another meeting at Ahmedabad, she requested the people to unite, for, "without co-operation among the different communities we can't liberate our country or live peaceful and honourable lives."[39]

In February 1922, she visited Patna and Bhagalpur. At Bhagalpur she was not permitted to meet the political prisoners and as a protest the prisoners and their relatives refused to see one another.[40] She collected sixty thousand rupees from Darbhanga (Bihar) for Khilafat Committee and she was offered a purse of twenty thousand rupees at Mongyr[41] (Bihar).

The question of prosecuting Bai Amman for provoking speeches also emerged before the government. But her arrest was not advisable.[42]

Mahatma Gandhi, sending a special message to Bai Amman on the eve of his arrest in March 1922, said: "Tell Bai Amman to pray for me and for all of us and to carry on the work which we have left behind. Her prayers and work will be quite sufficient to ensure our quick release and success."[43]

Bai Amman carried out the political work so dear to her till she died in 1924. Mahatma Gandhi paid an emotional tribute to her. He stated : "She realised that the freedom of India was impossible without Hindu-Muslim unity and Khaddar. She, therefore, ardently preached unity which had become an article of faith with her. She had discarded all her foreign or mill made clothing and taken to Khaddar . . ."[44]

Women in almost all the provinces were trying their best to encourage people to participate in the movement and were assisting to carry on the campaign. Mrs. Motilal Nehru, when she heard of the conviction of her only son, Jawaharlal, said: "I am happy Jawaharlal has the courage and bravery to stand for his conviction for the cause of liberty and truth . . . "She appealed to all women to consider the touch of foreign cloth as polluting. "This cloth has blood of our brothers and sister, how can we wear it?"[45] She said that the work for which Jawaharlal had gone to prison could not be prevented. If the men of India have lost strength, she said, "we women will do it. Are the jails of mother India meant only for men?"[46]

Lucknow also was a place of activity at this time. Meetings under Section 144 were for bidden but such weapons of the Government did not worry the people. They held their meetings in the Congress Committee's Office which were addressed to by Mrs. Abdul Qadir. Women have appealed to take to wearing *Khaddar* and to exhort men to join the national movement. A committee was formed, with Mrs. Abdul Qadir as president, to perform the work among the women.[47]

Women of Sind marched in processions and moved through the main markets and streets singing national songs and delivering motivating lectures.[48]

The non-cooperation movement daily gained momentum. The writer of the Simon Commission noticed that "Defiance of authority became widespread, an extraordinary development in Indian districts, where the power of Government had never been questioned within living memory."[49]

The government accepted this challenge by arresting people by *lathi* charging on processions and announcing the organisation as unlawful. When the Congress met in 1921 some thirty thousand Congress workers were in prison.[50]

The movement at this time was also growing violent. Riots in Bombay resulted in fifty deaths and three hundred and seventy-nine injured.

These riots were followed by a tragic action in *Chauri Chaura* in Gorakhpur district, United Provinces, where twenty-one police constables were assassinated with revolting cruelty by a mob acting under the impulse of the anti-Government movement.

Gandhiji could not tolerate the movement changing its creed of non-violence and consequently suspended the movement. He was arrested and sentenced to six years' imprisonment.

Apparently the movement did not succeed; but it had created the interest of the masses and also gave the first lesson in *Satyagraha* to the nation. Gandhiji provided a new foundation to the new movement. Emerson observes: "Gandhi has, I believe, done his work. He has made India self-conscious. He has given India a new sense of self-respect. His programme has been characterised by many negative features . . . It has never put forward even a suggestive outline of the Government, it would substitute for the one, it would tear down . . . But Gandhi has given a moral basis and a spiritual standing to India's revolution."[51]

Formation of a National Convention

The National Convention, formally inaugurated in 1922 was supported by the liberals and the National Home Rule League. Besant was instrumental in producing such an organisation and deputed to visit Simla to present the scheme before the two Houses of Parliament having session then. An Executive Committee, from amongst the members of both the houses representing the several provinces, was framed. A conference was conducted in Delhi in 1923 reasserting itself. Besant launched a vigorous agitation for the recognition of this body and also commenced a private company in England for the foundation of a weekly newspaper *United India*. This was sent to the sorted list of Peers of the House of Lords and also to the Indian newspapers.

A deputation on behalf of the National Convention also was sponsored to England under the leadership of Besant on 26 April 1924, for the furtherance of the cause of self-government for India. Besant divided the activities of the deputation in England into three types : speeches and common discussions, wide demonstrations in Queen's Hall, London, and Free Trade Hall, Manchester, to influence public view in England and a special conference with the Indian Parliamentary Committee through which the members of the House of Commons were to be addressed, and interviews with the members of the government. The deputation produced a memorandum signed by Dr. Besant and others, presenting a united demand for Dominion Home Rule for India.

The National Conference met in Delhi in the early part of 1924 immediately after the general elections at the end of 1923. Mrs. Besant was elected the General Secretary. Dr. H.S. Gour proposed her name for this office and said: "I am sure that when the work of the convention is fulfilled and achieved, she will live in our hearts as a lady who had done far more for the emancipation of the people of this country than any political thinker or statesman of our race and blood, who has striven and worked for the achievement of the Self-Government for India."[52]

The convention divided itself into seven committees to deal with different sections of the constitution to be prepared for India. A draft was prepared on these reports and the convention sat in Bombay in December and considered and modified it. It printed the fruits and distributed them among political parties, inviting further amendments. Later the draft was deposited to a sub-committee appointed by a Committee of All Parties presided over by Mahatma Gandhi. Its sub-committee incorporated a number of amendments and these accompanied by the others were submitted to a Drafting Committee in Madras having the Hon'ble C.P. Ramaswamy Aiyer, Mr. Shiva Rao, Sir Ram Yadunandan Prasad and Dr. Annie Besant with powers to correct it's language where necessary and to see the Bill through the press and publish it in the name of the Convention.[53]

The Bill[54] was carried to England in July 1925, and was introduced in the House of Commons as a private member's Bill in December 1925, and again in 1927. It received a great support of the Labour Party. For more than three years it remained the first and the only constitution for India drawn by responsible representatives in a National Convention and it was in itself a sufficient answer to those who thought that Indians lack national unity and that its leaders could present no outline of an agreed constitution.

The Bill known as the Commonwealth of India Bill, was passed in its first reading but failed to become an Act as the Government of England was subsequently approached by some leaders who opposed this Bill.

While supporting the boycott resolution at the Indian National Congress on 26th December 1927, she stated: "We want men who know India's needs and Indians' wrongs, men who can understand Indian problems. You have boycotted us, we boycott you. You have said no Indian shall sit on the Commission, we say let no Englishman judge India's fitness."

Throughout the next year Besant requested for unity and asked India for a single bill to be sent to Parliament as India's demand. She attended the first meeting of the All Parties Conference (1928) where she began discussion leading to the appointment in May 1928, following a motion by Mrs. Besant, of the Nehru Committee.

During this time the Government kept on intercepting her letters. So, she demanded her prosecution if they had evidence against her."[55]

While supporting the resolution on Dominion Status in the All Parties Conference, she urged the formation of a parallel government on Sein Fein[56] rules. She reported: "Make many

Bardoils all over the country and I tell you that the English people are very practical people and before many Bardolis are established they will come to you for settlement. This is the kind of agitation they understand."[57]

Besant was seventy-two years old but yet very active. She began her campaign favouring the Nehru report and went to Lucknow, Banares, Bombay, Poona and many other cities. In December the National Congress endorsed the report but she opposed Gandhiji once again when he moved a resolution stating that if the British Government did not accept the report in its entirety by the end of 1929, (the constitution drafted by the Nehru Committee), the Congress would again hold Non-cooperation.[58]

By now, Mrs. Besant's health was getting worse. Ceaseless public work performed by her for six decades affected the health of dynamic soldier. By 1933 she passed away, but her work in different spheres is always unforgettable.

In Mrs. Besant's work and efforts led slowly to the achievement of *Swaraj.* The Commonwealth of India Bill 1925, if agreed upon by all the political leaders, would have brought national freedom much earlier, and may be, without partition.

Again Annie Besant's agitation and aspirations led to the non-cooperation movement of Mahatma Gandhi. It was at her instance that the title of Knighthood[59] was denounced, and dissociation from governmental educational institutions was started.[60] The National Education Trust was also founded by Annie Besant. Sri Prakasa rightly said: "When we think of it, it might almost be said that Mahatma Gandhi who had been the undisputed leader of the Indian National Congress and as such of a major portion of political India since 1920 only intensified the programme that had been chalked out by Annie Besant in the days when she led the extreme wing of Indian Politics.[61]

Mrs. Besant had taken up issues like untouchables, education on Indian lines and suited to the Indian people *swadeshi* from an economic point of view, women's participation in the movement and Hindu-Muslim unity; and some issues emphasised by Gandhi later.

Mrs. Besant was a great person, who contributed a lot to this land and motivated the men and women of to realise their freedom.

Women Legislators

It was for the first time that women voted in the elections of 1926. The franchise granted to women was very restricted.[62]

In these elections 22 per cent women voted in Madras, 12 per cent in Bombay and in Punjab, 9.6 per cent in Bengal and 4.5 per cent in the U.P. The first woman to stand for elections was Kamala Devi Chattopadhyaya.[63] She secured 4,461 votes while her opponent 4,949, thus, losing by a narrow margin.

Amongst the Indian States, Travancore was the first to represent women. Dr. Poonan Ducose was the first woman health minister in India in 1925. Smt. Madhavi Ammal was nominated to the Cochin Legislative Council.

In British India, Madras led again by nominating Muthulakshmi Reddi to the Legislative Council. She was later elected as Deputy President of the Madras Legislative Council. Muthulakshmi Reddi[64] was also the first woman medical graduate of the Madras University. She related herself with Women's India Association from its very inception, i.e., from 1917, and was one of the members of the deputation which met the Secretary of State in association with the women's franchise.

Once Mrs. Reddi was in the Council, a staunch advocate of women's welfare, she saw to the enactment of the elimination of the *Devadasi* system; and for laws to close prostitution and save minor girls. She amended the Children's Act and worked for the creation of Health-Schools and Children's Wards. She also actively campaigned for the *Sharda Act* which was passed by the Central Legislature.

She also became the first Alderwoman of the City Corporation Madras for two years during which she displayed interest in problem like the child education and child welfare and beggary.

In 1928, Muthulakshmi Reddi was in England as a member of the Hartog Committee appointed by the Secretary of State to pressure women's educational development and problems in India. While returning to India she represented India at the Paris Congress of the Women's International Alliance as a delegate from India.

Occupied as she was with the uplift and education of women, the abolition of social evils and the reconstruction of

Indian society on an equivalent and democratic basis – Mrs. Reddi succeeded to be drawn towards political activity. Obviously the economic exploitation to which India was being subjected was an insuperable barrier in the way of attempts for a better society.

Mrs. Reddi visited America and attended the International Women's Council in Chicago in 1933. She also went to England to provide evidence before the joint select committee in connection with women's franchise.

Mrs. Reddi was instrumental in bringing about the setting up of the Cancer Hospital in Madras. She was the first organiser and Chairman of the Madras State Social Welfare Advisory Board (1954-1957). Muthulakshmi Reddi was awarded *Padma Bhushan* in 1956 for her distinguished services. She continued to participate in various organisations.

Bardoli Satyagraha—1928

A no-tax campaign was started in Bardoli[65] under the leadership of Sardar Patel. It was undertaken to correct an economic injustice. The Government of Bombay, against the advice of the Joint Parliamentary Committee and opposite to the resolution of the Bombay Legislative Council of the Bombay Presidency in 1924, considerably emphasised the rate of rural taxation, nominally at 20 per cent but actually, in some instances, over 60 per cent. The public felt that the increase was unwarranted and that an impartial committee to conduct enquiry be framed. The Government paid no attention.

The people refused to pay the taxes. The authorities met this challenge with the common *lathi* charge, imprisonment, fines, attachments and auctions of land. But none had much effect on the people. The women of Bardoli participated in this movement from its very inception but they had no leader. Smt. Mithuben Petit and Smt. Bhaktben Desai from Bombay greatly strengthened the movement amongst ladies. The women attended the meetings covering long distances on foot. They had composed motivating songs suitable to the occasion.

Sardar Patel arranged for Mithuben, Bhaktiben, Maniben Patel[66] and other ladies to camp on those very lands to be sold by fixing their tents and huts on it. The women in the area assisted in the collection of funds also. A lady, still unknown, donated two hundred rupees and promised to send this amount regularly every month till the fight was over. The Bardoli *Satyagraha,* besides proving an eye opener to the people, exhibited the large measure of coinage among women. However, it served as a training ground for the women of Bombay and a motivation for women all over the country. It was for the first time here that the literate and the illiterate and ignorant women participated in the movement. "The heroism of the simple unsophisticated women of Bardoli", observed Mr. Desai, "was an inspiration to all women outside Bardoli."[67]

The Bardoli *Satyagraha* was successfully completed in September 1928, after five and a half months of struggle. It made the Government aware of the strength of an organised and combined attempt.

Simon Commission

The Simon Commission arrived in India in 1928. Since no Indian was represented on the Commission, it was boycotted by the nationalist Indians. The Dominion State Constitution (commonly known as the Nehru Report) was adopted by the All-Parties Conference. The Calcutta Congress adopted this constitution if the British Parliament accepted it in its present form before December 31, 1929, failing which civil disobedience was to ensue.

References

1. Gandhi, M.K., *Women and Social Injustice*, Ahmedabad, 1945, p. 169.
2. *Mrs. M. Cousins and Her Work in India*, p. 14.
3. The Indian National Congress in its session held in December 1918 passed a resolution unanimously on the franchise of women, "that this Congress urges that women possessing the same qualifications as are laid down for men in any part of the scheme, shall not be disqualified on account of their sex." (Proceedings of the thirty-third session of the Indian National Congress held at Delhi in December, 1918, p. 5, *Modern Review*, January, p. 652.
4. *Modern Review*, *ibid.*, p. 652.
5. About 11cablegrams were sent, giving the text of the resolutions passed at the public meetings to prominent people in England emphasising the need for women's franchise.
6. Mrs. Hirabai Tata was the General Secretary of Bombay Women's India Association. She organised a number of meetings in Bombay and popularised the women's suffrage movement.
7. Daughter of Hirabai Tata.

8. The reactionary element was however not in favour of granting the franchise right to women. The Women's Association busied itself in writing to the members of the Councils, appealing to them to accede this right to women. Its members also went from province to province to witness the debate on suffrage.
9. Chirol, Valentine, *India*, London, 1926, p. 183.
10. In part the resolution reads: "We shall refuse civilly to obey these laws and such other laws as a committee to be hereafter appointed may think fit, and we further affirm that in this struggle we will faithfully follow truth and refrain from violence to life, person or property." (Report of the Disorders Enquiry Commission, *The Hunter Report,* London, p. 61).
11. Sitaramayya, Dr. Pattabhi, *The History of the Indian National Congress*, Vol. I, p. 164.
12. For details see Appendix G.
13. *India in 1920* (Official Report published every year), p. 238.
14. Sitaramayya, Dr. Pattabhi, *The Nationalist Movement of India*. Bombay, 1950, p. 45.
15. The Khalifa is the spiritual head of the Muslims; Khilafat is that which pertains to him.
16. This draft treaty was in one way lenient. In fact no consideration was given to the feelings of the Muslims in this country. By virtue of this treaty the Straits were internationalised. Turkey was also deprived of her rights in Egypt, Tripolitania, Morocco and Tunisia and the territories of Arabia, Palestine, Mesopotamia and Syria were taken away. In addition, Greece was temporarily to administer Smyrna and South Western Asia Minor and add Eastern Thrace (predominantly Turkish) to her realm. However the treaty of Lausanne offered better peace terms to Turkey by 1922.
17. The first Satyagraha was suspended on 18 April 1919.
18. Proceedings of the Indian National Congress, 1920, Quoted in Post Wheeler, *India Against the Storm*, New York, p. 177.
19. *Independent*, December 22,1921 (unregistered paper edited by Mahadev Desai, A.I.C.C. Library).
20. *Amrita Bazar Patrika*, July 7, 1922.
21. *Ibid.*, July 9, 1922.
22. Independent (unregistered paper edited by Mahadev Desai) December 27, 1921.
23. *Amrita Bazar Patrika*, January 10, 1922.
24. *Ibid.*
25. *Amrita Bazar Patrika*, January 1, 1923.
26. *Ibid.*, April 16, 1922.
27. *Ibid.*, May 30, 1922.
28. *Ibid.*, May 20, 1922.
29. *Ibid.*, December 9, 1922.
30. She was the daughter of Lala Karam Chand of Lyallpur (West Punjab), a rich man of the area. She was born in April 1888. Parvati was educated in the Kanya Maha Vidyalaya, Jalandhar, from which institution she passed her middle class examination. It was her father who broke the caste barrier by marrying her in 1905, to Dr. Milkhi Ram Bhatia employed in the Railway Service, thus setting an example of an intercaste marriage,

an unknown thing in those days. Her father also had two scheduled caste servants in the house who later took a prominent part in the Ghadar Party. The family therefore was far ahead of the times. Parvati was not fated to enjoy the married life for long as her husband died after two and a half years of her marriage in an accident. She, therefore, came to live with her father and decided to devote her life, working for the country. She qualified in Sanskrit and became a teacher in Delhi. She later came to Amritsar as a teacher and was in this city at the time of the Rowlatt Act Agitation. (This information was supplied by Shri Chander, brother of Parvati Devi).

31. *Amrita Bazar Patrika*, December 17, 1922.
32. Mohammed Ali and Shukat Ali.
33. *Civil and Military Gazette*, August 31, 1922.
34. *Amrita Bazar Patrika*, January 9, 1920.
35. In fact "one noticeable feature of the general excitement" observed *India 1919*, "was the unprecedented fraternization between the Hindus and the Muslims. The union between the leaders had now for long been a fixed plan of the nationalist platform. In this time of public excitement even the lower classes agreed for once to forget their differences. Extraordinary scene of fraternization occurred. Hindus publicly accepted water from the hands of Muslims and vice versa. Hindu-Muslim unity was the watchword of processions indicated both by cries and banners. Hindu leaders had actually been allowed to preach from the pulpit of a mosque."
36. A place near Lahore in west Punjab (Pakistan).
37. *Amrita Bazar Patrika*, September 2, 1922.
38. *Ibid.*, December 12, 1922.
39. *Ibid.*, January 5, 1922.
40. *Ibid.*, February 5, 1922.
41. *Ibid.*
42. *Home Political Proceeding*, 1922, File No. 933, p. 1.
43. *Amrita Bazar Patrika*, March 21, 1922.
44. *Ibid.*, May 23, 1922.
45. *Ibid.*
46. *Ibid.*, January 13, 1922.
47. *Ibid.*
48. *Ibid.*, June 25, 1922.
49. An Indian Statutory Commission was appointed to go into the question of constitutional development of India under Sir John Simon, which is popularly known as Simon Commission.
50. *Report of the Indian Statutory Commission* (Simon Commission), 1930, Vol. I, p. 250.
51. Emerson, *Non-Violent Non-Cooperation in India*, Asia, August 1922, p. 674; quoted in Walterbank T. Walter, *A Short History of India and Pakistan*, p. 157.
52. Aiyer, A. Rangaswami, *Annie Besant—Her Work for Swaraj*, p. 48.
53. Besant, Annie, *India Bonded or Free*, Second Edition, 1930, p. 237.

54. For details of the Bill, see Appendix to *India-Bonded or Free* by Annie Besant, p. 225.
55. *Amrita Bazar Patrika*, May 19, 1928.
56. Irish revolutionaries.
57. *Bengalee*, December 25, 1928.
58. *Proceedings of the Indian Congress*, 1928.
59. Sir Subba Rao Iyer denounced his title.
60. Mrs. Shiva Kamu, later sister-in-law of Mr. Arundale left the Medical College.
61. Prakasa, Sri, *Annie Besant*, Bombay, 1954, p. 144.
62. The following table showing the province-wise proportion of electors in the general constituencies to population, for the 1926 electorate, testifies the statement:

Province	*Population of the electoral areas in 1921*	*Electors male and female Male electors in brackets*	*Proportion of electors to population*	*Proportion of male electors to adult male population*	*Proportion of female electors to female population*
Madras	4,23,19,000	116,000 (18,65,000)	3.2%	11.6%	1.0%
Bombay	1,92,92,000	39,000 (7,59,000)	3.9%	13.4%	0.8%
Bengal	4,62,14,000	38,000 (11,73,000)	2.5%	9.7%	0.3%
United Provinces	4,53,76,000	51,000 (15,89,000)	3.5%	12.4%	0.4%
Punjab	2,06,75,000	21000 (6,97,000)	3.4%	11.9%	0.5%
Bihar & Orissa	3,38,20,000	None (3,73,000)	1.1%	4.6%	
Assam	67,35,000	About 3,000 (25,000)	3.7%	14.2%	0.2%
Central Provinces including Berar	1,27,80,000	None (1,69,000)	1.3%	5.2%	

63. Her account appears in the next chapter.
64. She was born in 1886 in Pudukottah State (now merged with the Madras province).
65. A place near Surat in Bombay Province.

66. Maniben Patel was the daughter of late Sardar Vallabhbhai Patel known as the Iron Man. She was born in 1904 at Gana near Bombay and received her early education at Queen Mary's High School and St. Joseph's Convent at Bombay. She later studied at Gujarat Vidyapith, Ahmedabad.
67. Desai, M., *The Story of Bardoli*, p. 154.

7

Civil Disobedience Movement

The failure of the Government to accept the Nehru Report and pay attention to the demand of the people within the stipulated period compelled the Indian National Congress to proceed with its designs of launching *Satyagraha* as had been decided at its session in December 1928, at Calcutta.

Therefore, the Indian National Congress which met in December 1929, at Lahore announced on the midnight of December 31, 1929, the objective of the Congress to have complete freedom instead of Dominion Status.[1] Thus, the new year was ushered in with new expectations, a changed creed and the prospect of an active struggle ahead.

The Congress members of the legislature were directed to boycott elections and 26 January 1930, was announced as Independence Day which was to be celebrated throughout the nation every year. Gandhiji was empowered to initiate the Civil Disobedience Movement according to his manner.

Gandhiji chose the breaking of Salt Laws as the centre of gravity. He experienced that since salt was a thing of common use, salt tax was unfair for the poor in the land.

Salt Satyagraha

Gandhiji commenced his historic march to Dandi on the sea coast near Jalalpur on 12 March 1930, formally inaugurated the propaganda[2] and was arrested on the 6th of April.

His arrest was the long-awaited indication and the campaign began with countrywide strikes. It specially electrified the patriotic enthusiasm in women which not only gave a two-fold courage and support to the cause but also invited attention and appreciation from the outside world.

At first, women had not been permitted to participate as Gandhiji had felt they would complicate matters. But the ladies of the land, coveting a place of equality with men, could not sit silently at the call of the country. They protested that in these crucial days there should not be any watertight compartments of services. They demanded that "no conference, no congress or commission dealing with the welfare of India should be held without the presence on them of their kind. Similarly, they must ask that no marches, no imprisonment, no demonstrations organised for the welfare of India should prohibit women from a share in them." Subsequently, they were permitted to participate in all phases of the campaign.[3]

They began their march on the road to freedom by breaking salt laws, forest laws, taking out *Prabhat Pheries,* processions, picketing schools, colleges, legislative councils and clubs. The Government faced the just demand with *lathi* charge, shooting, arrests, Section 144, Press Ordinance, Unlawful Instigation Ordinance and Intimidation Ordinance.

They were determined to participate in the movement bearing various official punishments inflicted. The Provincial Secretary of the Bengal Congress Committee alleged that sex was no protection. Two women had been caned on their bare backs.[4] In another incident at Allhabad the police did the most heinous thing by *lathi* charging a procession led by Smt. Swaroop Rani, also received a lathi blow as a consequence of which she felt unconscious.[5] In Delhi ten women were injured due to *lathi* charge; while in Madhya Pradesh three women murdered as a result of firing in connection with the violation of forest laws.

These atrocious acts did not discourage the women, but ignited their desire to suffer more, to sacrifice more and to obtain more.

As a protest against the tough measure of the government the women in high designations resigned their posts. Muthulakshmi Ammal resigned her seat in the Legislative Council and her post as Deputy President of the Council. Mrs. Hansa Mehta and Kamalbai Lakshman Rao resigned their offices as Honourary Magistrates. Miss Dickson, the first woman member of the Central Legislative Assembly resigned her seat and refused *Kaiser-i-Hind* medal.[6] Besides, various women took active part in the Civil Disobedience Movement.

Sarojini Naidu

Sarojini Naidu, the poetess, politician and peace-maker, was born in Hyderabad on February 13, 1879. Her father Dr. Aghonath Chattopadhya, a Bengali gentleman, founded the *Nizam* College and till his death, worked hard in the sphere of education. He was a reputed scientist. After matriculating at Hyderabad, Sarojini was sent to England in 1895, for higher studies on a scholarship sponsored by the *Nizam.* She studied at King's College, London, and then Girton College, Cambridge University. She could not study further due to ill health and returned to India in 1898. She passed a few months in Switzerland and Italy before returning to India. The rich historic past of Italy appears to have kindled her heart for freedom. She married Dr. Naidu in 1898, breaking that wall of caste and religion.

Mrs. Naidu requested in 1909, the students in the Byramji Jeejabai Institution, Bombay, that "The highest ideal, the climax of modern spirit should be the unification of the races of India, the unity, which of mutual industry of a common education, of disinterested labour, of breaking up ancient barriers, of eliminating ancient hatred and of the recognition of common brotherhood, that bound the Hindus and Mohammedans, the Mohamedans with *Parsis* and the *Parsis* with Christians."[7]

In the same year she attended the Social Service Conference and moved a resolution for saving the Hindu widows. Subsequently, she dwelt upon the female education. "Until and unless," she said, "they raise the fallen women in this country and make their voice heard, India's salvation was only a distant dream."[8]

She appeared for the first time on the political scenario as the "ambassador of Hindu-Muslim unity" in 1913 when she attended and addressed the Muslim League session.[9] After three years in 1916, Mrs. Naidu lectured from the Congress platform sponsoring the resolution on self-government. Then onwards she took distinguished part in the country's political life. The period that followed was full of difficulties and as such of ceaseless activities for the people determined to serve the nation.

Sarojini Naidu, who witnessed the salvation and happiness of life in the service to the nation, fought for self-government on the one hand and women's rights on the other.[10]

Mrs. Naidu led the deputation of leading ladies in social and political sphere in December 1917. This deputation waited on Montagu to secure female voting rights.

Next year in September 1918, she attended the special session of the Congress at Bombay and was instrumental in securing the resolution on women's franchise passed, whereby they were not to be disqualified on ground of sex.[11]

Mrs. Naidu visited England in 1919 as a member of Home Rule League Deputation to provide evidence before the Joint Parliamentary Committee. She used this opportunity to put forward women's case for franchise as well. She felt that without effective propaganda the Montagu-Chelmsford Constitution was likely to be suppressed with sex disqualifications. Hence, she organised a powerful agitation in England. She also headed a Joint Deputation of all the different Indian political organisations then in England and made a strong claim of the Indian female for franchise. She demanded that the provinces should be left free to settle whether or not special arrangements were needed where veil existed.[12]

Early in 1919 when Gandhiji inaugurated the *Satyagraha* Movement, Sarojini Naidu, was one of the first to take the promise. Then she went to Bombay, Madras and Ahmedabad and worked constantly to propagate the cause, Sarojini Naidu made special requests to women against the Rowlatt Act. She also sold prescribed literature and participated in the *Satyagraha* demonstrations in Bombay.

At a public meeting at Ahmedabad she condemned the Montagu-Chelmsford Reforms. Speaking about the arrival of the Secretary of State, Montagu, she stated, "His sentimental journey through the length and breadth of the land in the company of Lord Chelmsford and their expression of sympathy bore no fruit, for in one hand they had the sword and a cup of poison in the other and seemed to say : 'Here is bread for you but before you reach out for it you must drain this cup of poison to the dregs'." But she insisted: "As long as Indians have rectitude and strength in them, as long as they have any sense of self-respect they will stoutly refuse to empty the cup of poison."[13] She was in England, in 1920, for treatment and carried out her work there. She acquainted the people in England with the highhandedness of the Martial Law authorities, Her lecture in Kingsway Hall, London, produced Naidu-Montagu controversy.[14]

Unmindful of her ill-health, this brave soldier kept on working for the redress of the Punjab and *Khilafat* wrongs. She attended the discussion on the Punjab issue in the British Parliament and feet pained at the indifferent attitude of the attendants.[15]

The same year Mrs. Naidu attended the International Conference in Geneva. She was asked by people as to why she joined politics. Her answer was a symbol of her will to bring the Hindus and Muslims closer. She said: "I think it is inevitable that one should become interested in politics if one is a true Indian. The importance of Hindu-Mohammedan unity appealed to me. I lived in a Mohammedan city and you see, I had so many Mohammedan friends. Very few Hindus have had such intimate relations with Mohammedans as I, for I have taken part in all their political and educational movements. I have presided over their meetings and spoken at mosques. That is the thing which counts most among men and women, especially men. The first political speech I made was at a meeting of the Moslem League."[16]

Unity was important for her. Whether she spoke to the students, women or the politicians or the people at large, her point was unity among the races, quicken the achievement of freedom.[17]

She had hardly recovered from her heart malady when she returned to India. Those were the days of Non-Cooperation Movement launched by Gandhiji in 1920. Like a painful follower she followed Mahatma Gandhi's programme and was once again in the fight.

Riots in Bombay were followed by the visit of His Royal Highness, the Prince of Wales, in 1921. Mrs. Naidu personally approached the affected fields to disperse the crowds and to make peace.

Then came the Moplah outbreak. Mrs. Naidu approached Malabar to quieten the atmosphere. She condemned the Martial Law authorities operating in the area. The Government of Madras warned to prosecute her if she did not apologise for her statements and criticism but failed. She invited the Government's attention to many more statements made in this connection by other people which corroborated hers. So she challenged the Government to withdraw the remarks or make good the threats.[18] Sarojini returned the *Kaiser-i-Hind* Medal to the Government. Gandhiji was arrested in 1922 and his parting message was: "I trust the unity of India in your hands."[19]

Heavy work again affected her health and Sarojini had to leave for Ceylon in 1922. But she could not withdraw herself from political activities for long. Even there she delivered a number of speeches pleading India's cause and on her way back to India she stayed at many places to campaign for the cause and to shake the country from its slumber.

Mrs. Naidu stood for unadulterated Gandhian non-cooperation and opposed the idea of the Council entry. She attended the All India Congress Session at Calcutta in November 1922 and opposed in strong terms the resolution favouring the Council entry. The Akali movement[20] also invited her heed and she moved a resolution[21] in the Indian National Congress of 1923-24 criticising the stand taken by the Government. She stated: "I feel that I am but discharging a very small portion of the debt of inspiration that I owe to the ideals and the achievements of that dauntless little section of Indian humanity who, in their black robes and their black turbans, stand in the vanguard of the army of India's freedom. So great was the inspiration... when I rose from my sickbed almost unable to walk, I, none the less re-entered public life by marching at Amritsar in the 'Unlawful' Akali Dal as a protest against the tyranny of the Government and as a practical token of my resolution not merely to stand by and support but to participate if necessary in the activities of the Akalis."[22]

Early in 1924 Mrs. Naidu visited South Africa to study and modify if possible, the deplorable condition of Indian people. She spoke against the Anti-Historic Bill (1924), which was calculated to exterminate the Indian community in South Africa. She also addressed the East African Congress. She urged the audience: "You must with one united voice give an answer to the Government and say though in natural history rivers don't flow backward, we shall make the river of your decision flow backward."[23] She participated over the Indians question with the Government and members of the Parliament of South Africa and thus understood well the viewpoint of all concerned and hence succeeded to present the matter to the Government of India in all its details.

Mrs. Naidu's services were duly rewarded when elected President of the Indian National Congress in 1925. She was the first Indian woman to be assigned such an exalted office. Her election to the Presidentship was honouring womanhood and recognition of their rights. She herself referred to this fact in her Presidential address at the 48th session of the Congress at Kanpur in 1925 and said: "I am fully aware that you have bestowed upon me the richest gift in your possession... but rather ingenerous tribute to Indian womanhood and as token of your loyal recognition of its legitimate place in the secular and spiritual councils of the Nation."[24]

Sarojini Naidu outlined a plan creating different departments relating to divergent requirements of the people like a department for the re-organisation of villages, for the industrial workers and for education. According to her the education system of the time did not suit the special trend of our racial genius. She felt that military training should be an integral part of education. She favoured having a national militia by voluntary conscription of which the nucleus might be the present volunteer organisations. The question of providing aerial and naval training was also considered.[25]

Her message of the new year as President of the Congress was: "Mine, as becomes of a woman, is a most modest domestic programme merely to restore to India her true position as the supreme mistress in her own home, the sole guardian of her own vast resources and the sole dispenser of her own hospitality. As a loyal daughter of *Bharat Mata,* therefore, it will be my lovely though difficult task, through the coming year, to set my house in order, to reconcile the tragic quarrels that threaten the integrity of her old joint family life of diverse communities and creeds and to find an adequate place and purpose and recognition alike for the lowest and highest of her children and foster children, the guests and strangers within her gate."[26]

From 1923 to 1929 she was in America approaching parts of the United States and Canada. She delivered two hundred speeches during her tour and made the people aware of the conditions in India.[27] Speaking at a banquet given in her honour by the Hindustan Association of America, in New York, on

November 10, 1928, she said: "It was futile to aspire for the freedom of the world without a free India."[28]

Sarojini's speeches in these countries for the major part referred to "Interpretation of Hindu Womanhood," "An ultimate study of Mahatma Gandhi", and "Interpretation of the spiritual life of India."

In April 1929 Mrs. Naidu sailed for England and performed interviews with the members of the Government. Presiding over the First Provincial U.P. Youth Conference, she encouraged young men to follow the meaning of "give me liberty or death"[29] as the only option before them in the interest of the country.

She was specially nominated by Gandhiji to launch raid upon Dharasana[30] Salt Works in May 1930. Before taking charge of the raiding party she announced in a public speech, "The time has come in my opinion when women can no longer seek immunity behind the shelter of their sex, but must share equally with their men comrades all the perils and sacrifices for the liberation of the country.[31]

On May 15, 1930, she raided the Salt Works. Sarojini and her companions were arrested, but were freed the same day. Sarojini Naidu led another group of twenty-five hundred raiders upon the same Salt Works on May 21, 1930. Webb Miller, an eye-witness to the happenings at Dharasana, referred to her calling the volunteers for prayers before the march. She motivated them thus: "Gandhiji's body is in jail but his soul is with you. India's prestige is in your hands. You must not use any violence under any circumstances. You will be beaten but you must not resist; you must not even raise a hand to ward off blows."[32]

After the prayer the volunteers commenced marching towards the salt deposits surrounded by ditches filled with water. A group of volunteers arrived near the barbed wire stockade, guarded by the police. This group was ordered to disperse but the volunteers did not obey the command due to which the "police rushed upon the advancing marchers and rained blows on their heads with their steel shaft lathes."[33] The wounded men were removed and then many a batch of volunteers appeared to meet the same destiny. Ultimately the volunteers altered their tactics and sat on the ground near the salt pans.

The authorities could not even tolerate their assembling in this way and order to disperse them were directed again. They as usual, paid no attention to this order. As a result the police "commenced savagely kicking the seated men in the abdomen and testicles." The wounded men writhed and squealed in pain, which appeared to inflame the anger of the police... The police then dragging the sitting men by the arms or feet, sometimes for a hundred yards and throwing them into ditches.[34]

Mrs. Naidu was arrested the same day, i.e., May 21, 1930. In a message to her associates, she said thus: "Whatever happens, strictly adhere to the law of non-violence. Don't budge an inch from the place you have taken."[35]

Mrs. Naidu was freed following the Gandhi-Irwin Pact[36] signed on March 5, 1931. During the year the Second Round Table Conference was conducted in London. Mrs. Naidu attended it as an official representative of the Indian ladies.

The Gandhi-Irwin Pact was not honoured by Lord Irwin's successor, Lord Willingdon, with the consequence the most of the national leaders were again imprisoned.

Gandhiji returned to India on December 28, 1931, after attending the Round Table Conference at London. He was arrested on January 4, 1932, and was detained in the Pune jail.

Mrs. Naidu became the acting President of the Indian National Congress in 1932. The Reception Committee of the Congress was announced as unlawful. This did not deviate her from her determination to conduct the conference and she transferred the venue of its session to Delhi.[37]

On April 20th, Mrs. Naidu was ordered directing her not to act in furtherance of the Civil Disobedience Movement and not to cross the city without the consent of the Commissioner.[38] She paid no attention to this order and left for Bombay by Frontier Mail. The train was stopped at Bandra, ten miles short of Bombay. She was arrested[39] and sentenced to one year's imprisonment.

BOMBAY

Kamala Devi Chattopadhyaya

Smt. Kamala Devi Chattopadhyaya did outstanding work for the furtherance of the cause of India's freedom.

She was born in Mangalore in 1903 and was married while in school. Her husband died and Kamala became a child widow. She continued her studies contrary to the prevailing customs and subsequently joined the Queen Marry's College at Madras. She remarried Harindranath Chattopadhyaya, brother of Mrs. Naidu, setting an example to inter-caste, inter-provincial and widow remarriage.

Kamala decided to join active politics in 1922 and joined the Congress. She always remained in the thick of the struggle for independence. This bold lady was the first woman to contest election for the Legislative Assembly of Madras in 1926.

Kamala Devi was linked with many women's organisations and attended the International Congress of Women's League for tranquility and independence, held on August 23, 1929, in the city of Prague. She informed the gathering there with the Indian conditions.[40]

Presiding over the Youth Conference at Ahmedabad in 1929, she complained : "We are very fond of holding ourselves as ready for martyrdom but when the time comes for baring our necks we retreat and say wait till the next blow. Each time the coward gets the better of it. Start Civil Disobedience, declare an independent republic, establish a parallel Government, do it at any cost."[41]

During the Civil Disobedience Movement of 1930, Kamala Devi addressed meetings, prepared salt and picketed foreign cloth and alcohol shops. In one of the meetings she addressed at Esplanade Maidan, Bombay, she motivated the people to follow the lead provided by Gandhiji by violating the laws as that would paralyse the Government.[42]

Kamala Devi gave passive resistance and guarded the salt bowls when the police raided the Congress House, Bombay. Salt was publicly manufactured by her and sold openly. She even selected High Court premises for selling salt at a high price.

While it was the privilege of Sarojini Naidu to raid the Dharasana Salt Works, it came to Kamala Devi to plan a raid on the Salt Fields in the precincts of Bombay city.[43] Before realisation of her dream, she was arrested. Her parting message was : "Carry on the fight until British Imperialism becomes only a dark shadow of the past; India's freedom will open the gate for world freedom."[44]

Kamala Devi was taken to Court for trial. Instead of witnessing her trial, the fearless soldier invited the magistrate to buy salt and started selling it in the Court Room. She also invited the Magistrate to resign the job and join the *Satyagraha* Army of she was sentenced six months for imprisonment and imposed a fine of Rs. 150, and three months more under the Salt Act and a fine of Rs. 20 in default of two week's imprisonment. Both the sentences had to run concurrently.[45]

Kamala was freed in 1930. This was the time for the preparation of a large fight ahead. She, therefore, made a whirlwind journey of the country and for opening branches of the *Hindustani Seva Dal.* This organisation was an autonomous body and for the last seven years had been training workers for the service of the nation. In the beginning it had only recognition from the Congress but subsequently it was administered and controlled by the Congress itself.

Kamala Devi was in charge of women's organisation under the *Hindustani Seva Dal.* She organised camps for the training of women workers. The training course was separate for the girls. The course of training contained literary education, training in household hygiene, child rearing, sewing and spinning, in arranging meetings and course of study in Indian history and geography. The course was designed to make ladies fit for all that the country hoped them to do.[46]

During the year Kamala Devi addressed the students also. She was the Vice-Chairman of the Bombay Youth League. She presided over the Student's Conference at Lahore in October 1931. She criticised the education system and said, "It is a frame that ill fits us for it is cast in a sinister mould and that we have slipped it round our neck, it is strangulating us in slow, deliberate manner."[47] Kamala Devi inspired the students to arrange study circles, study the political and economic difficulties and describe them to the masses.

Kamala Devi was arrested in 1932 and sentenced to one year's imprisonment. She joined the Congress Socialist Party in 1934.

A large number of other women in Bombay participated in the great fight. But Jaishri Raiji, Hansa Mehta, Perin Captain, Sofia Somjee, Lilavati Munshi, Maniben Patel and Khurshedben, the grand daughter of Dadabhai Naoroji worked in several ways

– led processions, held meetings, picketed cloth and alcohol shops and organised classes for ladies to prepare them for the national struggle.

Picketing of shops was tough; but these courageous ladies had great patience and determination at their command. They asked the shopkeepers and traders to stop selling foreign cloth. Since picketing cloth shops was announced illegal, women had to face rigorous imprisonment, *lathi* charge and inhuman behaviour of the police. In the prison they harassed Maniben Patel, arrested in connection with the *Satyagraha* Movement, was treated as 'C' class prisoner. Many political prisoners were kept along with the criminals. Seventy-seven prisoners accompanied four babies including fifteen ordinary criminals and were locked up in a single barrack. There were no proper bathrooms and they had to clean the barracks and verandahs twice a day, wash the vessels and clean latrines.[48] But these difficulties did not shatter their belief. Many more were taking training to enlist themselves for the national service. A class to train women to participate in the Satyagraha campaign of Gandhiji for breaking salt laws was commenced under the supervision of members to the *Satyagraha Ashram* and Khurshedben. These trainees were trained to sing propaganda songs and to arrange village meetings, to display how to preserve peace and order at the meetings, sanitation, first aid to the wounded, nursing and spinning.[49]

Rashtriya Stri Sabha, another organisation of women, launched an intensive propaganda for the propagation of *Swadeshi* throughout the city. Members of this organisation visited house to house and secured signatures for the pledge of *swadeshi.*[50]

Gujarat was the citadel of this propaganda. The province was well-trained under the direct teaching of Gandhiji. The womenfolk exhibited remarkable power of organisation and steered the movement successfully. In Gujarat most of the dictators were ladies. The men were rounded up in the first few days and it was left to women to come out as dictators one after the other.

The women of Gujarat informed the Governor that they favoured Gandhiji's policy and action. They were determined to fight for prohibition and *Swadeshi* because the two questions affected them individually.[51]

BENGAL

The women of Bengal not only participated in Mahatma Gandhi's Civil Disobedience campaign but also in the revolutionary activities. They were motivated to adopt the revolutionary creed by Subhas Chandra Bose and many young girls entered into the fold of the revolutionary party.

An annual report of the Police Administration said that "Organised attempts, seldom successful, were made to hoist the Congress Flag on Government buildings in the mofussil. An increasing share of the work was taken up by women, both because it was becoming more difficult to find male recruits and because the presence of women-folk was calculated to prove an embarrassment to the police."[52]

This, of course, was a twisted statement. Ladies did not join the ranks primarily to embarrass the police. The women never worried the police authorities much, as the women were often punished the same way as men, i.e., dragging, lathi-charging and having life sentence on some.[53]

Despite such treatment, women went along their selected path, and picketed colleges, schools, clubs and courts. Women's organisations, like *Ladies Picketing Board, Nari Satyagraha Committee, Nikhil Jatiya Nari Sangh* and *Mahila Rashtriya Sangha* were announced unlawful.[54]

Mahila Rashtriya Sangha

Lotika Ghose was entrusted with the organisation of women. She with the assistance of Subhas Chandra Bose, founded the *Mahila Rashtriya Sangha* and Subhas Bose's mother was the first president. This body had its branches in other districts as well. Women joined the Salt *Satyagraha* by manufacturing salt in the seaside districts. Rashtriya *Sangha* was able to send groups for nearly six months for picketing and courting arrests.[55] The picketed schools and colleges were supervised by Lotika Ghose while another member of the *Sangha,* Arunbala Sen, performed the work of picketing the foreign cloth shops in the Bara Bazar and various women's organisations visited this place to stop the sale of foreign cloth. The trade in foreign cloth virtually came to a standstill for the time being.

Nari Satyagraha Committee

Another institution which played a distinguished part during this period was *Nari Satyagraha* Committee. Smt. Urmila Devi, sister of Deshbandhu C.R. Das, was its president and amongst its vice-presidents were prominent Congress women workers of standing like Mohini Devi, Jyotirmoyi Ganguli, Hemprabha Das Gupta and Ashoklata Das. *Samiti* Das and Bimal Pratima Devi were the secretaries. They marched in procession refusing government orders. They were harassed and intercepted by the mounted police, but nothing prevented them, so they were arrested by police.

The *Amrita Bazar Patrika* of May 25, 1930, alleged that for the first time in the annals of Calcutta the sports grounds of football had to be deserted on Saturday owing to lady picketers appearing at ciub tents.

Ladies Picketing Board

In May 1931, a Picketing Board was commenced by the women of Bengal.[56] This Board had to propagate against the use of foreign articles; to popularise home industries and to assist develop cottage industries; specially those of spinning and weaving *Khadi;* to agonise processions and meetings; stress the importance of liberty and equality of nations; the need for abolition of untouchability; to enlist members of the Congress, who would follow the instruction of the National Congress stipulating that the Bengal Provincial Congress Committee work in close cooperation with the National Congress.

Boycott and Picketing Section

This section had to carry out quiet picketing in various markets and shops against the sale of foreign articles, especially cloth.

Swadeshi Prachar Section

To popularise and preach for the use of *Swadeshi* articles specially *Swadeshi cloth* and *Khadi* in private houses, and to employ women workers to join the Board and enlist as members of the National Congress.

Prabhat-Pheri Section

To carry *Prabhat-Pheries* in several parts of the city in compliance with the instructions of the Board and to members for the Picketing Board.

Constructive Workers Section

To demonstrate the use of *Charkhas* and *Taklis* and to assist spinners to get in touch with weavers for the yarn spun by them. To assist manufacture a variety of handmade articles and to get markets for the same; to set *Ashrams* where little girls and boys are directed to spin yarn. These works were performed by this section.

General Section

This section was involved in conducting and taking out processions. The forementioned plan was very comprehensive and the women of Bengal performed a lot of work in different parts of Bengal.[57]

Meetings of the ladies was the order of the day in Bengal. In a meeting at Comilla, presided over by Urmila Devi, the following resolutions were passed :[58]

(i) The formation of *Mahila Samitis.*
(ii) Boycott of foreign articles.
(iii) Hindu-Muslim unity.
(iv) The abolition of untouchability and *purdah*.
(v) Motivating the ladies to support the Congress cause.

The distinguished worker at this place (Comilla) was Hemprabha Majumdar. She was afterwards arrested for her anti-government activities, i.e., taking out processions. She was awarded one years' rigorous imprisonment for leading a procession.[59]

Revolutionary Activities

The cult of violence which perhaps never died in Bengal was revised with the Civil Disobedience Movement. The organisation of the revolutionaries was very active in Dhaka, Comilla and Chittagong and young college girls appeared into its fold. The popular group of the women revolutionaries included Samiti and Suniti, Bina Das, Kalpana Dutta and Preetilata Waddedar.

The Chittagong Armoury was raided by the revolutionaries on April 13, 1930. This produced a clash between the revolutionaries and government officials in the village of Dhalghat near Chittagong. Two of the revolutionaries and Captain Cameron of the Chittagong Armoury were murdered. An old Brahmin lady of the village provided shelter for the absconding revolutionaries. She was arrested and tortured in different ways for eliciting facts of the case. Afterwards she was joined in the prison by Kalpana Dutta whom she warned not to be weak by police tricks. She said: "They might torture you but even then you must never tell them anything, they might even threaten you with hanging, but you must never give way."[60]

This lady authored a poem on the police tortures :

"The wicked men come politely
And sit close to you;
They extract words by giving threats
And take away your life at the end."[61]

She was mal-treated in prison. But she was not much aware about the rules and regulations of the prison. Her son died in jail and she could not get consent to see him. She was freed at the expiry of her sentence in a desperate condition. Later she joined the *Nari Samiti* when a branch was opened in Dhalghat.[62]

Kalpana Dutta and Preetilata Waddedar were revolutionaries of a high order. Both of them studied in the same school and in their youth had opposed the British domination. While studying in the senior class they wished to change the pledge "to be loyal to god and King" into "to be loyal to God and Country."[63] After their studies Preetilata joined the Dhaka University and attended *Deepwali Sangha,* an organisation to train the patriots in lathi and sword game. Kalpana Dutta joined the Calcutta University and became a member of the Ladies Association. They met the revolutionaries in 1931-32.[64]

It was on September 24, 1932, that Preetilata Waddedar led a raid on the Pahartali Railway Officers Club. As a consequence one European lady was fired. In an effort to shoot the gathering in the club she had to commit suicide by taking potassium cyanide.[65] Some revolvers, live cartridges and red leaflets threatening the authorities were discovered in her pocket.

Preetilata was the first woman to die in action. She was a courageous lady and had many interviews with Ramakrishna Biswas, a revolutionary who was hanged. She also faced the machine gun of Captain Cameron who was fired at Dhalghat. She was doubted of anti-government activities but the police failed to catch her as she went underground.

Kalpana was another active worker of the revolutionary party. She was seen very often, dressed in male outfit, in the vicinity of Pahartali. She was doubted of revolutionary activities, so a police watch was kept on her. But the authorities found no proof to put her on trial. When the Pahartali Club was raided, the police became convinced of her being a party to the raid and this kept the authorities from taking any action against her. So she was sent for trial under Section 109.[66] She was afterwards released on bail. Kalpana escaped while still on bail before the trial was over. She was again arrested after three months and tried by a special tribunal in relation to the Chittagong Armoury Supplementary trials.[67] She was sentenced to life transportation.[68]

Suniti, daughter of Uma Charan Choudhry, and Samiti, daughter of Debendra Lal Ghose, a professor in the Comilla college, fired the magistrate of Comilla, on December 14, 1931.[69] They were arrested and awarded a life sentence.[70]

Miss Bina Dass[71] was a student of Diocesean College. She moved from her house to the college hostel pretending that it would enable her to devote more attention to her studies, but this was to perfect her designs for the forthcoming University Convocation.[72]

On February 6, 1932, the day Calcutta University had its convocation, Bina was one of the recipients of Bachelor of Arts degree. As the governor stood to address the convocation, she fired five shots to kill him.[73] She was caught immediately. Then a number of arrests were made. A search of her belongings at the Diocesean College was held and various documents were discovered by the police. She was found to be member of the terrorist party. In a written statement to the Court she pointed out:

> I fired at the Governor impelled by my love of the country which is being repressed. I thought that the only way to death was by offering myself at the feet of my country and thus make an end of all my suffering. I invite the attention of all to the situation created by the measures of the Government which faced even a frail woman like me, brought-up in all the best tradition of Indian womanhood. I can assure all, that I have no personal feeling of animosity against Sir Jackson, the man who is just as good as my father and the Hon'ble Lady Jackson who is as good as

my mother. But the Governor of Bengal represents the system which has kept enslaved three hundred million of my countrymen and country women.[74]

She was sentenced to nine years' rigorous imprisonment.[75] Another girl, daughter of deceased Bankim Chandra Gupta of village Mirzapur, district Mymensingh, was caught because a suitcase consisting of seventy-eight packets marked dynamite, three coils of fusewire and various revolutionary books were found in her possession. She was awarded five years rigorous imprisonment under Sections 5 and 5 A of the Explosive Substances Act. Her mother was also arrested for harbouring announced political offenders.[76]

There were many more women who participated in the revolutionary activities and served different terms of imprisonment. Kamla Chatterjee, Bimal Pratibha Devi, Shobharana Dutta, Ujjala Devi, Parul Mukerjee, Jyotikanta Dutta and Banala Das went to jail. Santishda Ghose of Barisal was arrested while trying to encash a forged cheque of twenty-seven thousand rupees in Grindlays Bank, Calcutta to carry on revolutionary activities.[77]

PUNJAB

The women of Punjab inaugurated the Civil Disobedience Movement by marching in a procession of five thousand ladies at Lahore in 1930. Processions, meetings, picketing and in defiance of Section 144 became order of the day. Daily they held demonstration before the doors of the Council Chamber. The police and their lathi charge no more scared them. When the Viceroy came to address the Council members, they raised like "Long Live Revolution," "Up! Up! the National Flag", Long Live Bhagat Singh", "Gandhi Ki Jai".[78] The life and soul of the movement were Mrs. Lado Rani Zutshi, Parvati, daughter of Lala Lajpat Rai, Smt. Kartar Kaur, Atma Devi and many others.

Lado Rani Zutshi was the leading women of the period. She was married to the late Pandit Ladli Prashad Zutshi, a leading advocate of Lahore. Her interest in politics started in the Martial Law days in the Punjab in 1919; and ever after, she was an active Congress worker. During this movement she achieved importance for her singular activities and was appointed the eighth Dictator of the War Council and carried out the movement successfully.[79]

This bold woman and her daughters accompanied by other women offering *Satyagraha* picked the cloth shops, law courts and the quarters of Members of the Legislative Assembly. She had organised a uniform of red trousers, green shirts and white Gandhi caps matching the National Emblem[80] for volunteers.

Addressing a meeting outside Mori Gate, Lahore, she requesting to women to follow the example of those of Bombay: "The arrests of women show the weakness of the Government. "She went on to say, "Government imprisons persons for one offence or another because it wishes to prevent those people from carrying on Congress work outside jails."[81]

In another lecture on June 23, 1930, she motivated the people "to bear the tyranny of machine guns and *lathi* blows. How much can the government tyrannize us?"[82] she asked. She also circulated sedious matter though publication was punishable under Section 124 A or 153 A of the Indian Penal Code.[83]

Speaking at the death anniversary of Bal Gangadhar Tilak, she mentioned the highhandedness of the government. "These people," she said, "are wild beasts and devoid of humanity. Their civilisation is only temporary. They have come into power only temporarily, and have forgotten what humaneness is. They are now to learn to what extent this tyranny can go."[84]

As a consequence of these activities she was called upon to explain why she should not be ordered to execute a bond of ten thousand rupees with sureties of rupees five thousand each for good conduct for a period of one year.[85] She was sentenced to one year imprisonment but was freed under the Gandhi-Irwin Pact in 1931 before the expiry of the punishment, only to be re-arrested in 1932. Now she was sentenced to eighteen months' imprisonment. She had to be freed before the expiry of her term due to ill-health.

Lado Rani had infused patriotic enthusiasm in her daughters also, and they all shared her responsibilities in this moment. Seventeen women were arrested on October 9, 1913, including Prof. Janak Kumari Zutshi and Swadesh Kumari Zutshi[86] for picketing educational institutions. For the first time such a large number of women were apprehended in a single day. The Lahore Women's College students did not attend the college as a protest."[87]

Afterwards when the Zutshi sisters were put on trial, they denied to attend it unless their relatives were given permission to witness the proceeding. The case had to be adjourned. They were fined and to realise the fine, the police attached the clothes and beddings of the convicts, to be returned later.[88]

Mrs. Manmohini Sehgal (then Manmohini Zutshi), daughter of Lado Rani, also joined the freedom fighters. She began her career in the political sphere by becoming Chairman of the Reception Committee of the Second All Punjab Students Conference, presided over by Subhas Chandra Bose, in October 1929.[89] She afterwards became President of the Lahore Students Union founded by Bhagat Singh of the Lahore Conspiracy Case, in December 1929.[90] Manmohini was threatened by her college authorities with expulsion if she did not resign from the Students' Union. Afterwards her degree was withheld by the university. Only with the good offices of Dr. S. Radhakrishnan[91] she was able to obtain the degree of Master of Arts.[92]

She was arrested for picketing educational institutions on October 8 and followed her mother to prison. She was sentenced of six months' imprisonment. Manmohini was freed from prison but was re-arrested in January 1931 accompanied by her sister for picketing shops. This time she was sentenced to one years' imprisonment. She was freed under Gandhi-Irwin Pact. Manmohini was re-arrested in March 1932, for violating a notice served on her by the Punjab Government and sentenced to an year's rigorous imprisonment.[93] She had to undergo her full period in prison.

Manmohini had become one of the Punjab delegates to the *Swaraj* Party Conference conducted at Ranchi by Shri Bhulabhai Desai and Dr. M.A. Ansari.[94]

Manmohini worked as Headmistress of *Bihar Mahila Vidyapith* till she was married in 1935. She had to leave her political activities after her marriage and occupied herself in social work. Manmohini became the General Secretary of the National Council of Women (affiliated to the International Council of Women) in 1945. Manmohini provided evidence before the Cripps Mission in 1946 representing the National Council.[95]

Another important woman was Parvati Devi, daughter of Lala Lajpat Rai. Parvati participated in all the programmes of the *Satyagraha* Committee. She was arrested under Section 124A Criminal Procedure Code (Sedition) for her patriotic activities. She was ordered to execute a bond for rupees ten thousand with two sureties of rupees five thousand each. During the pendency of the case she was further asked to execute another bond of two thousand rupees to ensure her attendance. She preferred jail. She was sentenced to two years' rigorous imprisonment, and was fined twenty thousand rupees.[96]

Laxmi Devi, the wife of Mr. Trikha, also took a leading part in the several activities of the freedom movement. She was Speaking at a public meeting on July 30, 1931, she reported that "the government had started committing such tyrannies that we can't find any peace."[97] In another lecture she observed that the government only listens to the police and punishes innocent people.[98] She criticised the death sentence passed on Ranbir Singh, Durga Das and Chuni Lal, in connection with the plot to shoot the Governor.[99]

Laxmi Devi was convicted for her activities and asked to pay two thousand rupees or undergo one year imprisonment. She preferred the latter.[100]

MADRAS

In Madras Smt. Rukmini Lakshmapati[101] had the honour of being the first lady to be arrested in connection with the Salt *Satyagraha.*

The women of Madras played a significant role in organising youngsters into the *Vanar Sena*[102] or the Monkey Army, as called in the memory of the monkey who in the Hindu mythology, joined together to help Lord Rama. The dynamic energy of these youngsters was thus used into systematic and disciplined activity.

Durgabai Deshmukh

Another popular lady was Mrs. Durgabai Deshmukh who became the war dictator in the city of Madras and continued the movement.

Durgabai was born in 1910 in a village near Rajamundry, Andhra Pradesh. She was married at the age of eight into a conservative family. She became a child widow. "Durgabai was not an ordinary child. She was the daughter of liberty, the nursing of not just her cultured parents but of the peerless, powerful sea, the intrepid winds, the master of her own thoughts. In the midst of limitations she never faltered, freedom and light were stored in her heart, and when the time came these became her inspiration and strength."[103]

Her interest in politics can be traced back to the year 1921 when she was merely a child. During this year when the Non-Cooperation Movement was at its peak that she accompanied her mother, went around the town selling Khaddar.

She was at home in Hindi, a knowledge which came in very handy at the time of the Kakinada Session of the Indian National Congress 1923. She had taught nearly six hundred volunteers who were to work for this session in this language. Her interest in politics was further increased after meeting Gandhiji at this session. She participated in processions and manufactured salt openly during the 1930-31 movement. Later she was nominated as the second War Dictator after Sri Prakasham. She was arrested for her activities on May 25, 1930, at Arcot and was sentenced to nine months imprisonment.[104]

Durgabai joined the *Hindustan Seva Dal* and was re-arrested for her political activities. Now sentenced to three years' imprisonment.[105] While in jail she studied English. After her release, she wished to join the men's college of the Andhra University to study Political Science as a subject. She was refused admission on the ground that there was no hostel arrangement for the girls. As a challenge to the authorities she began a hostel for women. She obtained her Master's degree in Political Science and a Bachelor's in Law as well.

The year 1942 saw her as a practising advocate and she was the first woman to appear and argue in a killing case. In 1946, while a practising advocate, she became a member of the Constituent Assembly and afterwards a member of the provisional Parliament.

Durgabai was taken as a member of the Planning Commission. She went to China which further expanded her horizon. She married C.D. Deshmukh, then Union Minister, in 1953.

Women's cause remained dear to Durgabai Deshmukh. She began the Central Social Welfare Board and remained its chairman from 1953 to 1963.[106]

DELHI

In this great city twenty-four girl guides refused to salute the Union Jack and their names were struck off the rolls.[107]

Mary Campbell, a temperance worker in India, writing in the *Manchester Guardian* of June 1931, described the valour of Delhi women in the following words: "I was in Delhi when Mr. Gandhi, on his way back to jail, sent word—'I leave the work of picketing and drink and drug ships to the women of India.' I thought he had made a mistake this time that the Delhi women, so many of whom lived in *purdah,* could never undertake the task. But to my astonishment, out they came, and they picketed all the shops in Delhi, sixteen or seventeen in number. I watched them day after day. They stood there saying nothing but politely *salaaming* each customer who approached. The same thing happened repeatedly. The man would stop and say: 'I beg your pardon, sister. I forgot myself in coming here, and go away. That went on for some days until the licensees appealed to the Government. The hefty policemen arrived with police vans and warned the women to go away. I thought those delicate sheltered women would give in now; they would never endure being touched by a policemen. But they did, and as fast as one was arrested, another took its place. Altogether about sixteen hundred women were imprisoned in Delhi alone. But they had done their work. Though the shops were opened no one went in . . . At last the licensees themselves closed them, and so far as I know they are still closed today."[108]

Again in this historic city, a thousand women went to the court for persuading the lawyers and the authorities to close down the courts. Mrs. Sahni was among the wounded on that day. Pandit Motilal Nehru witnessing the scene, penned that the police officer announced the assembly unlawful. When he was asked for a order to this effect, he had none. No magistrate was accompanying him. He threatened to open fire, if the crowd did not disperse. In the meantime five armoured cars arrived at the scene. The women refused to leave the premises unless the police was withdrawn and they were permitted to return in procession. The police afterwards withdrew to the farthest end of the courtyard and made the road free when the ladies and others marched back to the city.[109]

Satyawati

The great city of Delhi also watched a martyr's death. Satyawati, grand-daughter of Swami Shradhanand, was another significant leader of this movement in Delhi. She was a revolutionary. Defending social taboos, at the age of twenty-three, she devoted, to the Congress movement, her heart and soul, in 1930. She conducted meetings, led processions, picketed foreign cloth shops not only in the market but also on the river Jamuna where usually the *Marwari* ladies in their foreign clothes came to bathe.[110] As a consequence of her attempts some fifty per cent of women took to wearing *Khaddar*.

Speaking at a public meeting on May 3, 1930, Satyawati inspired the audience to remain steadfast in their effort and boldly face the machine-guns parading the streets. On May 12, 1930, at the mourning procession of Ami Lal, who died of a gun shot, pointed out "such things do happen in attaining freedom and that flames of such fire would reduce the tyrant to ashes."[111] She was arrested under Section 108 of the Indian Penal Code (to furnish security to cease dissemination) and was asked to furnish security of five hundred rupees or demonstrate good behaviour for six months. She denied to furnish the security and was sent to jail.

At her trial in Delhi Satyawati remarked : "We have abandoned our homes and children to redeem our motherland from foreign bondage, and neither the threat of the dungeons nor of bullets and the merciless beatings can deter us from the duty which we owe to ourselves and the coming generation. I and thousands of my sisters are ready to suffer, but we must win India's freedom."[112] She was awarded six months imprisonment. In a parting message to India, she said: "So long as there was even a single child, she would not let the government rest, nor would she rest herself."[113] She was released only to be re-arrested in 1932. Now she was sentenced to two years' imprisonment. During her incarceration she contacted pleurisy which subsequently developed into tuberculosis but she remained unaffected and continued political work.

Satyawati was again active in 1937 in anti-government activities and arrested. She was attacked by the police. This question emerged before the Assembly producing a successful adjournment motion. She was asked to execute a bond for good behaviour, but her refusal sentenced her to one months' imprisonment which was later reduced.[114] The moment Satyawati was emerged she was again active. She attended the Punjab Political Conference convened in April 1938. She was ordered to desert Punjab within twenty-four hours, and her entry into the Punjab without consent was forbidden for one year. She violated the order and was arrested.

During 1940 and 1941 Satyawati was tried twice for sedition and jailed. She had hardly been freed when she was arrested again in August 1942, and detained as a security prisoner until her condition became so critical that the doctors lost all hope of her life. She was freed but was instructed by the authorities not to enter Delhi. She naturally denied to obey and even Gandhiji supported her. She violated the order and was arrested. She was afterwards released and the case against her was withdrawn.[115]

Satyawati was admitted to the hospital. Just two days before her expiry in 1945, Pandit Jawaharlal Nehru approached. She said to him: "My only desire is India's freedom."[116]

UTTAR PRADESH

In Allahabad, Swaroop Rani, wife of Motilal Nehru, inaugurated the campaign by manufacturing salt in front of the police station. Here the police *lathi*-charged a procession led by her and Swaroop Rani got a blow on her head and fainted.[117] The spirit of patriotism was infused in the Nehru family. Pandit Jawaharlal Nehru, penning about the activities of his wife and sister, refers to their part in this struggle. He writes: "Salt suddenly became a mysterious word, a word of power. Long before the movement began volunteers were being given necessary training. Krishna[118] and Kamla[119] had joined the ranks of the volunteers. The volunteers, of course, were unarmed, the idea was to make them more efficient in their work and capable of dealing with large crowds. Krishna Nehru along with Shyam Kumari Nehru were arrested for taking out a procession. They were fined fifty rupees or in lieu of it to undergo one months' simple imprisonment. The fine was paid by some unknown person and they were released the next day."[120]

Kamla Nehru went about like a whirlwind, managing women volunteers and the students. She played a significant part in organisation of No-Tax campaign in the province. Presiding over the U.P. Women's Political Conference she made a fervent request to women to prepare for the future struggle and asked them to use *Khaddar.*[121] Kamala became the dictator of the war council and the acting President of the Congress Working Committee.[122] She was arrested on January 1, 1931 and a pressman asked her for a message. She stated: "I am happy beyond measure and proud to follow in the footsteps of my husband. I hope the people will keep the flag flying."[123]

Another women active in this age was Mrs. Mukund Malviya, daughter-in-law of Pandit Madanmohan Malviya. An effort to hold the District conference at Allahabad failed. The police guarded all the public premises to stop any meeting. Mrs. Mukund Malviya advanced to defy the authorities and to hold the meeting near the Clock Tower in the city of Allahabad. She was arrested and awarded one years' rigorous imprisonment.[124] Chandravati Lakhanpal[125] played an important part in this struggle. Her interest in politics dates back from her student days. She participated in the movement of 1930. Chandravati visited village to village organising villagers to make them politically aware till she was arrested in 1932 and awarded one years' imprisonment.[126]

Uma Nehru,[127] who had been interested in the rising of women for many years, now approached to take her place in the *Satyagraha* Army. The part so boldly played by women in the freedom struggle attracted heed and was praised not only within the country but outside as well. Writing in the *Asiatic Review*, Mrs. Gray observed: "If the women are to be judged by deeds rather than by words . . . They have picketed, walked in processions, gone to prison and thus have proved their courage in many a dangerous riot."[128]

Desh Sevikas or Storm Troops amongst Congress women were in the forefront of the movement. They were first enrolled in 1930 and formed a band of volunteers ready to do active work. Some fifty of them went to jail during the first year. Most of these ladies had never deserted their homes before. "They had first to learn the courage necessary to be seen abroad in the streets. Presently, they learned to walk long distances, to stand in the sun all day, to picket cloth and toddy shops, to hurry to danger points when summoned by the Congress, or the police, to remove stones, pipes and other obstacles placed in the middle of the road to obstruct traffic, even to shed their fear at night and of hooligan crowds."[129]

Besides, active *Desh Sevikas* who courted arrests, thousands more joined in processions, flag salutations and strikes, cooked and nursed in the hospitals, and sold *Khaddar.* Many of these sacrificed their life of ease and comfort to suffer imprisonment and picket shops and went from town to town involved in needful campaign and unmindful of the heat or cold.[130]

Margaret Cousins writing under the heading 'Towards Progress and Freedom' remarked : "The response to the call of Mahatma Gandhi was magnificent. Within the next three years over five thousand women had served terms of severe imprisonment, they had suffered *lathi* charges, loss of property, loss of livelihood from ill health, loss of caste, loss of reputation. They willingly faced publicity of the most trying kind in picketing liquor shops and foreign cloth shops, in walking in public processions, in proceedings in law courts. They sacrificed all kinds of cherished privileges of caste, ceremonial purity and privacy."[131]

The police had adopted all kinds of ways in dealing with women. It was alleged from Andhra that "the police seems to be mean enough not to spare women even from their undignified behaviour." The report describes nine cases of ill-treatment.[132] While in Karnataka in Siddarpur Taluka "they were dragged along the road, beaten with lathis and canes and even whipped. Their sarees were pulled and torn and they were abused in the foulest language."[133]

The Kerala authorities had adopted a fine way of punishing the ladies. They were carried by night trains to remote places and deserted uncared for, at midnight at wayside stations. Fifty or sixty-days' old babies were often separated from their mothers.[134] The darkest part of the repression was the treatment received by the female *Satyagrahis.* "This appears to be a general lack of the sense of respect for women in all provincial governments. Abuses, beatings of women and even raping have been calmly allowed to be practised."[135]

But this repression however did not worry the women and they remained unyielding and constant to the stand they had selected. Thus, women displayed that gaining national freedom was not the responsibility of males alone and that when charged with a responsibility, they were able to steer through as successfully as men. This provided strength to the movement. During the Civil Disobedience Movement of 1930-31 twenty thousand women were jailed. For every six persons who courted arrest, included one woman."[136]

The movement which started in 1930 continued till April 1934. It was one long constant struggle except for a short period when Gandhiji was attending the Second Round Table Conference in London in 1931. During this period the Simon Commission's report was also published; but failed to satisfy the aspirations of the people. Even this report had recognised the courage of the women. It says: "No document discussing India's constitutional system and the directions in which it can be developed and improved could omit the women of India today."[137]

The period also watched three Round Table Conferences convened by the British Cabinet to reconcile different shades of viewpoints in the political sphere of India for giving a new constitution to the nation. Finally, the British Parliament passed the Government of India Act 1935, thereby providing a new Constitution to India.

References

1. *Congress Bulletin,* January 9, 1930.
2. The programme was embodied in the following seven points :
   - (i) All-India Satyagraha at Dharasana Salt Works and technical breanches of salt elsewhere.
   - (ii) Appeals to government servants, students and lawyers to make sacrifices.
   - (iii) Intensive boycott of foreign cloth.
   - (iv) Initiation of campaign for non-payment of land revenues and taxes in certain provinces and areas.
   - (v) Breaches of forest laws.
   - (vi) Boycott of British goods and British banking, insurance, shipping and other institutions.
   - (vii) Boycott of liquor shops.

3. *Stri-Dharma*, Vol. 13, December 1929 to October 1930, p. 247.
4. *Congress Bulletin,* May 30, 1930, p. 4.
5. *Amrita Bazar Patrika,* April 10, 1930; Nehru, J., *An Autobiography,* p. 334.
6. *Stri Dharma,* Vol. 13 October to December 1930, pp. 336-84.
7. *Hindoo Patriot,* March 8, 1909.
8. *Indian Ladies Magazine,* Vol. VIII, 1908-1909, p. 262.
9. *Modern Review,* Vol. 39, January-June 1926, p. 104.
10. She seems to have been greatly influenced by Gokhale to take up political work. Naidu describes herself how one evening he spoke to her. He said, "Stand here with me, with the stars and hills for witness, and in their presence consecrate your life, your talent, your song and your speech, your thought and your dream to the motherland. O'poet, see visions from the hill tops and spread abroad the message of hope to the toilers in the valley." (*Modern Review,* Vol. 39, January-June 1926, p. 104).
11. G.A. Natesan & Co., Madras, *Speeches and Writings of Sarojini Naidu*, p. XVII.
12. *Modern Review*, Vol. 27 January-June 1929, p. 45.
13. *Amrita Bazar Patrika*, April 4, 1919.
14. For correspondence see Appendix G.
15. In a letter to Gandhiji she wrote: "I am in a very bad health. But the twin question of the Punjab and the *Khilafat* absorb all my energies and emotions. But it is in vain to expect justice from a race so blind and drunk with the arrogance of power, the bitter prejudice of race and creed and colour, and betraying such an abysmal ignorance of Indian conditions, opinions, sentiments and aspiration. The debate on the Punjab in the House of Commons last week shattered the last remnant of my hope and faith in British justice and goodwill toward the new vision of India. The discussion in the house was lamentable and indeed tragic. Our friends revealed their ignorance, our enemies their insolence, and the combination is appalling and heart-braking."

    In another letter she wrote : "The specialists think that my heart disease is in an advanced and dangerous state but I cannot rest till I stir the heart of the world to repentance over the tragedy of martyred India." (G.A. Natesan & Co. Madras, *Speeches and Writings of Sarojini Naidu*, pp. xxi-xxii).
16. *Modern Review,* July to December 1920, Vol. 28, p. 342.
17. Moving a resolution in the 38th session of the Congress she exclaimed: "Here are we with you in that independent commonwealth of common human responsibilities, in which united India dares to be one with you—not isolated, not ringed round, not separated by that refuge of the weak called independence, but without partition, without walls, without barriers but on a common ground of endeavour sharing the common heritage of a common dream realised by a common constitution by the progress of humanity." (*Proceedings of the Indian National Congress*, 38th Session, 1923, p. 134).
18. G.A. Natesan & Co., Madras, *Speeches and Writings of Sarojini Naidu*, p. XIII.
19. *The Indian Review*, Vol. XXIV, January-December 1923, p. 322.

20. Akalis were an enlightened section of the Sikh community who worked to bring reforms in their places of worship. The Sikh places of worship had fallen under the hands of disreputed Mahants (preachers) who refused to abdicate them. The Government sided with the Mahants as a result of which the Akalis started an active movement.
21. The resolution reads : "This Congress declares that the attack made by the Government on the *Shiromani Gurdwara Prabandhak Committee* and the Akali Dal is a direct challenge to the rights of free Associations of all India, for non-violent activities and being convinced that the blow is aimed at all movements for freedom, resolves to stand by the Sikhs and calls upon Hindus, Musalmans, Christians, Parsees and all people of India to render all possible assistance with men and money." (*Report on the Indian National Congress session*, 1923-24, p. 174).
22. *Report on the Indian National Congress session* 1923-24, p. 174).
23. G.A. Natesan & Co., Madras, *Speeches and Writings of Sarojini Naidu*, p. XXIV.
24. *Congress Presidential Address from 1911 to 1934*, Madras, p. 772.
25. *Congress Presidential Address*, *op. cit.*, p. 774.
26. Sitaramayya, Dr. Pattabhi, *op. cit.*, p. 290.
27. *Times of India*, November 29, 1929.
28. *Times of India,* January 1, 1930.
29. Mittra, N.N., *Annual Register*, Vol. II, 1929, p. 401.
30. Dharasana Salt Works are about 150 miles north of Bombay.
31. *Times of India*, Bombay, May 8, 1930.
32. Webb Miller, 'I Found No Peace', pp. 190-196; quoted in Jack A. Homer, *The Gandhi Reader*, Bloomington, 1956, p. 249.
33. *Ibid.,* p. 252.
34. *Ibid.*
35. *Amrita Bazar Patrika*, May 22, 1930.
36. Gandhi-Irwin Pact whereby the Civil Disobedience Movement was suspended by the Congress and the Government agreed to release the prisoners.
37. *Advance*, April 6, 1932.
38. *Ibid.,* April 21, 1932.
39. *Ibid.,* April 23, 1932.
40. *Stri Dharma*, Vol. 12, November 1928 to November 1929, p. 565.
41. *Annual Register,* Vol. II, 1929, p. 401.
42. *Advance,* May 19, 1930.
43. Kamala Devi described the raid which was planned by her: "A similar raid (referring to Dharasana Salt Works) was planned on the salt fields in the precincts of Bombay city. It fell to me to plan it, but unlike Dharasana, where only a small group was entrusted with the task of the raid, here I visualized a mass raid embracing a large part of the city two million population. I was sure that no force, not even machine-guns, could stop this raid. On the eve of the raid I was arrested but my parting message to my colleagues and the vast populace was to execute this plan. I was represented by my son of seven who proudly carried the banner and engaged in the drama of this first battle." (Publications Division, Delhi, *Women in India,* p. 21).
44. *Stri Dharma*, Vol. 12, Nov. 1928-1929, p. 565.

45. *Amrita Bazar Patrika,* May 17, 1930.
46. *Amrita Bazar Patrika,* November 19, 1931.
47. *Advance,* November 5, 1931.
48. For details of the treatment accorded to women see Appendix H.
49. *Times of India*, March 24, 1930.
50. *Ibid.,* May 2, 1930.
51. *Amrita Bazar Patrika*, May 2, 1930.
52. *Annual Report of Police Administration*, Bombay, 1932, p. XI.
53. Smt. Hem Nalini was hit on the head by a lathi while attending a meeting, Samiti and Suniti and Kalyani Das were sentenced to transportation for life.
54. *Amrita Bazar Patrika*, January 5, 1932, p. 5.
55. *Modern Review,* 1930 (Article by J.C. Bagal), Vol. 94, p. 56.
56. *Amrita Bazar Patrika,* May 14, 1931.
57. *Ibid.,* May 14, 1931.
58. *Ibid.,* April 29, 1931.
59. *Ibid.,* April 2, 1931.
60. Dutta, K., *Chittagong Armoury Raiders Reminiscences,* p. 41.
61. *Ibid.*
62. *Ibid.*
63. *Ibid.,* p. 51.
64. Kalpana Dutta came in contact with the revolutionaries in 1929 but did not accept their creed till 1931. Preetilata came into the fold to this group in 1932.
65. Dutta, K., *Chittagong Armoury Raiders Reminiscences*, p. 41; *Annual Register*, Vol. II, 1932, p. 10.
66. This Section is applied only in case of those who conceal their identity for immoral purposes.
67. Dutta, K., *Chittagong Armoury Raiders Reminiscences,* p. 41.
68. *Annual Report of the Administration of Bengal*, 1932-33, p. 20.
69. *Amrita Bazar Patrika*, January 20, 1932.
70. *Modern Review*, 1953, Vol. 94, p. 57.
71. She was the daughter of a Government pensioner, the former Headmaster of Sanskrit Collegiate School, Calcutta.
72. *Annual Report of the Police Administration of the Town of Calcutta and its Suburbs*, 1932, p. 11.
73. *Amrita Bazar Patrika,* February 16, 1932.
74. *Annual Register,* Volume I, January-June 1932, p.11.
75. *Modern Review,* Vol. 51, January-June, p. 344.
76. *Annual Report of Police Administration, op. cit.,* 1933, p. 16.
77. *Ibid.,* pp. 16-20. *Modern Review*, 1953, Vol. 94, p. 57.
78. *Amrita Bazar Patrika*, July 11, 1930.
79. *Ibid.,* August 19, 1930.
80. *Ibid.,* July 16, 1930.
81. *Ibid.*
82. *Ibid.,* September 2, 1930.
83. *Ibid.*
84. *Ibid.*
85. *Annual Register*, Vol. I, January-June, 1932, p. 22.

86. Two daughters of Lado Rani Zutshi.
87. *Amrita Bazar Patrika*, October 10, 1930.
88. *Ibid.*
89. Papers obtained from Manmohini Sehgal.
90. *Times of India*, Bombay, February 5, 1930.
91. He was the 2nd President of India.
92. Papers obtained from Manmohini Sehgal.
93. Papers in possession of Manmohini Sehgal.
94. *Ibid.*
95. This Council was started in 1925.
96. *Amrita Bazar Patrika*, October 15, 1930.
97. *Ibid.*
98. *Ibid.*
99. *Ibid.*
100. *Ibid.*
101. Rukmini Lakshmipati was born in 1892. She graduated from Madras University and was associated with all the activities of Women's India Association. She was the Secretary of the All India Women's Conference (local branch). She was elected as Municipal Councillor and also served as a Health Minister of Madras Government for 1946-47.
102. The *Vanar Sena* was originally started in Bombay by Shri Johri from among the Bombay Youth League leaders, and was later taken up by the All-India Youth League leaders, over the whole country. Active women participants were Kisan Dhumatkar in Bombay. Remeswaramma in Madras, Vidya Killewala and Mrs. Kamala Devi in Bombay, while at the tender age of 12, Indira Gandhi, daughter of Pandit Jawaharlal Nehru organised six thousand children in Allahabad. (Publications Division, New Delhi, *Women in India*, p. 21).
103. *Illustrated Weekly of India,* January 27, 1957, p. 39.
104. *Amrita Bazar Patrika*, May 27, 1930.
105. *Social Welfare*, Delhi, 1959, p. 5.
106. She resigned from the Board in 1963.
107. *Amrita Bazar Patrika*, March 11, 1930.
108. Zacharia, H.C.E., *Renascent India*, pp. 263-64.
109. *Annual Register*, January-June 1930, Vol. I, pp. 150-51.
110. *Amrita Bazar Patrika*, June 4, 1930.
111. *Ibid.,* May 29, 1930.
112. Brockway, A.F., *Indian Crisis*, London, p. 163.
113. *Amrita Bazar Patrika*, May 27, 1930.
114. *Congress Bulletin*, May 13, 1937.
115. *Modern Review*, Vol. 78, July to December 1945, p. 260.
116. *Ibid.*
117. *Amrita Bazar Patrika,* April 10, 1932.
118. She was the sister of Pandit Jawaharlal Nehru.
119. Wife of Pandit Jawaharlal Nehru.
120. Nehru, Jawaharlal, *An Autobiography,* p. 210.
121. *Amrita Bazar Patrika,* November 5, 1931.
122. *Advance*, November 4, 1931.
123. Nehru. J., *op. cit.,* p. 334.
124. *Annual Register*, Vol. I, January to June, 1932, p. 24.

125. She was the daughter of Pandit Jainarian Shukla. She was born in 1904 and received her education at Allahabad and Banaras. She is at present a member of the Council of States.
126. *Women on the March*, December 1957, p. 22.
127. She is the daughter of Pandit Niranjan Nath Huku and was born in Agra in 1884. She was educated in St. Mary's convent at Hubli (Karnataka). She was married to Pandit Shamlal Nehru in 1901. She was a member of the *Lok Sabha* and was associated with many a women's organisations and educational institutions.
128. *Asiatic Review*, Vol. XXVIII, 1932, p. 565.
129. *Ibid.*
130. *Ibid.*
131. Chattopadhyaya, K. *The Awakening of Indian Womanhood*, p. 56.
132. *Congress Bulletin*, October 15, 1932, p. 3.
133. *Ibid.*, p. 25.
134. *Ibid.*, p. 27.
135. *Special Bulletin* issued by the All-India Congress Committee, March 15, 1933, p. 1.
136. Modern, E., *The Women in Gandhi's Life*, p. 182.
137. *Indian Statutory Commission*, Vol. I, p. 49.

8

The Quit India Movement

> There was no power in the world that could set any limitation to women's achievements. There was no *Salic* Law which would hold good in the world when women were determined that they would rise to the full height and statute of their capacity.
>
> —*Sarojini Naidu*[1]

Political Conditions of the Period

The year 1939 watched the beginning of the Second World War in Europe. England announced war on the German Reich on September 3, 1939 professedly in defence of democracy and the weak countries. And yet Britain was reluctant to free India of her dependency. India lacked the independent foreign policy and hence to follow the one laid out by England. Lord Linlithgow, the then Governor-General of India· of India, proclaimed India to be at battle with Germany the same day (September, 3, 1939). The Congress ministries in office were not consulted and as a mark of protest, they resigned.

The Indian National Congress had cleared in the election manifesto, as far back as 1936, its "opposition to the participation of India in an imperialist war."[2] This stand of the Congress was further strengthened by the Working Committee of the Indian National Congress meeting in September 1939. The Working Committee pointed out that the declared wishes of the Indian people . . . have been deliberately ignored by the British Government," and while the committee "unhesitatingly condemns the latest aggression of the Nazi Government in Germany against Poland . . . the issue of war and peace for India must be decided by the Indian people."[3]

The Congress Working Committee also demanded from the Government a clear announcement of its war aims and a pledge of freedom for India. India would be prepared to render help to the British Government in her dangerous hour if these demands were accepted. The demands of the Congress were rejected. The Congress then decided to campaign against and to stop people from rendering any help in the battle effort. To intensify its campaign Mahatma Gandhi commenced an individual *Satyagraha.* It was "to carry on non-violently and openly anti-war propaganda" and "to preach non-cooperation with the Government in their war efforts."[4]

As a consequence of this campaign, opened by Vinoba Bhave on October 17, 1940, thirty thousand men and women courted arrest.[5] It continued till the closing of the year when the Government had to free the political prisoners in view of the existing situation. The Japanese were knocking at the door of India and the destiny of the British was in jeopardy.

Sir Stafford Cripps was sponsored to India with new proposals to win over the famous support. But Cripps's proposal was rejected by all the parties. All expectations of a settlement receded to the background and Cripps's Mission, instead of goodwill and quiet atmosphere, left ill-will and bitterness among the Indian people. In a desperate mood the Congress Working Committee passed a resolution in July 1942, asking the British to withdraw from India.

The people were in a defiant mood and they were inspired by the British reverses at the Japanese hands. The suffering of the battle refugees and the cruel treatment received by them further incensed them. Force and intimidation had been used against those exhibiting reluctance in contribution to battle funds.

Gandhiji was arrested on August 9, 1942 and he left a short but significant message to the nation in three words: "Do or Die". It became a target for the millions and a source of courage and sacrifice increasingly demanded at the altar of independence.

The news of Gandhiji's arrest was followed by strikes in Bombay, Ahmedabad and Poona. By August 11, 1942, this infection had affected all the country. Alongside also people marched in processions, conducted meetings and demonstrations; the universities closed down for lack of students. Industrial labour in Ahmedabad, Bombay, Kanpur, Indore, Bangalore and Mysore, struck work.[6]

The movement did not spare the rural areas. In various places people announced themselves free, courts and offices were seized, police stations were fortified. Flags were on secretariat buildings, courts and other Government offices. The Government machinery was paralysed in various districts, mainly in Bihar, Central Provinces, Andhra, Uttar Pradesh, Gujarat, Karnataka, Assam and parts of Bengal.

The Government emerged with counter-measures. It enacted "the Penalties Enhancement Ordinance, Collective Fine Ordinance, the Special Court Ordinance, the Whipping Ordinance." These ordinances legalised certain shapes of plunder, loot, flogging and even murder of political offenders Searches were held and properties confiscated. Congress offices and its funds became the property of the Government. Whole of India had become a "big prison".[7]

Leaders were arrested in the first round-up and in their absence women continued the movement and bore the brunt of the British wrath.

The women not only took out processions and held demonstrations but also organised camps for training in civic duties, first aid, education, democracy and the Indian constitution. Training in *lathi* and drill was also given in these camps.[8]

The women arranged Political Prisoner's Relief Fund and collected large sums. Some women became underground and operated the movement from there. In every province there were tales to tell about the female heroic part.

ASSAM

The women of this province played a prominent role in this movement. It was probably the sudden unbounded attachment for liberty which made them take over the command of the freedom struggle, "The struggle waged by Assam to break down the shackles of slavery", observed Mitra and Chakraborty in *Rebel India*, "is largely a struggle for Assam's womanhood."[9]

On September 20, 1942 Kanak Lata Barua, a girl in her teens, marched towards Gohapon Thana,[10] alongwith five hundred people to occupy the Thana building. She was called upon to leave the spot by Rabati Mohan Shome, the Officer-in-charge, Police Thana,but she boldly responded: "Unless the

Thana_Officer and his men wanted to act as the servants of the people, they must clear out and allow the people to take possession of the place."[11]

The Daroga threatened her of firing if she did not move. She remained firm and told him to perform his duty and she would perform hers. She was shot dead and the flag was taken by her male comrade Mukunda also shot dead.[12] Many more were murdered including a pregnant woman and six others were wounded.[13]

The women's organisation sprung up under Smt. Annupriya Barua and Sudhalata Dutta, as a result of atrocities committed by the military and police. The women visited the terrorised fields and encouraged and cheered the people. Again it was left to the women to face the military and armed police and to lead processions in Gohpur, Barapujjia, Teok and Barhampur.[14]

It was in Assam that "Free India's Fighting Force" was organised. Women also joined this facilities and they took charge of providing army. They organised the Red Cross First Aid parties and provided warm clothing, bandages and many other goods to the workers and countrymen all over Assam. The Government later broke up the organisation but the women continued their work.[15]

In Tezpur in Assam, women from surrounding villages paraded the streets sang songs, shouted slogans and unfurled the tricolour.

In some premises the women were treated cruelly when they denied to disclose to the police the whereabouts of the underground relatives who Mrs. Anna Prava Barua endured police atrocities for two long years. Unable to arrest her husband the police confiscated all her possessions including the image of the family deity. The police would approach in the night and lift the mosquito net to search her. As a consequence it became impossible for the female members and specially Anna Parva Barua to sleep in comfort[16] and privacy.

Ten thousand women of village Bajali appeared *en masse* on October 7, 1942, to meet at the Pata Churkuchi Police Station platform. The ladies sang national songs and unfurled the national flag. The police tried to disperse them, but failed. They also requested the police officials to resign their posts.[17]

On January 26, 1943, one thousand women assembled to celebrate the Independence Day. Since public meetings were prohibited they called a prayer meeting at Kirtan Ghar. Chandra Prabha Saikiani was pulled out and arrested while lecturing. The *prasad* was mixed with dust and the police also attacked some of the women of whom Sita Bhuwaneswari Devi was the worst affected.[18]

BENGAL

The women of Bengal had been taking part in the freedom struggle ever since the beginning. The people of Midnapore District played a notable part in the movement of 1942.

The Tamlauk sub-division had organised itself against the Japanese attack. They raised troops of volunteers including men and women. Various camps were opened to impart training to those who joined the ranks. Local relief committees were helped. A *Khadi* Centre was also arranged where four thousand spinners were working, most of these being women.[19] A National Government was formed. It was helped by the various Ministries. The National Government kept on working till August 8, 1944 and was dissolved at the instance of Gandhiji.[20] The women of Tamlauk division marched in procession and in one of these seven women were arrested and two years rigorous imprisonment was sentenced to each.[21]

One procession was led by a seventy-three-year old lady Matangini Hazra. The processionists had to occupy the Thana. The police hit her hands but she remained firm holding the flag. Instead she instigated the officials to stop firing and to bare their jobs to join the freedom movement. Finally she was shot dead.[22]

Seventy-four women of this division were raped by the Government employees, and one of them died. Women with daggers tried to offer resistance collectively which worked out.[23]

It was alleged on November 7, 1942, that forty-three persons were murdered and seventy injured in the Tamlauk sub-division. The houses of people involved in political activities were burnt. In some cases, the women were not permitted to leave the houses. After setting fire to the houses, the police or military remained on guard. The women had to be rescued by the volunteers through back doors or by ladders thrown over the roof.[24]

On January 9, 1943, six hundred soldiers surrounded three villages of Masuria Dalmasuria and Chandipur in Mohishadal Thana. They not only looted the villages but also committed criminal attack on 46 women in a single day.[25]

The women commenced an organisation called *Bagini Seva Sangha* for protecting their chastity and honour. Some of them faced the soldiers and the police with arms. Two ladies were prosecuted under the Arms Act for using daggers in self-defence.[26]

Kalpana Dutta

Kalpana, arrested for her revolutionary activities in 1932, was freed in 1937, when the Provincial Autonomy was started in the country. Special efforts for her freedom were made by Rabindranath Tagore, C.F. Andrews and Mahatma Gandhi. In the Midnapore Jail, Gandhiji contacted her. In her book *Chittagong Armoury Raiders Reminiscences,* she wrote : "Gandhiji came to meet me in the Presidency Jail. After a little conversation, Gandhiji spoke to me 'Nazimuddin[27] is extremely angry with you and says none of the Chittagong Armoury Raid would be released, but yet I am trying for you."[28] She was freed in 1939. She occupied herself in studies and also involved in communist compaign. She worked in labour areas and Dhobi Para. Kalpana worked in the *Kisan Sabha* Office and afterwards joined the Tramway Workers Union Office as a whole time worker.[29]

Kalpana joined a post-graduate course. By this time the Second World War started, the authorities ordered her to desert Calcutta within twenty-four hours and interned her in her house in Chittagong. Her activities at this time were to continue the confidential work of the party and see to its efficient running. It included the despatching of all Provincial Committee and Central Committee leaflets, books and papers to various areas, establishing shelters and dumps in the town, organising distribution of pamphlets, etc. In 1941, the bans on her activity were relaxed.[30]

UTTAR PRADESH

Groups of girl students journeyed the districts and provided whatever relief and succour to the people. Women of respectable

Hindu families were ordered to leave their houses at the point of bayonets including the mothers carrying babies. They were asked to part with their jewellery which was removed from their bodies forcibly. In Samanwal village of District Ghazipur, an *Ahir* woman was shot down while running away from the soldiers.[31]

It was alleged from Banaras that the ladies who had suffered at the hands of police, related lamentable fables. In some cases the women were pulled by their long hairs; they were asked to do sit-ups; no food was provided to them. In one case a child was roasted alive before his mother's eyes. Some women were tortured to reveal the whereabouts of their husbands.[32] Nine students were externed from Banaras Hindu University for actively taking part in the movement.[33]

PUNJAB

Punjab energetically answered to the call of Mahatma Gandhi—students, both boys and girls, unscrupulous advanced in the field. Lahore on November 10, 1942, one hundred and four students were arrested, including twenty-two girls. The girls were bold, they distributed the badges. The girls even did not pay any attention to the presence of the police and did not get into the police van till they were asked by their principal to do so. At the police station they were cross-examined and they replied in this manner:

Q. What is your name?
A. Bagi No. 1, 2, 3, ...22.
Q. What is your father's name?
A. Gandhiji.
Q. What is your mother's name?
A. Bharat Mata.[34]

In Amritsar the girl students were provided a highly objectionable treatment.[35]

Rajkumari Amrit Kaur

During the movement Rajkumari Amrit Kaur played a role in organising processions and protest meetings. Rajkumari belonged to the royal family of Kapurthala State. She was the daughter of Sir Harnam Singh and was born in 1886 in Lucknow,

Uttar Pradesh. Her mother was one of the leading social workers and the daughter learnt to fight for social as well as political freedom of the nation.

She had most of her education in England and was a keen sportswoman. On her return to India she engaged in organising sports and games in the Punjab.

Gokhale was a great friend of Amrit Kaur's father, said: "The flames of my passionate desire to see India free from foreign domination were fanned by him."[36]

Rajkumari Amrit Kaur first met with Mahatma Gandhi in the crucial days of Martial Law in 1919. She afterwards became his secretary, a designation she occupied for sixteen years.[37]

Amrit Kaur proved instrumental in bringing about the birth of the All India Women's Conference in 1926 and remained its secretary for many years. In 1932, she gave evidence before the Lothian Committee on Indian franchise and afterwards, as a member of a delegation of Women's Organisation, she testified before the Joint Select Committee of Parliament on Indian Constitutional Reforms.[38]

Rajkumari took a leading part in the Salt *Satyagraha* and was arrested in Bombay. Afterwards when the Communal Award was declared, she criticised it.

She visited Bannu in the North-West Frontier Province to champion the case of the Congress. She was convicted on July 16, 1937, by the Assistant Commissioner, Bannu, on an allegation of sedition and was awarded imprisonment till the rising of the Court and to pay fifty rupees fine.[39]

Amrit Kaur was most active during the Quit India movement in 1942. She led processions every day. One procession was meted ruthless *lathi* charge in Simla. From August 9 to 16 the processions led by her were *lathi* charged fifteen times.[40]

The Government could not let her remain free and finally she was arrested at Kalka. She was carried by car to Ambala Jail and was permitted to carry a bedding roll, a bag consisting her spinning wheel, her *Bible* and *Gita,* which she insisted on taking, and her brass bowel for drinking water. Her suitcase of clothes was not allowed with her and she had to manage for more than one month with one pair of clothes. The filth in the prison was indescribable. Pigeons and rats were her constant companions. There was a foul smelling latrine in the living room which she refused to use on hygienic grounds. She had to bathe in the open.

The food was worse. She was unable to eat it. Within a week she was hospitalised. In eight weeks she lost one stone weight and had to be sent back to Simla where she remained interned for twenty months. She lost her brother while in prison. Her letter to her sister-in-law was not even sent.[41]

After independence, she became Cabinet Minister in the Government of India.

Amar Kaur

Amar Kaur, wife of Mohan Lal, a lawyer of Gurdaspur who left his practice responding to Gandhiji's call in 1921, entered public life at the same time.

Amar Kaur and Adarsh Kumari and many others discovered a novel way of molesting the authorities. While coming from Lyallpur to Lahore on August 23, 1932, they pulled the chain in the running train at Badami Bagh Railway Station, some miles from Lahore. After the train stopped, they shouted slogans like "Inquilab Zindabad", "Videshi Mal Boycott" and "Gandhi ki Jai". They asked other passengers to join them in their efforts to free the country.[42]

Amar Kaur and others were tried[43] and awarded five months imprisonment and a fine of forty rupees each. Amar Kaur was sentenced one month's extra imprisonment for pulling the chain.[44]

The Lahore Bar filed a revision and the High Court directed that they could be freed on paying a security of five hundred rupees each pending the decision of the case. Amar Kaur and Adarsh refused to come out on bail and decried the action of the High Court Bar.

Amar Kaur did not limit her activities to Punjab only. She went to North-West Frontier Province. She was arrested and jailed at Bannu for her political activities.

Following the policy of individual *Satyagraha* commenced by Gandhiji in 1940, Amar Kaur offered *Satyagraha* at Kasur in Lahore District. She was freed from jail only to be rearrested in September 1942. She organised women's training camps in Lahore and Amritsar and arrested therefor. The treatment meted out to the political prisoners was insult. So she, accompanied by Satyawati, decided to hold demonstrations in jail. They succeeded to unfurl a national flag on the jail gate on October 9, 1942. Jail authorities lost their temper and these two ladies were shifted to Ambala District Jail.[45]

Amar Kaur's husband was not permitted to see her. While in Ambala jail she fell ill. Her husband again visited the authorities to see her but failed.[46]

She was freed in April 1944 due to declining health after one year and four months in prison.

Pushpa Gujral

Pushpa Gujral[47] of Punjab took a leading part in the movement of 1942.

Her interest in political work started in 1919, but she became active only during the movement of 1930. She was elected President of the City District Congress Committee. She gathered funds for the families of political prisoners.[48]

Pushpa Gujral went to prison for the first time in 1940 for offering *Satyagraha* and awarded six months imprisonment.

1942 watched the passing of the popular Quit India resolution and the family was re-active. Pushpa was arrested along with the entire family and was awarded six months' imprisonment.[49]

Pushpa Gujral was linked with many other social work agencies. She was member of the Punjab State Social Welfare Advisory Board. She is no more with us.

NORTH-WEST FRONTIER PROVINCES

The freedom movement had became so famous amongst the women that even veiled Bannu was no exception. They marched in procession proudly, shouting slogans against the alien usurper, as a mark of protest against the arrests of Hindu-Muslim merchants for providing food and asylum to the Khudai *Khidmatgars.*[50] It was the first demonstration assigned by the women in the history of the province and it had far reaching impact on the people.[51]

Sind

The women took out processions. The police of Karachi adopted new measures to harass them. They were abused and carried to far off places and freed in the middle of the night. The City Magistrate, Rup Chand, while dealing with the case of a girl, slapped her on the face as she refused to apologise. Two girl volunteers entered the City Magistrate's Court and ordered him in writing to resign the post as he proved incompetent. Its copies were circulated in the court. Both of them were arrested, tried and convicted to long imprisonment.[52]

MADHYA PRADESH

In every province novel measures were being tried to overthrow the foreign rule. Women approached officials and members of the bar on *Raksha Bandhan* and appealed to the former to resign and the latter not to attend the courts.

Women of the village Chimur[53] had to suffer a lot at the hands of the police and military. On August 19, 1942, a special train coming with 200 European soldiers and fifty Indian constables arrived at Wardha. The sepoys and soldiers looted the property of the residents. Women were raped. In many cases they succeeded to save themselves by putting a united front. Sometimes women in mature pregnancy or in confinement or in menses, and girls of tender age were raped by them.[54]

Enquiries were made into the events at Chimur by a committee consisted of officials and non-officials. It was disclosed that thirteen women were actually raped and some of them by more than one European. Four girls were also molested, one of them by one European soldier and later by one Indian soldier. They seized her ring and ten rupees from mother.[55] The pregnant wife of the *sarpanch* was also raped.[56]

Anasuyabai Kale

Her interest in public work started in 1920 when she organised *Bhagini Mandal*, a women's organisation. Anasuyabai Kale became a member of the Central Provinces Legislature in 1928 and was its Deputy Speaker. But she resigned as a protest against Gandhiji's arrest in 1930 associated with the Salt *Satyagraha.*[57]

Anasuyabai took active part in the Civil Disobedience Movement of 1930 and imprisoned for her political role.

The Quit-India Movement witnessed her in the sphere of active politics. Due to her efforts the lives of twenty-five young men,[58] associated with the Ashti Chimur chapter of the annals of the freedom struggle of 1942,were protected.[59]

In free India Anasuyabai became a member of the Central Legislature.[60]

BOMBAY

Bombay was the first province to be affected by the political upsurge and it was in the vanguard of the freedom fight.

Sarojini Naidu

Mrs. Naidu of the fame of Dharasana Salt raid was again active during this period.

In these few years Sarojini Naidu worked hard to bring the two communities closer. She addressed conferences and spoke from several platforms. Addressing a political meeting at Vellore (Madras) she said: "The Hindus and Muslims are the two eyes of the nation and if both eyes were to be focused together on the *Swaraj* image under the leadership of Mahatma Gandhi, freedom would be theirs ere long."[61]

She was arrested on December 3, 1940, for participating in the individual *Satyagraha* inaugurated by Vinoba Bhave. She became ill and had to be freed on December 11, 1940.

As soon as Sarojini recovered, she resumed her political work. She was re-arrested immediately after the Quit-India resolution was passed on August 9, 1942. Sarojini appeared from the Aga Khan Palace in ill-health and remained inactive for ten months after her release in March 1943.

Sarojini came in public again on January 7, 1944, and addressed a conference at Bombay. On January 26, 1944, she approached Delhi on her way to Lahore. As soon as she reached Lahore railway station, a notice was issued to her by the Punjab Government forbidding her from delivering any public speech or participating in a procession, or writing to the newspapers. She returned the notice remarking that she was already under the direction of her doctor, whom she was obeying and was not addressing any public conference or joining any procession. Therefore in her connection the order was non-existent.[62]

Immediately after India achieved independence, Sarojini became the first woman Governor of Uttar Pradesh in 1947, one the largest Indian States. She occupied this office up to March 1949 when she passed away. She was a great ambassador of Hindu-Muslim unity and the champion of female's rights.

Kamala Devi Chottopadhyaya

Kamala Devi, active participant of the Salt *Satyagraha* away, now reined the movement again. In fact, she was never tired and carried out her work throughout the period. She was arrested for her political work many times between 1939 and 1944. She left for the United States for acquainting the people of that country about the Indian conditions.

After India achieved independence, she directed her interest from politics to cooperative movement. She sponsored the Indian Cooperative Union. She established the Theatre Centre of India, a federation of theatre organisations all over India. She was honoured with Padma Bhushan in 1955.

She made great contribution in reviving the traditional cottage industries of India.[63] She is no more.

Miraben (Madeleine Slade)

Madeleine Slade was not an active participant in the political struggle, but supported the cause of the freedom of India.

Born in 1892, she was the daughter of Sir Edmund Slade. She came from an aristocratic family of Great Britain. She had a good education, but she changed her interests very often. In 1923, she moved to Paris and "was living a life of thoughtless luxury in those days, idling away the time between London, Paris and Berne. Her parents were well-to-do and she had nothing to worry except the pursuit of pleasure and the ways to appreciate and enjoy the life that was bestowed by her parents."[64]

She read a book of Romain Rolland, a French philosopher, on Gandhiji and was greatly influenced. She has herself narrated how the change came about: "Then something happened one night. I had never thought of religion before but it came all of a sudden. I read this book and I decided then and there that if possible I must give life to Gandhi and to India. Accordingly she wrote to Gandhiji requesting him if she could join the *Ashram* in India and serve for the rest of her life."[65]

Slade took one year to really approach her new master. She sent for *Khadi* so to get the necessary garments made before her coming to India. She also spent her days and nights reading the Hindu scriptures. After she was fully prepared, she approached her new home. Her parents tried to refrain her but failed. She came to India in 1925 and received a new name, Miraben.

Miraben accompanied Gandhiji to England in 1931 to attend the Second Round Table Conference. She sent news releases regarding Gandhiji's campaign to the press in England, America, France, Germany and Switzerland. The Government warned that unless she stopped sending news to foreign countries she would be arrested but failed.

As soon as Miraben returned from England, she started on a *Khadi* selling tour throughout India. When she returned, her entry in the city was banned by the government of Bombay. She violated the order and was arrested. She was charged under Section 21 of Emergency Ordinance and awarded three month' imprisonment.[66]

Miraben visited England again in 1934 to educate its people on Gandhiji's philosophy. She was again arrested during the Quit-India Movement of 1942 accompanied by Gandhiji and confined to the Aga Khan Palace for twenty-one months.

In 1946, she was appointed Special Advisor to the Government of Uttar Pradesh for "Grow More Food" campaign. From 1947 to 1960 she remained Advisor for Development. She was running an *Ashram* at Rishikesh in the *Himalayas.* She expired some time back.[67]

Khurshed Behn

Khurshed Behn, a famous organiser of the Volunteer force in 1930, went to the North-West Frontier Province in 1940 to propagate the gospel of non-violence amongst its public. She went from village to village contacting the *Pathans, Pirs, Maliks* and *Khans* and made them aware of the cruelty of abducting people. She contacted the members of the Hindu community also, infusing in them the spirit of strength and valour. At the end of the year she desired to go to Walo Tangi, a tribal territory, and sought the Government's consent to cross the border. When the Government did not give its consent she informed the Government of her intention. In an effort to cross the border she was arrested on December 4, 1940, and was prosecuted. She had to pay a fine of one thousand rupees or in default thereof to three months' imprisonment. She preferred imprisonment rather than fine.[68] After the expiry of her sentence she was externed from the Frontier Province and was interned in Bombay.

Khurshed challenged the validity of this order in letter dated March 31, 1941. But the Government paid no attention to her protest. She was later permitted to move within the Bombay Presidency. But she remained unsatisfied as she wanted to leave Bombay. Khurshed wanted to accommodate the Government as regards its policy of extricating her from North-West Frontier Province, but she could not be extricated from various parts of the country. Khurshed Behn finally decided to violate the Government orders and accordingly informed the authorities on July 31, 1941 of her desire of leaving for Wardha on August 1, 1941.[69] She could not reach Wardha.[70] Khurshed was arrested on the day of her parting and sent to Central Jail, Yerwada, (Pune).

Khurshed also participated in the Quit-India Movement. She perused carefully the atrocities of the police.

Bombay was greatly affected by the 1942 movement. Apart from the usual processions, Women's Day was celebrated. Three processions were held in Ahmedabad. A procession was lathi-charged and seventy-six women were arrested.[71]

On a similar occasion in the month of October, processions of women from the various parts of the city began. The police assaulted one such procession and seized the tricolour. As a consequence the women squatted on the road and refused to move unless the flag was restored to them. The police responded with ruthless teargas attack. Some fainted while others were wounded. One Satyawati Mehta got serious injury on her head with the bursting of a gas cylinder and had to be rushed to hospital. About eighty men were wounded but volunteers were forbidden from providing water to the wounded.[72]

The women of Bombay took out processions on the 9th of every month, being the day of Gandhiji's arrest. The police had made arrangements to meet them. Exactly at the fied hour, Jayshriben appeared. No sooner did she appear than she was arrested accompanied by other ladies. As they were being arrested a procession of *Desh Sevikas* emerged on the scene. They were arrested and their arrest served as indication for spontaneous processions. The procession was lathi-charged. A girl of fourteen years tried to unfurl the tricolour but was beaten by the police. Another girl, Manfule, was also beaten for a similar effort. The police opened fire on these women processionists five times and made two hundred and fifty arrests.

Usha Mehta

Usha Mehta[73] was one of the leading workers of the Radio Conspiracy Case. When the famous Quit-India resolution was passed, she was present, a witness to this important decision. She had a great desire to make this resolution a success. She disliked picketing of foreign cloth shops and liquor shops. She wished to do something different. Usha Mehta's dream wish came true when some friends decided to run a transmitting station confidentially. "It appealed to me immensely and I jumped at the idea and plunged into the movement in spite of staunch opposition from my father who being a government servant did not approve of my idea and who wanted me to finish my education"[74] Nothing stopped this brave girl, not even the peril it presented to her father, a Judge at the time.

The distinguished leaders were in jail by August 9, 1942 and from this day preparations for starting a radio in the name of "Voice of Freedom" speaking from somewhere in India, were taken in hand.[75] A transmitter was must for successful continuation of the movement. It was felt that the press would be censored and as such the required campaign could easily be launched through the radio for the cause. Babuhai and Usha first started working for the radio. Money was needed. A woman relative of Usha offered her ornaments. Usha was reluctant to accept it. Ultimately Babubhai Khakar got the required amount and a transmitter was set up with it.[76]

Another group led by Vithalbhai K. Jhavari, now one of the editors of the birthday volume on Gandhiji, also established another transmitter. Besides these two, there were various other groups. Dr. Rammanohar Lohia, a popular socialist leader, was aware of these groups and attempted to coordinate the work. The most active group was Babubhai's in which Usha worked.

Usha narrated how they camouflaged their moves. "Fortunately for us, one uncle from upcountry or our sister or some other relative would come to our rescue. Uncle wanted a flat for one month. One of his nephews would go and hire it, take all the luggage there and would anxiously wait for him. But by the time uncle was expected, another flat would have to be hired for some other fictitious purpose. Every time the process was to go from the broadcasting station to the railway station and from there again to the new transmitting station. This had to be done every fortnight or so. Once Babubhai and I found a very good place; quite safe according to us. We were extremely happy at the idea that we would be able to carry on at least for a month or two. We went to the owner to pay the rent. A queer apparatus was lying there. We said 'Sethji, what is this supposed to be?'[77] 'A detecting machine to catch the illegal radios,' came the reply. 'Detecting machine', I exclaimed in my mind, but I took care to see that the face did not betray the expressions. Babubhai cleverly joined him in abusing all those who did such illegal acts and we were off. We thanked our stars for having been cautioned in time. The first words of Babubhai were 'Behn, we are saved from the tiger's jaws.'[78]

"Babubhai had warned me not to wear white *Khadi* sari that day but I had insisted on it. Since that day, however, I changed my dress only slightly so as to be less conspicuous."[79]

Usha Mehta was primarily assigned the work of broadcasting news and delivering talks in Hindustani. This broadcasting station first provided the news of Chittagong bomb raid, Jamshedpr hartal and the news about tortures in Ashti Chimur. In the lectures, attempts were made to clarify and describe the Congress stand, both from the national and international viewpoints.

Illustrating the Quit-India Movement the remarks were : "So far we were conducting a movement, but now we are conducting a revolution, there is victory or defeat. This revolution is not of one party or community, but of the whole of India, we hope you will not rest content till the British Empire is burnt to ashes."[80] The lectures were mostly given by Dr. Lohia.

However, this Radio could not work long. The Government came to know of it and raided the premises on November 12, at night. The Superintendent of Police and his military technicians and a force of fifty odd policemen came to possess the belongings of this broadcasting station. The entry of the Deputy Commissioner did not make the brave soldiers curious and they did not even move from their seats. Babubhai and Usha Mehta accompanied by many others were arrested in this Radio Conspiracy case. The police tried its best to extract the details from Usha Mehta but she answered no question relating to this topic. During the interrogation period she was also put in the lock-up. Explaining life in the police custody she says : "The lock-up period is perhaps the most trying time in the life of a prisoner. During the day you have to face the policemen and at night your only possible activity could be either to kill the bugs or to kill time. Again it is humanly impossible to sleep in a cell full of filth, dirt and nauseating smell."[81]

"In spite of six months' continuous interrogation, the police could not get any information from her and finally charged her with agreeing in conspiring among and between ourselves and others, to do or cause to be done illegal acts like possessing, establishing, maintaining and working illegal wireless telegraph without lawful . . . authority or excuse prejudicial acts and spreading prejudicial reports."[82]

The case was *Emperor versus Babubhai Khakar, Vithalbhai Jhaveri, Usha Mehta, Chandrakant Jhaveri, Nanak Motwant.* "Throughout the trial," says Usha Mehta, "we enjoyed so much that I am tempted to say that it was a golden period of my jail life. All along, we used to chew chocolates or peppermints unperturbed by the efforts of the Prosecutor who was hard at proving the case against us. The revelations of the approvers likewise failed to disturb our equanimity."[83]

The case was decided and Usha Mehta was awarded four years' imprisonment.[84] She remained in prison till April 1946.

After her release in 1946 she adopted teaching and later achieved doctorate degree on a thesis on the "Social and Political Thought of Mahatma Gandhi."

Kasturba Gandhi

Bombay watched a martyr's death in prison. Kasturba Gandhi had shared the responsibilities of the freedom struggle with Gandhiji but she died as a prisoner on February 24, 1944.

She could not even get the needed medical help. After a great deal of correspondence by Gandhiji, the doctors of her choice were permitted to attend her.

Hansa Mehta

Hansa Mehta joined the freedom struggle early in life. Greatly motivated by the leaders of the day she journeyed all over India, meeting women to produce awareness among them. This, however, was opposed by the British Government. On August 30, 1930, the railway authorities played a trick and sent down engines to drown the public voices shouting 'Inquilab Zindabad' on reaching of Kamala Nehru and Hansa Mehta at Delhi Railway Station. The engines were made to hoot non-stop.

As educationist and a devoted social worker, Hansa believed that without improvement in the quality of life of women, social reform was impossible. Her wonderful contribution in the sphere of education won her many distinctions. She was the first woman Vice-Chancellor in India (Baroda University). *The Times of India*, in its issue of August 15, 1947, explained the unprecedented scenes of zeal on the ushering of the independence of India at the hour of midnight. In the Constituent Assembly, "Pandit Nehru made a speech which was at once notabie and a masterpiece of literature." After the oath of devotion, the report says, "Smt. Hansa Mehta presented a national flag to the Constituent Assembly on behalf of the women of India."

Mridula Sarabhai

Mridula Sarabhai was a famous political and social worker. She was the daughter of Sarla and Ambalal Sarabhai, the fabulously wealthy Industrialists and Philanthropists of Ahmedabad. She became a leading worker in the cause of freedom, in 1927. Like her contemporaries, she was deeply moved by Gandhiji's message and participated in the Salt *Satyagraha* (1930), the Rajkot *Satyagraha* (1938), and was in and out of prison marry times. She worked actively during the INA Trials in 1946. She played a prominent role in the restoration of kidnapped women during the communal riots, which shook the country in the wake of the partition of India in 1947.

MYSORE

Resultant upon the arrest of Gandhiji the leaders of Isur and neighbouring villages framed *Panchayats* and asked officials to resign. The Patil[85] of Isur refused to resign. A party of children took over the papers and other articles and thus freed him of his duty forcibly. As a consequence, the village was raided by the Police Inspector. The children summoned the police officials and invited them to wear Gandhi caps and take off their hats. The Sub-Inspector ordered a *lathi*-charge on children. A girl, the daughter of Shanker, removed his hat and replaced it with a *Khadi* cap. The Sub-Inspector shot at the girl and she was wounded. This enraged the villagers, and they assaulted the police party and killed the Sub-Inspector and Amildar. A trial followed. Fourteen persons were awarded death sentence and twenty-three, including three women, lifetransportation. The High Court confirmed the death sentence of five and the transportation sentence on three women.[86]

KARNATAKA

The students participated actively in the movement. The share of the girl students in these activities was great too. The government made lathi blows and indiscriminate beatings on these law-violating students. Thirty-two girls were severely beaten at Kumtha Adoni[87] (Karnataka).

Balamakki Bamakka, the old mother of two influential merchants, led a procession with a tricolour and Gandhiji's photograph. She appealed to the Sub-Inspector of police to prevent the procession his resignation and lead the movement against the government. She was arrested.

At Dharwar, on October 23, 1942 two lady students, Hemlata Shenolikar and Gulvadi, entered the District Courts and unfurled the flag on the Judge's seat. Gulvadi addressed the members of the Bar in the court and summoned the Judge and called upon him to resign and dissolve his court within eight days, or he would be tried as a traitor. The police appeared on the scene. Gulvadi escaped, Shenolikar was ordered to pay a fine of fifty rupees or to suffer imprisonment for one month. She didn't pay the fine and preferred to go to jail.[88]

Gulvadi again visited Dharwar Bar and addressed it again, asking them to support the cause of freedom. She was arrested and sentenced to pay a fine of one hundred and fifty rupees or three months' imprisonment.[89]

Sucheta Kriplani

Sucheta Kriplani's[90] interest in politics dates back to the days she was a lecturer in Banares University in 1934. Her marriage to Acharya J.B. Kriplani, then General Secretary of the All India Congress, further increased her interest. She resigned her job in the Banares University and entered political field. Individual *Satyagraha* was started by the Congress in 1940 and she was one of the selected ones who was allowed to take part in this *Satyagraha* and was arrested.[91]

By the time she was freed, another movement was under way. Most of the leaders were in the jail. She did not find it proper to surrender to the police and went underground. She had to face many troubles to carry on her activities, but escaped arrest by the police.[92]

During this period a women's department of the Indian National Congress was commenced in 1943 with Sucheta Kriplani as Secretary-in-charge. She issued leaflets to organise women's department influentially. It was felt that women must be given correct information to protect them from getting panicky over trifles. With this aim it was decided to hold meetings at regular intervals in *mohallas* to keep uneducated, ignorant women informed regarding battle. The information could be provided through hand bills and bulletins.[93]

Another work done by this Department was to organise a Volunteer Corps. The volunteers were trained on simple drill, first aid and the art of self-defense in an emergency. The Corps were also required to assist the refugees when they came to the town or left it.[94]

In the towns they form a Central Committee with branches in each *mohalla* was framed. The Committee through its branches had to (a) convey to each house about the daily instructions. (b) gather information regarding the difficulties of the *mohalla.* (c) organise to teaching spinning to the *mohalla* women, (d) arrange speeches on useful general information, (e) arrange a brief course of physical culture with special stress on how to evade personal attacks, (f) find out cases of attacks and oppression on women, describe to victims that such incidents were not to be kept confidential under false note of modesty and honour, give publicity to such events and provide help in bringing criminals to books, be they civil or military, and (g) keep in touch with men's Volunteer Corps to be able to ask for help in any emergency.[95]

The *Mohalla* Committee had to make preparations to teach carding, spinning, etc. It had to supply *charkhas* and cotton, take the spun yarn and arrange for the weaving of cloth.[96]

Apart from this work, the Women's Department was to undertake to (i) study the problems of women and their reasons and cures, (ii) attempt to increase the membership of women (iii) coordinate the work of women workers, (iv) suggest ways and sources of increasing the capacity of women workers to share more responsibility when asked to do so, (v) suggest ways and means to the women representatives for their effective working in local government bodies, assemblies and institutions for constructive work like Khadi, village industries, labour, kisans, and (vi) to keep in touch with women's activities in India.[97]

Sucheta Kriplani was arrested in 1944. After her release in 1945 she occupied herself mostly to the social and relief activities. She visited East Bengal during the communal riots in 1946 to save the women and children from Muslims. When Mahatma Gandhiji went to East Bengal and adopted to work for rehabilitation of the refugees, Sucheta joined him.

During 1947, when India was partitioned, there were riots, in Punjab. Sucheta Kriplani rushed to the affected areas and organised relief operations.

She was a member of the Uttar Pradesh Legislative Assembly and afterwards became a member of the *Lok Sabha*. She had been the Chief Minister of Uttar Pradesh.

Aruna Asaf Ali

Aruna[98] has been a staunch soldier of the army of freedom fighters. She became distinguished during the Salt *Satyagraha*. She addressed meetings prepared salt and also led processions. The Chief Commissioner of Delhi was deeply alarmed by her activities. As a result he prosecuted her not for sedition "but for being a vagrant having no ostensible means of livelihood."[99]

She was asked to provide security for good conduct, which she refused. Aruna was arrested and awarded one years' imprisonment. A few months later most of the political prisoners were freed under the Gandhi-Irwin Pact. The government did not release Aruna in Lahore jail. Her women co-prisoners refused to leave saying that unless Aruna was released they would not move. Gandhiji had to interfere and the prisoners left Aruna in jail.[100] Later in response to a strong public protest, Aruna was released after a few days.

Aruna was re-arrested in 1932. Apart from imprisonment, she was fined two hundred rupees. Failing to get the find, the police resorted to a novel way of taxing her patience. They seized her most costly sarees.[101]

This time Aruna was put in the Delhi District jail. The political prisoners were being treated callously as a result of which Aruna started the lead and observed a hunger strike. The authorities conceded to the demand of the political prisoners, but Aruna suffered heavily. She was shifted to Ambala jail and was placed there in solitary confinement.[102]

After Aruna's release she refrained from active politics and for the next ten years she witnessed the developments in India with interest and made her own plans about the programme and measures of achieving freedom.

Aruna presided over the national tricolour hoisting ceremony at Gowalia Tank Maidan, Bombay, on August 9, 1942. A large crowd had assembled to witness the function. The police tried to interrupt the function and lathi-charged the gathering. Teargas and bullets were also utilised. "The sight of so much innocent blood and suffering lit the fire in her. It was Aruna's baptism in the politics of revolution."[103]

Aruna was one of the most significant figures of the movement of 1942. For all this period of four years she escaped arrest and succeeded. She continued her activities underground. On September 26, 1942, the property of Mrs. Asaf Ali and Jugal Kishore Khanna was confiscated by the Delhi Administration after the expiry of one month's notice during which they were directed to surrender themselves.[104] Aruna's property was auctioned for twenty thousand rupees and her car for three thousand and five hundred.

The attitude of the government did not demoralise Aruna. She published bulletins, participated in the freedom movement, visited from place to place for her work. She even contacted Mahatma Gandhi during this period but the police failed to get her. She was a leading leader of the underground movement.

Aruna edited *Inquilab*, a monthly journal accompanied by Ram Manohar Lohia. In the March 1944 issue of *Inquilab*, Aruna asked the fighters for independence "to choose his field of work and if the aim is common do not allow any academic and therefore futile arguments on questions like violence and non-violence to divert your attention from the stern realities of today . . . This revolution is the most opportune moment for taking stock and making preparation for our next effort. I want every student and youth to think and feel as soldiers of the revolution that is to come."[105]

Aruna earned the praise of many government servants for her strength and resourcefulness. Pyarelal writes: "An Englishman who was also a government servant meeting her accidently at the house of a friend, after hearing from her the story of her adventures, instead of informing the police complimented her for her courage saying, he himself would have done the same thing in similar circumstances."[106] A prize of five thousand rupees was declared by the authorities for capturing her.

Aruna fell ill. Hearing of her shattered health Gandhiji wrote to her: "I have been filled with admiration for your courage and heroism. I have sent you a message that you must not die underground. You are reduced to a skeleton. Do come out and surrender yourself and win the prize offered for your arrest. Reserve the prize money for Harijan cause."[107] Aruna could not surrender and kept on working despite her bad health. She appeared in the open when warrants against her were cancelled on January 26, 1946.[108]

Aruna illustrated in a public meeting at Calcutta that she underground mainly for the reason that she had to go various places to preserve and promote the spirit of national organisation that was being invaded by the Government.

In February 1946, Aruna advised the creation of a new *Azad Hind* Army in India. She said, "We have no place for mere intellectuals, we want practical people who can carry the message of independence throughout the whole length and breadth of the country."[109]

Yusuf Mehrally, observed in the *Tribune*, "The heroine of 1857 was the Rani of Jhansi, that of the 1942 revolution is undoubtedly Aruna Asaf Ali."[110]

Aruna Asaf Ali became the Mayor of Delhi Corporation in 1958, a post she occupied with distinction.

Women in the Indian National Army

About the first decade of the century, the revolutionary and militant activities were at their peak in India. Some of the revolutionaries fled to other countries such as Japan, China, Siam and Malaya to avoid repression by the British Government and for perfecting their designs for liberating nation. The most important was Ras Behari Bose who sought shelter in Japan after throwing a bomb on Lord Hardinge in 1911.

The number of revolutionaries increased with the passage of time, and the local population of South-East Asia containing three million people strengthened the revolutionary movement with men and funds.

There were various organisations set up by the Indians in this area. The Gadar party was active in Shanghai. In Bangkok, Thai Bharat Cultural Lodge[111] was the centre of revolutionary activities. The leading revolutionaries were S. Amar Singh, Pritam Singh and Chanda Singh.

Japan announced war on Britain and America in December 1941. On December 15, 1941, Captain Mohan Singh of the Indian Army, now known as General Mohan Singh,[112] with fifty-four associates, met Pritam Singh near Jitra Cantonment. Mohan Singh and his associates pledged to sacrifice their lives for the national freedom.[113]

The Indian Independence League was framed on January 16, 1942, at Kuala Lumpur. Subsequently branches were founded in Thailand and other places. By now the number of Indian prisoners at Kuala Lumpur became five thousand. Captain Mohan Singh addressed them and motivated them to join the Indian National Army to fight the British in Malaya and elsewhere.[114]

Ever since the framing of the Indian Independence League the Indian women in East Asia assisted to further the cause of

India's Independence League. Indian women helped in the preparation and collection of bandages, first aid dressings, collection of funds and goods needed by the troops and motivating young men and women to do their duty in the crucial hour.[115]

In March, 1943, the Women's Section of the Indian Independence League was inaugurated. Mrs. M.K. Chidambaram was elected Chairman and Miss Saraswaty as Secretary of the Women's Section of Indian Independence League, Singapore, Dr. Lakshmi Swaminathan was appointed Secretary at the Headquarters. These ladies journeyed the several parts of Malaya, Thailand and Burma to open branches and to enlist volunteers.[116] Finally all branches of the Indian Independence League commenced the Women's Section. The main work of the women was of collecting funds and providing facilities to the soldiers. But with the reaching of Subhas Chandra Bose there emerged a revolutionary spirit in the organisation.

On July 9, 1943, Subhas Chandra Bose addressed a meeting and demanded men and women volunteers. He felt that women must be prepared to share the onus of freedom's war. "This caught the imagination of the Indian womenfolk" and a beginning to start a Women's Regiment was made, which later popularly came to be known as the "Ranee Jhansi Regiment."[117]

A women 's camp was commenced on October 23, 1943, in Singapore which was followed by many more in Malaya and Burma. They were imparted training in nursing, social service and general welfare work. The military part of the training contained (1) drill, (2) arms training, (3) tactics, (4) map reading, and (5) general topics. They were trained to use machine guns, bayonets, sub-machine guns, revolvers, rifles, grenades, swords and daggers.[118]

The women wore the soldiers uniforms and had to maintain strict military discipline. They were taken out on route marches and had to cover between 6 and 40 miles at times. Their day started with the singing of the National Anthem and common prayer for the national liberation. They would, each day, re-affirm their promise too—"I shall fulfil my objective in the face of all difficulties, I shall sacrifice myself, my body, soul and properties, all for the fulfilment of my pledge. I promise I shall not do any such thing which may besmear the name of Hindustan and Netajee. I shall obey all the orders of superiors with heart and soul. I shall keep in good condition all the weapons Netaji has given."[119]

The women of Ranee Jhansi Regiment were eager to go on active service. So they sponsored a representation to Subhas Chandra Bose, the Chief Commander of the Indian National Army, "It is you, who taught us that there is no distinction between men and women. It is you who gave us training, fit for menfolk, have inspired us with courage and moral stamina required for actual warfare. We have received complete training. In these circumstances why should we not be sent to the battlefront without delay?"[120] This was signed with the blood drawn from the fingers of the signatories.[121]

The first group was sent to Burma in the beginning of 1945. The members of the Jhansi Regiment could not participate in actual battle as the Indian National Army was retreating at that time. Before Netaji left for Malaya, he gave orders that the regiment be disbanded and members sent to homes.[122]

Dr. Lakshmi Swaminathan (Mrs. Sehgal)

Lakshmi Swaminathan[123] was a significant woman of the Indian National Army. She was in Singapore at the time when Netaji called. She answered to this call with wholehearted zeal. She was the Commander of the Ranee Jhansi Regiment and also the Minister of Social Welfare and Medicine in the Azad Hind Cabinet.

As the Commander of the Ranee Jhansi Regiment, Lakshmi was designated as Lt. Colonel. When the Indian National Army declined she did not surrender to the British, she was captured and afterwards placed under arrest. Her Regiment was disbanded in 1946 and most of the girls were sent away to Singapore from Rangoon. Lakshmi Swaminathan was sent to Rangoon prison. There was a great deal of campaign for her release and the government had to bend and released her on the terms that she would make no public speech.[124]

Lakshmi, however, violated the order and spoke on the anniversary day, October 21, 1945, of the *Azad Hind Fauj*. She also campaigned and supported the cause of the Indian National

Army at Delhi. Her activities disappointed the authorities and she was issued a notice and asked to go to Kalawe.[125] On November 14, a second notice was issued and the next morning she was flown to Meiktila from where she was carried to Kalawe in a military car.

Lakshmi was freed the next year. She visited India and married Captain Sehgal of the Indian National Army.

Towards the Aim

Throughout the war period, most of the Indians, wherever they were, continued their attempts to liberate themselves. The leaders of the major political parties were in prison for two years between 1942 and 1944. The Government was still un-willing to start negotiations with Indian leaders on the constitutional set-up. The Labour Party of England condemned the policy of the British government regarding India and criticised it for its failure to find some workable solution. In December 1944 the Labour Party passed a resolution urging the government for the resumption of discussion with Indian leaders for securing a place for India as a self-governing member of the British Commonwealth.[126]

The next year was important for it watched a new British offer[127] which was declared by Lord Wavell, the then Viceroy, general elections in Great Britain (July 1945) with Labour Party in power, and the closing of the Second World War.

During this period Indians became more significant than ever before. The battle had caused a lot of dislocation in the routine life of the people. The food was expensive and scarce. Some places were affected by famine. The war also provided an opportunity to Indian soldiers to tackle new machinery and armament. The trial of the men of the Indian National Army further ignited the fire of nationalism. There were wide spread demonstrations and clashes with the government against the trials.

Early next year emerged the uprising of the sailors of the Indian Navy at Bombay which gradually spread to other seaports. This claimed the lives of many people.

By now Clement Attlee had replaced Winston Churchill, the war-time Minister. Attlee made a declaration in February that a Cabinet Mission would visit India to help the Indian leaders to draw up a new constitution. The Cabinet Mission[128] reached India on March 24, 1946, and held negotiations with the several political parties and the Indian government. The Indian leaders could not arrive at a common understanding. As a result, the Cabinet Mission had to give their own pattern for solving the constitutional deadlock.

The Cabinet Mission offer was accepted by the Muslim League in its entirety by resolution on May 6, 1946 but the Hindu leadership agreed only with the portion associated with constitution making in June 26, 1946. The government, therefore, had to declare that the interim government could not be framed on account of the problems arising out of the stand adopted by political parties.

The decision of the government enraged Jinnah and the Muslim League passed its popular Direct Action Resolution in which both the Congress and British Government were criticised for the breach of trust. Serious riots between Hindus and Muslims took place in many parts of the country.

On August 12 Lord Wavell invited Pandit Nehru, the President of the Indian Congress, to frame the National interim government. Elections to the Constituent Assembly were also conducted and it met for the first time in New Delhi on December 9, 1946. It contained fifteen women members. The Muslim League refused participation. The Constituent Assembly went on with its work.

Attlee made the following declaration on February 20: "His Majesty's government wishes to make it clear that it is their definite intention to take necessary steps to effect the transfer of power to responsible Indian hands by a date not later than June 1948."[129]

Lord Wavell was replaced by Lord Mountbatten on March 24, 1947, as Viceroy. The condition at this time was very tense as a strong agitation for partition was moved by the Muslim League. It became clear that the unity of India could not be maintained and Jinnah and the Muslim League would have Pakistan.

The Mountbatten plan amongst other things providing for the partition of India was accepted by the Muslim League on June 9, 1947 and by the All India Congress Committee on June, 15 1947. The Indian Independence Act was passed by the British

Parliament on July 18, 1947, marking the end of the British domination in India.

References

1. Women's Indian Association, Madras, *Women's Work in Madras – Reminiscences*, p. 7.
2. Nehru, Jawaharlal, *The Unity of India, Collected Writing – 1937-40*, London, 1941, p. 401.
3. Nehru, Jawaharlal, *Toward Freedom*, New York, 1941, p. 432.
4. Diwarkar, R.R., *Satyagraha in Action*, Calcutta, p. 96.
5. *Ibid.*, p. 98.
6. *August Struggle Report*, Part II-Prepared under the aegis of All India Satyagraha Council, U.P. Branch (unpublished), All India Congress Committee Office, Delhi, p. 5.
7. Sahai, Gobind, *42, Rebellion*, Delhi, 1947, p. 9.
8. *Hindustan Standard*, 27 July, 1942.
9. Mitra, Bejin and Chakraborty, P. (Edited), *Rebel India*, Calcutta, 1946, p. 3.
10. *Ibid.*, p. 4.
11. A place in Darrang District.
12. The Congress report says that one after another four stepped into her place and defied the bullets by laying down their lives, (*August Struggle Report* prepared under the aegis of All India Satyagraha Council, U.P., p. 157.
13. Mitra, Bejin and Chakraborty, P., *Rebel India*, 1946, p. 4.
14. *Ibid.*, Calcutta, 1946, p. 5.
15. *Ibid.*
16. *August Struggle Report* prepared under the aegis of All India *Satyagraha* Council, U.P. Branch (unpublished), A.I.C.C. Office, New Delhi, p. 5.
17. *August Struggle Report* (Assam) (unpublished), A.I.C.C. Office, Delhi, p. 62.
18. *Ibid.*
19. Mitra, Bejin and Chakraborty, P., *The Rebel India*, Calcutta, 1946, p. 22.
20. *Ibid.*, p. 22.
21. *Ibid.*, p. 25.
22. *Ibid.*, p. 25.
23. Mitra, Bejin, *op. cit.*, p. 22.
24. *August Struggle Report* prepared under the aegis of All India Satyagraha Council, U.P. Branch (unpublished), A.I.C.C. Library, New Delhi, p. 120.
25. Mitra, Bejin, *op. cit.*, p. 28.
26. *August Struggle Report*, *op. cit.*, p. 120.
27. Nizamuddin was Home Minister of Bengal.
28. Dutta, K., *op. cit.*, p. 25.
29. *Ibid.*
30. *Ibid.*
31. August struggle, *op. cit.*, p. 88.
32. *The Report of the Banaras August 1942 Disturbances—Enquiry Committee* (unpublished), A.I.C.C. Library, New Delhi, p. 3.
33. *Ibid.*

34. *August Struggle Report, op. cit.,* p. 173.
35. *Punjab Congress Committee Report on Disobedience in Lahore,* August 9, 1942, p. 4.
36. Morton, E., *Women Behind Gandhiji*, London, 1954, p. 139.
37. *Illustrated Weekly of India,* January 1957.
38. *Women's Work in Madras-Reminiscences,* Women's Indian Association, Madras.
39. Award given by Ramsay Macdonald when Premier in 1932, regarding the political rights of major and minor communities in India.
40. *Congress Bulletin*, September 4, 1937.
41. Punjab Congress Committee—*Report on Disturbances in Punjab*, p. 8.
42. Sitaramayya, Dr. P., *op. cit.,* Vol. II, pp. 761-62.
43. *The Tribune*, Lahore, August 26, 1932.
44. The others with her were Smt. Yashodan Kumari and Krishna Kumari, daughter of Gobind Ram Khanna. Adarsh Kumari, daughter of Lala Pindi Das.
45. *The Tribute,* Lahore, September 1932.
46. "Brief Account of the National Activities of Bibi Amar Kaur Ahluwalia" – a hand bill.
47. Letter No. 5950-JL-42/54484, dated October 8, 1942; Letter No. 8245-JL-42/73492, dated December 31, 1942 (in the possession of Amar Kaur).
48. She was born in 1900 in Sanglai (Jhelum) now in Pakistan. She was educated at the village school and was married at the age of sixteen to A.N. Gujral, Advocate of Jhelum.
49. All India Congress Committee – *Women on the March,* April 1958, p. 7
50. *Ibid.*
51. Followers of Khan Abdul Ghaffar Khan, a leader of the national movement in the North West Frontier Province.
52. *Ibid.*
53. *August Struggle Report*, Part II, *op. cit.,* p. 145.
54. Chimur is a village with a population of about six thousand people in Chanda District.
55. *India Ravaged* – Being an account of atrocities committed under British aegis, over the whole sub-continent of India in the latter part of 1942, Chimur-Bhansali, Professor, p. 2 (A.I.C.C. Library, New Delhi).
56. *India Ravaged*, Bhansali, Professor, p. 13.
57. *Ibid.*
58. *Times of India*, October 8, 1930.
59. These men were to be hanged for taking part in the 1942 movement. They were responsible for the killing of some people in the two villages of Ashti and Chimur.
60. *Mahila Pragati Ke Path Par*, September, 1957, p. 13 (Hindi); *Women on the March*, September 1958, p. 4.
61. She died in 1958.
62. *Annual Register*, Vol. I, 1940, p. 79.
63. Sitaramayya, Dr. P., *History of the Indian National Congress*, Vol. II, pp. 577-78.
64. *Illustrated Weekly of India*, January 20, 1957.
65. *Amrita Bazar Patrika*, February 25, 1930.

66. *Ibid.*, p. 4.
67. *Advance*, February 19, 1932.
68. *Women on the March*, July 1957, p. 11.
69. *Congress Bulletin,* January 8, 1942, p. 42.
70. *Ibid.*, 1942, p. 44.
71. A district of Madhya Pradesh.
72. *August Struggle Report*, Part II, *op. cit.*, p. 59.
73. *Ibid.*, p. 62.
74. From papers in possession of Usha Mehta.
75. The Congress Radio Calling. Accused No. 3 in the Congress Radio Conspiracy Case (Papers in possession of Usha Mehta), p. 1.
76. *Ibid.*
77. The Congress Radio Calling, *op. cit.*, pp. 2-3. Mitra, Bejin and Chakraborty, P., (Ed), *The Rebel India*, p. 154.
78. *Ibid.*
79. *Ibid.*
80. *Ibid.*, p. 6.
81. Radio Calling, No. II (Papers in possession of Miss Usha Mehta).
82. *Ibid.*
83. *Ibid.*
84. Sahai, Govind, *42-Rebellion*, Delhi, 1947, p. 86.
85. A petty official in charge of collecting the land revenue in a village.
86. *August Struggle Report*, Part II, *op. cit.*, p. 184.
87. *Report of the Pradesh Congress Committee on the happenings in Karnatak*, August 9, 1942 to September 20, 1942, p. 3.
88. Karnatak Pradesh Congress Committee Report on the happenings in Karnatak, October 11, 1942 to October 31, 1942.
89. Karnatak Provincial Congress Committee, *Brief Report on Happenings in Karnatak*, November 1, 1942, to November 15, 1942.
90. Sucheta Kriplani came from a well known Bengali family settled in Punjab. She was educated at Lahore and Delhi. She took her Master of Arts degree from Delhi and became a Professor in Banaras University.
91. All India Congress Committee, *Women on the March*, August 1957, p. 13.
92. *Ibid.*
93. *Annual Register*, January to June, Vol. I, 1942, p. 301.
94. *Ibid.*
95. *Ibid.*
96. *Ibid.*
97. *Ibid.*
98. Aruna comes from a respectable Gangoli family of Bengal. she had her early education in Sacred Heart of Jesus at Lahore and then in a Protestant School at Nainital. After completing her education she took up work in the Gokhale Memorial School for Girls at Calcutta. She met Asaf Ali, a promising lawyer and a Persian scholar, at Allahabad and they became attached to each other. There was a lot of opposition, for they both belonged to different communities, Asaf Ali was a Muslim and Aruna a Hindu. She was almost 23 years younger to him. But Aruna clung to her decision and despite opposition married Asaf Ali in 1924.

99. *The Tribune*, February 1946.
100. *Ibid.*
101. *Ibid.*
102. *Ibid.*
103. *Ibid.*
104. *Advance*, September 29, 1942.
105. *Inquilab*, monthly journal of the Indian National Congress, Eastern Zone. Edited, Rammanohar Lohia and Aruna Asaf Ali, March 1944, A.I.C.C. Library, New Delhi.
106. Lal, Pyare, *Mahatma Gandhi, The Last Phase,* p. 37.
107. *Ibid.*
108. *Ibid.,* p. 43.
109. *The Tribune*, February 18, 1946.
110. *Ibid.*
111. This Lodge was opened by Swami Satyanand Puri, a great Indian scholar and philosopher and a disciple of Rabindranath Tagore.
112. General Mohan Singh originally comes from Ugoke in District Sialkot, West Pakistan. He was with the 1/14th Punjab Regiment in Burma fighting against the Japanese.
113. Giani, K.S., *Indian Independence Movement in East Asia*, Lahore, 1947.
114. *Ibid.,* p. 64.
115. *Ibid.,* p. 80.
116. *Ibid.*
117. *The Tribune*, March 7, 1946.
118. Benerjee, Bejoy, *Indian War of Independence*, p. 82; *The Tribune,* March 7, 1946.
119. *Ibid.,* pp. 85-86.
120. *Ibid.,* p. 116; Mehta (Mrs.) Gurcharan, *Azad Hind Fauj,* Amritsar, p. 173.
121. *Ibid.*
122. *Roshni*, Journal published by the All India Women's Conference. Delhi, May 1947, p. 41.
123. She was a civilian doctor in Singapore and is the daughter of Ammu Swaminathan of Madras who took prominent part in the various movements launched by the Congress. She passed her M.B.B.S. from Medical College, in 1937. Apart from being a Commander of the Ranee Jhansi Regiment, she had a portfolio in the *Azad Hind* Cabinet being in charge of Social Welfare and Medical Work.
124. Banerjee, Bejoy, *Indian War of Independence*, p. 116.
125. *Ibid.*
126. Wallbank, T. Walter, *A Short History of India and Pakistan*, p. 213.
127. In this offer it was made clear that the responsibility of making a new constitution rested with the Indians. Lord Wavell offered to make important changes in his Executive Council. For this purpose he convened a meeting to which twenty-two representatives of various political parties were invited. Differences among the major political parties took place over the representation of Muslim League nominees and Lord Wavell had to announce the breakdown of the talks.
128. The Cabinet Mission consisted of Lord Pethick-Lawrence, Sir Strafford Cripps and A.V. Alexander.
129. Banerjee A.C., *The Making of Indian Constitution*, Calcutta, 1948, p. 402.

9

Nationalism and Feminism

Subject, women will be incomplete unless and until we talk of their participation in the freedom movement through the Rani of Jhansi Regiment—the fruit of efforts of Subhash Chandra Bose. During the period of 1943 and 1945, 1,500 Indian women in Burma, Malaya and Singapore exchanged their colourful saris for the *khakis*, breeches, half caps and boots of the Rani of Jhansi Regiment, the all-female brigade of the Indian National Army (INA). In the leadership of Subhas Chandra Bose, Hindus, Muslims and Sikhs, members of the moneyed elite and the daughters of rubber plantation labourers shared the same food and fate to win a jungle war for India's freedom.[1] How should this unprecedented mingling of women from varied caste, religious and social backgrounds be understood? Was this merely a politically expedient nationalistic act or perhaps a nascent expression of Indian feminism?

In a narrower sense, the Rani of Jhansi Regiment was the child of the psyche, personality and politics of Subhas Bose. It has been explained as '. . . eloquent testimony to Netaji's[2] ideal of equality between men and women. It accomplished within the short span of a year what a movement for emancipation of women could not achieve in half-a-century. . .'[3]

Through an effort to make sense of the historical meaning and importance of the Rani of Jhansi Regiment, many questions must be raised. What was it about Bose and his ideas that prompted Indian women and girls as young as thirteen to leave the safe life of *purdah,* cut their hair, don fatigues and take up arms so readily? What allowed him to involve women in such a direct way? What influenced him to tap into ancient Indian symbols of women that were as encouraging as they were inspiring? Was Bose simply manipulating images to promote the idea of the Regiment for its symbolic value or was he genuinely committed to a larger role for women in Indian society? The drama of the Rani of Jhansi Regiment, with images of women trudging through the jungle wielding tommy guns and swords seems uncanny at least. To concentrate exclusively upon the apparent incongruity of Indian women 'guerrillas,' however, runs the risk of underestimating its historical significance.[4] What motivated these women and girls to join the Regiment with so much enthusiasm? Incredibly, among the most committed of the Rani of Jhansi recruits had never even set foot on the Motherland.[5] The purpose of this paper will be to show how elements of Indian nationalism and feminism and the personal psychology and charisma of Subhas Bose coalesced in the formation of the Rani of Jhansi Regiment.

For Subhas Bose, the mobilization of powerful women, whose models were rooted in Indian mythology and history was a prerequisite for national liberation. The complementarity of these old images with elements of Bose's personal psychological development motivated him to devote his life to the nationalist cause and wedded the attainment of that objective with the direct involvement of Indian women. By transmitting the ideals of traditional Indian sources, and his personal longings for a powerful Indian mother figure, Bose tapped into the collective psyche of Indian women in strong merging of historical consciousness, feminist initiative and nationalistic fervor.

By naming the Regiment after the Rani of Jhansi, Bose employed a powerful metaphor for resistance to colonial rule, evoking the memory of the 'first war of independence,' as it is known in the lexicon of Indian nationalism.[6] In the 'last and decisive War of Independence,' Bose dreamed of 'thousands and thousands of Ranis of Jhansi.' In announcing the formation of the Regiment, Bose stressed to women the honour and heroism attached with the Rani's example. 'It is not important how many guns you can carry or how many cartridges you can fire. It is the spiritual force which will be generated by your heroic example that is significant.[7] The Rani legend also had multiple sources in Hindu cultural and religious tradition, rooted in the prehistoric Mother, the primal Shakti, the most recognised force in all Hinduism,[8] and the female avenger Durga/Chandi/Bhavani.[9]

The warrior Rani as a freedom fighter provided a legitimate alternative to the Gandhian non-violent mainstream as modelled by Sita, the submissive female ideal.[10] In choosing the Rani as a symbol, Bose was able to wed strains of nationalism to imagery of powerful, effective women assuming roles of strong leadership and responsibility.

Symbol and Substance of the Regiment

With the goal to assess the true cultural and political meaning of the Regiment one must consult its members. The self-reports of Rani of Jhansi veterans reveal a variety of motivations, from school-girl euphoria among the very young volunteers, to the more considered politics of a Lakshmi Swaminathan, the captain of the Regiment.[11] The recollections of Swaminathan, a doctor from Madras who had settled in Singapore in 1940, also suggest a wider role for women than temporary mobilisation for the 'war effort.'[12]

It was Swaminathan's understanding that while her immediate task was recruitment, in peacetime the Department would be used to push and promote greater rights for women. Moreover, Bose made it clear to her that the Regiment was not a propaganda device. He wanted a group of women he could rely on to fight bravely and competently.

Undoubtedly the Rani of Jhansi veterans[13] memories of camp life suggest Bose was serious about this. Each prospect underwent a grueling three-month preliminary training to qualify and earn the INA imprimatur.[14] Once accepted for service, hard and fast routine and strict discipline were imposed. Days began with a 5 a.m. reveille, the raising of the National Flag, the chanting of the National Anthem, the offering of prayers and the taking the oath of allegiance to the Motherland and Bose. Following a strenuous workout 'perspiring and panting, they would . . . run back to their barracks for their plates and mugs' for a twenty-minute breakfast.[15] The day proceeded with drills for continuous soldiers and officers alike. The women learned how to handle rifles, bayonets, tommy guns, revolvers, grenades, and swords.

Twice a week marches were conducted, going as many as twenty-two miles in six hours. This daily regimen hardly sounds like the stuff of mere symbolism. There was a cerebral element as well, with courses on Roman Hindustani, history, geography, hygiene and ironically, a needed seminar on 'the great men of the world.'[16] In spite of the diffidence of some of the young recruits,[17] the testimony of Rani of Jhansi veterans displays the image of passive compliance by women to the rigid agenda and charismatic leadership of a man.

In fact the Ranis consistently took bold initiative and often challenged Bose to prove his commitment to including women in the nationalist cause. Before Bose arrived in Southeast Asia in 1943, women's activities in the Indian Independence League were confined to a sort of cheerleading role through speeches, songs, recitations and dramatic shows, primarily by non-*purdah*-observing middle class women. This limited role went on until January 1944, when Manawati Arya, a teacher from Rangoon and a Rani of Jhansi recruit, brought it to the attention of Bose. She complained that this was not compliant with his call for 'total mobilisation' of all classes of Indian women. Bose responded favourably and gave Arya a mandate to set up a full-fledged Women's Department at headquarters and called her First Secretary. Uneducated as well as *purdah*-observing women were brought into the INA fold.[18] The traditional reticence of the women composing the Regiment continued to dissolve when, in spite of its furious readiness, the unit's first assignment was the caretaking of wounded INA troops. Members of the Regiment objected. Perplexed and dismayed by this limited custodial duty, they proclaimed their disappointment in a petition signed in blood and presented it to Bose:

> "It is you who taught us that there is no distinction between men and women. It is you gave us training fit for men-folk . . . Why should we not be sent to [the] battle-front? It is our prayer that we be sent to the front without delay."[19]

While journalists and historians dispute its precise context and chronology, the petition episode reveals an unequivocal and documentary assertion of feminist sensibility.[20] In 1946, Capt. Swaminathan, in commenting on the growth from mere symbolism to direct military action by women, noted their full immersion in the traditionally male sphere of warmaking.

'I suppose we all forgot our sex. We were just automatons. We fired, refilled, and fired again, and yet again, endlessly . . .[21]

Moreover, in the spring of 1945, the Regiment 'anxiously orders to march to Imphal to fight shoulder to shoulder with our brothers.[22] As per Bose, Imphal was an 'all-out struggle to the finish for Indian liberation,' that would be the first step in reaching Delhi.[23] The willingness of the Rani of Jhansi Regiment to fight was a victory in the battle to involve women in the struggle for Indian Independence, but the campaign itself proved to be an all-out military disaster. The British had advanced relentlessly and were nearing Rangoon.

The Rani of Jhansi Regiment set up a frontline hospital to handle casualties, but 'dysentery, typhus, and dengue fever ravaged both armies. Leeches incessantly drained human blood, and maggots preyed on wounds.[24] By April the monsoons had started to raise heads and on the 24th of the month, Bose left with the Rani of Jhansi Regiment in a convoy amid the flames of a British air attack.

The Leader and the Led

Suppose, if there is common agreement on anything in the records of Rani of Jhansi veterans, it was the profound influence of Subhas Bose upon their thoughts, feelings and acts. Testimonials of Rani of Jhansi veterans and other observers of the period are veritable paeans to the selflessness, brilliance, organisational skill, charm and sheer endurance of Subhas Bose.[25] Swaminathan mentioned the Indians in Burma as 'transformed human beings' when Bose reached and recalled how a 'forest of hands would rise in response to Netaji's calls for soldiers.' 'The rich men in their posh cars, the poor in their rags, volunteered to Netaji.[26] Bose, in all respects, was larger than life.[27] British, Indian and Japanese biographers describe the 'glamour', 'charisma' and mesmerizing effect he had on those around him.[28] In his statement prior to the court martial proceeding at Red Fort after the war, INA General Shah Nawaz Khan proclaimed: "It will not be wrong to say that I was hypnotized by his personality and his speeches. He placed the true picture of India before us and for the first time in my life I saw India through the eyes of an Indian."[29]

These fundraising abilities in him bordered on the magical. Indian businessmen and traders in Southeast Asia donated rupees, houses, landed properties, lorries, cars and cows.[30] Women would hand over precious jewellery.

A wealthy Muslim from Rangoon contributed the money to start the National Bank of Azad Hind, much to the dismay of the Japanese.[31] These seemingly mythical powers were visibly complemented by a more down-to-earth affection for his troops and attention to small details.[32] Rani of Jhansi veteran Janaki Athinahappan remembers how Bose would often burst out sobbing when he visited his injured soldiers in the hospitals.[33] Sounding cautious after the first Imphal debacle, Bose's 'Special Message' to the Regiment in May 1944 reads more like the tender message of a concerned father than instead of the bold reassurance of a confident general.

He described the 'grave responsibility' he felt at having asked women to leave their homes to take up weapons. "I have been endeavouring to look after and to nurse this new Regiment in such a manner that every father, every mother and every guardian may feel that his or her girl is safe in our hands."[34] Here, the Rani of Jhansi veterans' memories of the retreat from Rangoon to Bangkok in April 1945 are the poignant descriptions of a dedicated leader shouldering the responsibility of a plan gone tragically failed.[35]

Among these Rani of Jhansi veteran one remembers leaving Burma, the roads, trees and grasses ablaze in the wake of the British scorched earth policy. Incendiary bombs dropped on their trucks, forcing the convoy to abandon them. At one point, they came upon the names of two girls from the Regiment scratched in the trunk of a tree. They had been killed by machine gun fire earlier during a retreat by train.[36] Capt. Janaki Athinahappan found Bose red-eyed, in severe pain, drinking endless cups of tea and worrying about the safety of the convoy. She convinced him to take his boots off, finding his feet covered with blisters. He spurned the Japanese offer of a car, denying to abandon his troops in the jungle. He reportedly told the Japanese to 'go to hell,' insisting he would not cross a treacherous river 'till the girls have gone across first.[37] Bose had seen them for the last time on 14 August 1945 in Singapore, when they staged a drama on the life of the Rani of Jhansi.[38]

The Leader and his Mythic Mother

Undoubtedly of the personal charisma and dedication that drew women to Bose's regiment, but less obvious is what inspired him to make the imaginative leap from the Gandhian notion of a Sita like role for women in the fight for national freedom to the more Durga-like role of the Rani of Jhansi unit. After touring Southeast Asia looking for able recruits and seeing such passion 'blazoning in the eyes of his sisters.'

Bose instilled the ancient symbol of Indian women as the resuscitators of a dying country and proudly declared that 'no power on earth could hold a nation in subjection which consisted of such intrepid women.'[39] Definitely, the critical conceptualization of the Rani of Jhansi Regiment is to be found in ancient Indian notions of women and mothers. Elements of personal life history, charisma and traditional aspects of Indian myth found in Bose's founding of the Regiment. Bose was a son of Bengal, which boasted a tradition of iconoclasm lasting at least a millennium. His father had grown up in Calcutta during the reform era of the nineteenth century and saw with his own eyes the first experiments in female education and the concurrent efforts to break the barriers of *purdah* and sex-segregation. Bose admired his father's early associations with the Brahmo Samaj[40] leaders and Vidyasagar, the champion of women's education and widow remarriage.[41] Alongwith this, the neo-Hinduism of Vivekananda and Ramakrishna, which emphasised the female aspects of Hinduism, had an even better and profound effect on Bose. From Vivekananda he adopted the goals of personal salvation with service to humanity.

From Ramakrishna, he decided 'to effect my own salvation and to serve humanity by abandoning all worldly desires and breaking away from all undue restrains."[42] Ramakrishna had popularized the idea of 'Supreme Mother' in the worship of Kali.[43] I worship all women as representatives of the divine Mother.[44] Bose took his prescription to heart, and envisioned this powerful prototype as the protector for India. Bose saw this dual sacrifice for Kali and for the Motherland as the formula for Indian independence. Fusing Kali, Mother India and powerful mother figures, Bose started to believe that it was up to Bengali mothers to extend their nurturance to all Bengalis and by extension save India.

As Geraldine Forbes has explained it: "Just as the Goddess turned no one way, so Indian women should learn to accept all men as their sons but in turn this extended nurturance must be their own sacrifice and devotion to the Goddess/Motherland."[45]

Through looking at three of Bose's most influential relationships with women, we can trace how his inventive views of women ultimately went into the 'mobilized' mothers and sisters of the Rani of Jhansi Regiment. Through a series of letters to his mother between the ages of fifteen and sixteen, Bose tried to shape her into an early version of the powerful Indian mother whom he would envision thirty years later as the indisposable source of water for the freedom of India.

In one letter he describes India as moving 'towards perdition' but only "if Bengal's mothers bring their sons up in an entirely different new way can Bengalis once again regain their manhood."[46] In another letter, he united the metaphor of Mother India with his own mother,

> "You are a mother, but do you belong only to us? No, you are the mother of all Indians—if every Indian is a son to you, do not the sorrows of your sons make you cry out in agony? Can a mother be heartless? . . . Then how is it that in the face of such a miserable state of her children, mother remains unmoved! . . . does not your heart bleed at the sight of the present deplcrable state of Indians? . . . a mother can never be selfish because a mother lives for her children."[47]

At this place, we have an adumbration of the reasoning that would later impel Bose to form the Rani of Jhansi Regiment. Finally, in the same letter, his deeply-felt conception of women's mission is spelled out uniquely.

> "But a mother's life is not motivated only by selfish considerations. Her life is dedicated to her children, to the country. If you read the history of India, you will see that so many mothers have lived for the sake of Mother India and have, when the need arose, sacrificed their lives for her. Think of Ahalya Bai, Meera Bai, Durga Bai—there are so many. We are reared on mother's milk—therefore nothing can be more educative and elevating than what instruction and guidance we get from the mother."[48]

While this is somewhat overwrought prose of an adolescent intoxicated, by a new idea, it contains the inchoate emotions and philosophy that were to reach their mature expression in the making of the Rani of Jhansi Regiment. As Bose moved from adolescene into young adulthood, he wished Smt. Besanti Devi to be his mentor and a guide to the nation.

After Das's sudden death in 1925 and Bose's now unambivalent embrace of the idea of activist Indian women in the nationalist cause, he wrote a number of letters to Basanti Devi imploring her to give the lead in Bengali politics. As she had done through her celebrated arrest in 1921, Bose wanted Basanti Devi to '. . . appear amongst us once again the embodiment of *Shakti*."[49]

In the early letters, sent from the Rangoon Jail, Bose expresses concern for her welfare and wonders whether seclusion is right for her.[50] By 1927, no longer in jail, he is getting impatient, and challenges Basanti Devi to behave as a true Indian Mother.

By now, he had accepted the need for fully mobilized mothers and was angry and confused by Basanti Devi's refusal to share his vision. In spite of his entreaties, she retired fully from public life.[51] In many respects, the creation of the Rani of Jhansi Regiment twenty years later was the final realization of Bose's yearnings for powerful mothers.[52] Bose was also close to his sister-in-law too, Bivabati, the wife of his elder brother Sarat. Krishna Bose suggests their relationship can best be understood in the context of the life-long attachment between Subhas and Sarat, whose lives were closely interwined politically.[53] Another explanation may be found in the *debar-boudi* relationship that often exists between a Bengali woman and her husbands younger brother.[54] Subhas and Bivabati were known to each other since she joined the Bose household when they were both fourteen. His letters to her from the Mandalay prison (1925-1926) display a humor, tenderness and intimacy, albeit platonic, that is lost from his other correspondence. His letters indicate that he clearly saw her as a person from whom he could expect unconditional support and direction. As per Krishna Bose, this role as confidante and peer advisor places Bivabati in 'an interesting middle place between the mother figures and the prominent friendships in his life.[55] It seems likely that she was the idealized prototype of the bold, competent, older sister as comrade, who was later to take up arms for the Regiment.

Bapu and Bose for Foundation of Feminism

We find ample evidence of Bose's expressed and actual commitment to feminism, always carefully phrased in the language of Indian myth and history and often laden with powerful symbols. His writings, speeches to students, and addresses during Provincial Conferences between 1928 and 1931 seem radical even today.

He cited the Code of Manu, one of the great sacred texts, in which it was proclaimed that Mothers should be worshipped, adding warning of Manu: "In a society where women are not respected, all efforts come to naught." His programme sought to abolish child marriage, *purdah,* and the prohibition on remarriage of widows. He stressed female education, economic independence for women and the option not to marry. In Bose's thinking, India had three oppressed groups who had been deprived of their human rights: women, the oppressed castes and labourers and cultivators. To achieve social redress, *Swaraj* or political freedom was wanted first, for "without the power to shape our own destiny—we cannot have either compulsory free education or social reform . . ."[56] In 1928, as President of the Bengal Congress, Bose acted as a catalyst and inspired young women to come forward as a female volunteer political force. As he would do later with Lakshmi Swaminathan, he enlisted an educated young women, Lalita Ghosh, to recruit women for political work.[57] Like the later Ranis, these women performed much more than merely enlarge the ranks or provide symbolic value. Some even committed daring revolutionary acts of violence.[58] The feminist bent of Bose's thinking can be seen in the early thirties when, while in Germany,[59] he acknowledged the women's movement and credited Gandhi with inspiring it.

In order to understand the progressive nature of Bose's thinking, it is meaningful to compare it to Gandhi's conception of the role of women. Gandhi's use of deeply-rooted symbols had mobilized women inside India in a unique fashion. It was not until Gandhi that women, most importantly rural women, left the seclusion of *purdah* in large numbers not to join a women's movement, but to help in the struggle for freedom from colonial rule.

There were, however, significant differences in how these two men perceived women's roles. While Gandhi said "Women alone can enter the hearts of men and transform them,"[60] it is clear his vision of women's power and role in liberating India was much more limited than Bose's. In 1930, Gandhi announced that same activities were meant only for women, namely organizing the boycott of foreign cloth and picketing foreign cloth and liquor shops.

According to one view, the acts themselves were less significant than the symbolic defiance of social taboos—the challenge to the rigid caste system as a disruption of social relations.[61] It was, anyway, a narrow departure and corresponded to Gandhi's limited religious and moral definition of women's roles. Gandhi's non-violent means and their application to women contrast clearly with Bose's perception of women as activists providing indispensable vitality and sustenance to the independence movement.[62] Like Bose, Gandhi tapped into an idealized picture of Indian women, but as religious and moral role models, not active combatants. Spinning and weaving were vocations he considered appropriate to the 'nature' of women.[63]

Women's role in the social and political arena was still Sita-inspired,[64] 'the passive resistance of their daily lives more suited to socially organised passive resistance and non-cooperation.[65] The essence of their role can be best captured in Gandhi's great belief in women's capacity to suffer. 'Women is the embodiment of sacrifice and suffering and her advent to public life should therefore result in purifying it, in restricting unbridled ambitions and accumulation of property.'[66] Like Gandhi, Bose employed ancient notions of women but chose historical figures who could best represent both his own image of the strong seminal woman as well as the most potent metaphor of Indian resistance to British rule, the heroine of the 1857 Revolt, the Rani of Jhansi, Lakshmi Bai. In so doing he articulated a new definition of female heroism in which the strings of nationalism and feminism were joined seamlessly. In announcing the formation of the Regiment.

"They have shown that when the need rises they could, like their brothers, shoot very well." Those responsibilities that Bose outlined for the Ranis were based upon accepted but greatly expanded roles for women as 'mothers' and 'sisters.'[67] As nurses, fundraisers, organizers and recruiters, 'mothers' could play inspirational as well as sustaining roles. While these might appear to be little more than traditional female occupations, Bose envisioned an enlargement of their universe and influence in which they would leave their safe homes to enter barracks, hospitals and army camps to join the men of the INA.

The younger women, physically stronger and not burdened by family responsibilities—the 'sisters'—would be asked to take up arms and fight shoulder to shoulder alongwith their brothers as equals.[68]

When Bose inaugurated the Rani of Jhansi Training Camp on 22 October 1943, he thought it appropriate that there 'should be a stir of new life among our womenfolk.'[69] In his address, Bose alluded to the ancient Vedic period (1500–500 B.C.,[70] whose historical records indicate that women were revered, were free to choose their husbands, encouraged to be intellectuals, and participated in prominent religious rituals.[71] The greatness of Indian womanhood had its roots in those early days when India had its Sanskrit culture.[72] Here one has the sense of a renaissance in the position of women that far outstrips Gandhi's conception of women providing moral strength through suffering.

Summary Findings

To conclude, the study of the Rani of Jhansi Regiment is burdened by the apparent novelty of Indian women bearing arms as well as the sheer paucity of source material. With a handful of exceptions (Forbes, 1984; Lebra, 1971) the Regiment is talked about only in passing as the curious innovation of Subhas Bose for total mobilization—an expedient public symbol used to encourage women to depart from their traditional roles for the 'war effort'.

The 'hey-day' literature from years 1946 and 1947 (Chandra, 1946; Roy, 1946; Saqui, 1946) is especially troubling. Mired as they are in the cult worship of Bose after his mysterious death in 1945 and the popular exoneration of the INA after the war, these initial interviews with Rani of Jhansi veterans represent lost opportunities. To one interested in assessing the degree of feminist and nationalist inclinations present in the women, even for self-reports of the veterans offer limited help.

Their recollections are couched almost entirely in the language of nationalism instead of the personal philosophies, experiences and reflections of women soldiers. These constraints make drawing conclusions a speculative undertaking at best. In spite of the scant records available, there would seem to be good reason to believe that the story of the Regiment represents a rare convergence of ancient myth, political history, nationalism feminism and the cult of personal charisma women in an enlightened, progressive leader. The practical outcome of these multiple influences was that women and girls left home, joined a women's regiment officered by women, became active in the fight for national independence, acted autonomously and related to men and women of different castes and religions in an unprecedented manner. The historical evidence shows that the Rani of Jhansi women often took initiatives and that initiatives were encouraged and responded to by Bose. Their freedom to set and act upon both a nationalist and feminist agenda suggests that the Regiment represented prominently more than a transient and expedient symbol of total mobilization.

As for Subhas Bose, it must be said that he succeeded in drawing a disparate flock of Indian women into the fight for liberation in a way that Gandhi never did, nor aspired to. In this respect, Bose's ideas and actions regarding women's roles in the national liberation movement were largely feminist in nature and revolutionary in their expression. To Bose, achieving a free India was dependent upon mobilising powerful 'mothers' and 'sisters.'His was not an effort to impute to women powers or abilities he did not already trust them to possess by their very nature. He acted rather to release that power, seeing the mobilisation of women's inherent strength as a prerequisite for Indian freedom. There is convincing evidence to suggest that Bose's public pronouncements were not mere rhetoric to swell the ranks of the INA. The recollections of Rani of Jhansi veterans prove Bose's commitment, and through the consideration of his early relationships with his mother, Basanti Devi, and his sister-in-law we have seen how his attitudes and beliefs about women evolved.

His commitment to women's rights seems indisputable, reflected consistently in his speeches from the late twenties and early thirties. He mobilized women, encouraged them to organise and even approved female involvement in the revolutionary movement. Bose's dedication, charisma and organising ability were certainly factors in pulling women to the Rani of Jhansi Regiment. Beyond this, Bose's genius lay in his capacity to fuse the experience of his formative relationships with women and his personal psychology to produce a vision of powerful mothers and sisters which found a profound resonance in Indian women.

In his charismatic fashion, he simultaneously celebrated Indian culture, promoted feminism and aided nationalism. The inherent strength and malleability of Indian myth and history allowed Bose to articulate this new definition of female heroism, and the demands of nationalism provided it with an urgency that made it tempting to Indian women in Southeast Asia.

References

1. This study will be observing women primarily through a Hindu lens, so will miss the specifics of Muslim women. While Muslims formed a large proportion of the Indian National Army, drawing its professional corps from prisoners-of-war of the British Indian Army, the women's regiment relied exclusively on Indian recruits—the majority of whom were (Hindu) Tamils.
2. This term, an appellation, was how Bose was referred to in India. It was not, as is frequently cited, styled after the German 'Fuhrer.' Most respected Indian leaders have had a title, as in 'Mahatma' (Gandhi) etc.
3. Jitendra Nath Ghosh, *Netaji Subhas Chandra,* p. 149.
4. Geraldine Forbes has noted that because women are generally regarded as passive, those who engage in violent activities are usually seen as acting unnaturally. Past literature has promoted this idea of aberrance, labelling these women either goddesses (the positive version) or social rebels (the negative one). See Geraldine Forbes, 'Goddesses or Rebels? The Women Revolutionaries of Bengal', p. 1.
5. See Manawati Arya, *'The Rani of Jhansi Regiment in Burma,'* p. 18.

6. This was a watershed event which ended in direct rule by the Crown instead of the informal empire structure of the British East India Company.
7. Subhas Chandra Bose, *Selected Speeches of Subhas Chandra Bose,* pp. 190-91.
8. Shakti is embodied in the Rani as a mother, guardian of her husband's heir and the town of Jhansi. See Lebra, *The Rani of Jhansi,* p. 145.
9. *Ibid.,* p. 124. The female goddess Durga was a skilled swordsman who trammled the demon Mahisha underfoot. The goddess Chandi, predominant in Bengal, was an aspect of Durga, part war goddess and part Great Mother. She slew the demon and restorted the gods' dominions to them. Both the metaphors for India vs. Britain. Thue Rani's wearing of military attire relates to the androgyne theme of Hindu deities, connoting wholeness. Shiva is an androgyne, his female facet representated in Parvati/Uma in Durga/Kali.
10. Gandhi's guiding image for Indian women was Sita, the heroine of the epic *Ramayana.* She represents the Hindu ideal of a chaste, self-sacrificing wife who dutifully follows her husband into exile. After being abducted and rescued, she is unable to convince her husband of her husband of her fidelity and eventually asks the mother earth to swallow her. Joyce Lebra, Joy Paulson, Jana Everett, *Women and Work in India,* p. 7. Actually, during the height of Gandhi's non-cooperation movement, the Rani was often cited as a model of patroitism, courage, and leadership. [Lebra, *The Rani of Jhansi,* p. 145.]
11. The author is grateful to Geraldine Forbes, who has interviewed many of the Rani of Jhansi veterans, for her informed and generous observations of the Ranis.
12. Swaminathan's background was unusually progressive compared to the other Rani of Jhansi veterans. She was reared to believe that women should receive the same education as men and be able to support themselves. She was taught to drive, ride horses and play sports as a child. Later on, it was her father who encouraged her ride horses and play sports as a child. Later on, it was her father who encouraged her to attend medical school. Geraldine Forbes, *'Mothers and Sisters: Feminism and Nationalism in the Thought of Subhas Chandra Bose,'* p. 29.
13. *Ibid.,* p. 29.
14. Rani of Jhnasi veteran Janaki Athinahappen remembers that women 'young and old, poor and rich, educated and uneducated, skilled and unskilled, mothers and daughters and sisters of varying walks of life thronged the Indian Independence League Office for

enlistment . . . In some cases, mothers left their children behind in the care of relatives and trusted friends so as to be able to answer the call . . . The . . . air was filled with hope, thrill and enthusiasm.' See Athinahappan, *'The Rani of Jhansi Regiment,'* pp. 29-30.

15. Ghosh, *Netaji Subhas Chandra,* pp. 147-48.
16. *Ibid.,* p. 146.
17. Though some had husbands in the INA, most of the Rani recruits young and single, with little education or experience outside the confines of *purdah.* Their initial shyness and awkwardness on the parade ground prompted a return to a type of seclusion and this area was fenced in. But after a few months, the Ranis were ready to march in public. See Forbes, *'Mothers and Sisters,'* p. 30.
18. Although the roles for these women were not as far-reaching as those who served in the Rani of Jhansi Regiment, many *purdah*-observing women did leave their homes in order to prepare provisions for soldiers, help the sick and injured, mend dresses and uniforms, and embroider armbands. Manawati Arya remembered that, 'Raising money and material for the movement and providing recreation and moral encouragement . . . became the sacred duty and moral obligation of those Indian women who once felt their field of work was only within the four walls of their homes.' Here one sees evidence of the confluence of social change in the roles of women and the larger freedom movement. See Arya, *'The Rani of Jhansi Regiment in Burma,'* pp. 18-40.
19. P.B. Roy, p. 37, *The Glory That is I.N.A.*
20. Some sources (Roy, 1946, Saqui, 1946) imply that it occurred early on, prompting Bose to prepare a contingent of women with advanced guerrilla training for the front. According to this version the women engaged British heavy weapons for sixteen hours near Moulmein in Burma in April 1944 and sustained injuries. One veteran of the Regiment, Janaki Athinahappan, confirms the advanced training in January 1944 but then implies that the women were waylaid by the mounting carnage from Imphal and pressed into service as nurses. Fifty of the women reportedly received decorations. See Athinahappan, My Life With the Rani of Jhansi Regiment,' p. 38.
21. See. P.B. Roy, *The Glory That is I.N.A.,* p. 38.
22. Saqui, *Facts About the I.N.A.,* p. 50.
23. Lebra, p. 139. *Jungle Alliance.*
24. *Ibid.,* pp. 154-55.

25. Rani of Jhansi veterans measured his daily endurance by his tea consumption. A Japanese escort officer remembered Bose as a sort of 'superman' who replaced three the Japanese were all impressed at his discipline, organisation, and expertise in his new-found calling as a soldier. See Fred Saito and Tatsuo Hayashida, 'To Delhi! To Delhi! 1943-1945,' Sisir K. Bose (ed.), *A Beacon Across Asia: A Biography of Subhas Chandra Bose,* p. 218.
26. Chandra, *Meet Col. Lakshami,* pp. 20B, 29.
27. Interestingly, as Joyce Lebra has pointed out, Indian and Japanese accounts consistently describe him as a towering figure, over six feet. Photographs and film footage also create this illusion. He was actually five feet eight inches. See Lebra, *Jungle Alliance,* p. 228.
28. Carr, *The War of the Springing Tigers* p. 178.
29. Shah Nawaz Khan had not joined the INA until the arrival of Subhas Bose. He had a traditional loyalty to Britain and a lack of confidence in the previous Indian Independence League leader, Rash Behari Bose. See P.B. Roy, *The Glory That is I.N.A.* p. 29.
30. Majumdar, *'Netaji Rani of Jhansi Regiment—Reminiscences,'* p. 21.
31. Mihir Bose, *The Lost Hero,* pp. 222-23.
32. He would make sure his most seriously wounded soldiers received their favourite meals. See Chandra, *Meet Col. Lakshmi,* pp. 43-43.
33. Athinahappan, *'The Rani of Jhansi Regiment,'* p. 31.
34. Subhas Chandra Bose, *'Netaji's Special Message for the Rani of Jhansi Regiment, May 1944,'* reprinted in *The Oracle* II, (Jan. 1980), p. 42.
35. What began as a convoy of trucks turned into a retreat by foot covering a thousand kilometers. Bose insisted on personally accompanying the Regiment and walked with them for twenty-three days, usually in darkness, through jungles and over difficult terrain, crossing turbulent rivers and streams, drenched from the monsoon rains 'under the constant vulturous eyes of enemy planes . . .' See Antinahappan, 'The Rani of Jhansi Regiment,' p. 30.
36. Majumdar, *'Netaji's Rani of Jhansi Regiment—Reminiscences,'* p. 23.
37. Mihir Bose, *The Lost Hero,* p. 244.
38. Forbes, *'Mothers and Sisters,'* p. 30.
39. See Arya, *'The Rani of Jhansi Regiment in Burma,'* p. 19.
40. 'Founded in 1828 by Rammohun Roy, this movement emphasized religious reform by embracing the rights of the individual. See Heimsath, *Indian Nationalism and Hindu Social Reform,* p. 7.

41. Subhas Chandra Bose, *'An Indian Pilgrim,'* Sisir K. Bose (ed.), *Netaji Collected Works* (hereafter *NCW*), Vol. I, pp. 15-18.
42. *Ibid.,* pp. 38-39.
43. Emphasis on the mother was not an innovation of neo-Hinduism. There are sixteen mother goddesses in the Hindu pantheon and in Bengal the Mother goddesses, particularly Kali and Durga, are most prominent. She is Uma, the child bride, the potential mother; she is Kali, the mother in her fearsome aspect, who can take life as well as give it. She is Durga, slayer of demons, protectress. See Manisha Roy, *Bengali Women,* p. VIII.
44. See J.M. Everett, *Women and Social Change in India* (New Delhi, 1979).
45. Forbes, *'Mothers and Sisters,'* pp. 23-24.
46. Letter from Subhas Bose to Prabhabati Bose, c. 1912-1913, *NCW,* Vol. I, p. 137.
47. *Ibid.,* pp. 141-42.
48. *Ibid.,* pp. 143-44.
49. Letter from Subhas Bose to Basanti Devi, 6.7.*25, NCW,* Vol. III, pp. 77-78.
50. Letter from Subhas Bose to Basanti Devi, 20.12.26, *NCW,* vol. IV, p. 118.
51. Krishna Bose reminds us that Bengal was splitting apart politically during these years and spectaculates that Bose's prodding of Basanti Devi had a much to do with his oven ambivalance about taking the lead as it did with sincere desire to have Indian women involved in the emancipation of India. See Krishna Bose, 'Important Women in Netaji's Life,' *Illustrated Weekly of India,* 13 August 1972, p. 35.
52. Krishna Bose suggests Westerners explore the specific Bengali 'mother cult' instead of applying to Bose a facile Freudian interpretation of a 'mother complex.' See Krishna Bose, 'Important Women in Netaji's Life,' pp. 34-35.
53. *Ibid.,* pp. 48.
54. According to Manisha Roy, the *debar* (brother-in-law) becomes the substitute brother or cousin, providing friendship and flirtation, both of which are missing from a young women's marriage. And the *boudi* acts as the patient listeners as the *debar* tells her about his friends, his dreams about the future and his loneliness. See Manisha Roy, *Bengali Women,* pp. 108.
55. Krishna Bose, *'Important Women in Netaji's Life,'* p. 49.
56. Quoted in Forbes, *'Mothers and Sisters,'* p. 26.
57. *Ibid.,* p. 298. Geraldine Forbes interviewed Lalika Ghosh in 1976. She explained how Bose's use of the 'house on fire' analogy in the late twenties mobilised even protected women in Bengal to

defy authority and the barriers of the caste system in a way only non-protected or poor women had done before. She admitted that Bose tried to avoid the radical language of social change that would alienate his constituency. He would use this same technique with the Rani of Jhansi Regiment.

58. *Ibid.,* pp. 26-27. As with the testimonies of the Rani of Jhansi Regiment, all mention the inspiration and model that Bose represented.
59. Subhas Chandra Bose, *'The Indian Struggle,'* Sisir K. Bose, ed., *NCW,* Vol. II, pp. 137-38. While en route from Germany to Southeast Asia, Bose mentioned to his aide, Abid Hasan, the need to get Indian women to join the INA, going so far as to dictate a speech for his female force. See Forbes, 'Mothers and Sisters,' p. 29.
60. Gandhi, 'Speech at Gujarat Women's Conference, Dandi,' quoted in Forbes, oddesses or Rebels', p. 1.
61. panikkar, *Hindu Society at Cross Roads,* p. 39.
62. Though in 1929, Gandhi insisted that he was 'uncompromising in the matter of women's rights,' his nine-point program mentioned only the equality of women. Women's rights per se were never a primary goal of his national movement. He was faithfulness. He remained against inter-caste marriage throughout the 1920s and only that national unity was dependent on the complete removal of class barriers. See Heimsath, *Indian Nationalism and Hindu Social Reform,* p. 345.
63. Mies, *Indian Women and Patriarchy,* p. 126.
64. *Ibid.,* p. 27. Mria Mies has noted that Gandhi 'was perhaps hardly conscious of the fact that his ideal of womanhood . . . contained in fact many traits of the puritan-Victorian ideal of women . . . preached by the English bougeoisie.'
65. Jayawardena, *Feminismj and Nationalism in the Third World.* p. 97.
66. Quoted in Mehta, *Indian Women*, p. 110.
67. Geraldine Forbes suggests that Bose viewed sisters as women with whom one could work closely because one's relationship with them was devoid of eroticism. See Forbes, 'Mothers and Sisters,' p. 24.
68. *Ibid.,* p. 30.
69. See Subhas Chandra Bose, 'Opening of the Rani of Jhansi Training camp, 22 October 1943,' *Testament of Subhas Bose,* pp. 211-12.
70. Some historians confine this golden age to the pre-Vedic period prior to 1500 B.C. when the mother goddess was worshipped and the male Shiva was less important. According to this view,

it actually was during the Vedic period that Aryan desire for superiority over the Dravidians produced the belief about ritual position and the caste system emerged, restricting women to the role of mother. Early marriage was institutionalised, women are unable to marry below their subcaste, and *sati* (cremating widows on the funeral pyre of their dead husbands) began to be practiced. All were designed tio insure fidelity and legitimacy of heirs. These restrictions were (and continue to be) the most rigid within the Brahmin caste, though lower castes mimicked higher castes to gain respectability. See Lebra, Paulson, Everett (eds.), *Women and Work in India: Continuity and Change,* pp. 5-7.

71. Ferminist historians have warned that these 'golden ages' of sex equality or matriarchy in pre-history are often based on myth and archaeological evidence of goddess worship, not necessarily on history. They warn that the universal dominance of men can be self-confirming because of the invariable return to patriarchy. See Randall, *Women and Politics: An International Perspective,* pp. 16-17.

72. Subhas Bose, 'Speech Delivered on Occasion of the Opening of the Rani of Jhansi Regiment Camp.' 22 October 1943, (Xerox from Base, original source known). Abbreviated versions or inconsistent translations exist in *selected speeches of Subhas Chandra Bose,* p. 208 *Testament of Subhas Bose,* p. 211.

10

Views of Eminent Persons

Swami Dayanand and his Satyartha Prakash

Through his *Satyartha Prakash,* published first in 1875 and revised in 1883,[1] Swami Dayanand was answering to the contemporary atmosphere of colonial rule, Christian evangelicalism, and consideration for socio-religious reform among the literate urban middle classes in North India.[2] He shared their consideration for improving the lot of Hindu women by abolishing the existing social evils like child marriage, polygamy, seclusion, enforced widowhood, prostitution, low position of women, and the common prejudice against their learning. In Swami Dayanand's conception of reform for the regeneration of *Aryavarta,* education, procreation and social control are interconnected.[3] His perception is based on his own explanation of the Vedas and some subsequent writings.

In Satyartha Prakash the girl's right to learning is as much stressed as the boy's.[4] Towards the end of his life, he was of the view that the *Shudras* should also read the *Vedas;* he substituted the idea of *varna* classification by birth with that of the four-fold division of society on the ground of talent and achievement.[5] Therefore, the *Shudra* girls, too, in his opinion became entitled to attain education. It appears, however, that they were not to attend the same school as the girls belonging to the families of the twice-born.[6] In any case, the girls had to attend the schools meant exclusively for them, to be situated a few miles away from any habitation or school for boys, and to be run exclusively by female teachers and servants.[7] The duration of schooling for girls was much lesser than for boys, the minimum being only eight years against the boy's seventeen years.[8] This discrimination determined also the degree of education for girls.

The contents of the syllabus suggested for girls indicated that they had to acquire some general education supplemented by special training fit for the sort of would be conjugal household.[9] They were not to be educated for any professional job, except for teaching in a girls' school.[10] Resultantly, girls were not supposed to learn any 'foreign' languages.[11] Their education was associated with domestic happiness.

Swami Dayanand's theory of social regeneration rested on his idea of monogamous married life *(grihasthashram)* marked by restriction, conjugal fidelity and compatibility.[12] After finishing her education and obtaining the minimum age of sixteen, the girl was free to give her consent for marriage to a person whose countenance and profession was made known to her by her teachers.[13] The compatibility was significant not only in physical and personal terms but also in more of special background and training of the prospective bride – a sort of 'home science' for a particular category of vocation.[14] The maintenance of *Brahmacharya* prepared the couple for producing superior children. Their blend was chiefly for procreation and woman could beget upon ten issues.[15] To rear the children well was a significant socialization of the offspring. She was to manage the domestic affairs in compliance with the desires of her husband.[16] Swami Dayanand champions rejection of certain classes of girls for matrimonial alliance, but he does not point out what those bachelors were to do.[17] This suggests his viewpoint as mainly the male angle. In other ways too, his bias in support of the male becomes known. The girl to be selected as wife should not be closely associated to any of the boy's parents; her own parents should stay in some remote town to avoid her frequent visits to the parental home. In this situation the girl's father would not have to part with something or the other upon her going, and she herself would fail to rush to her parents in real or perceived problem.[18] The wife could remain at home when the husband became recluse and in no case could she follow her husband.[19] Perhaps to reside at home was physically more convenient, but the implication was that she did not deserve to seek salvation through the sources open to man.

Swami Dayanand favoured remarriage but only if the concerned persons were virgin widows and widowers.[20] For the other widows, and widowers, he personified *niyoga* which in his presentation was a legally acceptable but temporary wedding. It was mainly for procreation. Through such a widow could beget two male children for herself, which would make them the legal successors to her husband's name and property. She could produce eight more male offsprings for four widowers, bring them up to the natural father who would treat them for some years and then entrust them as his legitimate heirs.[21] The idea and custom of *niyoga* was meant for the legalisation of sexuality, because illicit and uncompelled involvement in Swami Dayanand's view resulted in social deterioration.[22] The objective of *niyoga* to have male offsprings was closely linked up with the idea that property should exist in the family. The girl had no right to inherit property.[23]

From the detail of household life mentioned by Swami Dayanand it seems that he had the upper and middle class families of the *dwija* castes in mind. The round of a woman's life in such circumstances was to contain good upbringing as a child, learning in the home from the age of five to eight, schooling upto the age of sixteen, wedding by consent to a young man seen personally and of known profession and similar position, producing and bringing up offsprings, especially male offsprings, caring for the conjugal members, managing the home and supervising the servants, depending on sons after the husband's *vanprastha,* and dying without wishing for salvation. In the event of her husband's long absence or infertility or without a male child, she could contact *niyoga* to have two male offsprings. She was never to give up the hearth and conjugal home. Her role, thus, was limited to the home, as the wife and the mother. All her talent and dedication was to be exercised within the four boundaries of the house. Even if she went out to obtain male children for herself, it was for her first lawfully married husband, his family and property.

Manusmriti

Nearly all of Swami Dayanand's theories about the status of women are available in *Manusmriti*.[24] But he rejects as interpolations those of its verses that prohibit *niyoga* and *swayamvar,* recommend child marriage, prescribe control of woman by her male relatives, refrain her from the study of the

Vedas and from involvement in religious ceremonies.[25] Out of the available 2,685 verses a latest annotated edition of *Manusmriti* excludes 1,471 verses as 'inauthentic' as these did not stand the tests of inner consistency and conformity with the *Vedas.*[26] Manu and Swami Dayanand are thus made to resemble each other and present ladies as deserving respect, as the mistress of the home, and as the mainstay of its ecstasy.[27] Even the 'purified,' edition leaves no suspicion that Manu's consideration is for the preservation of the wife as 'the field' for production in the interest of the husband who is 'the owner of the field' *(kshetra-swami).*[28] In his revelation of *niyoga,* Swami Dayanand virtually reiterates this status. Manu also advises that to ensure that the woman does not go astray, she should be kept occupied with the several domestic responsibilities.[29] The underlying suppositions in the *Manusmriti* and *Satyartha Prakash* are that motherhood is the chief function of woman, dedication to husband her main duty, and his household management her prime responsibility, and that nature envisaged these roles for her.

Swami Vivekananda

Swami Vivekananda regarded women as the embodiment of *shakti*, the primeval energy in the root of existence. He regarded them as the salt of the earth itself, for they give man his earthly form and nourish him with personal charm and grace, with the milk of human kindness, and with their sweat and blood, in different societal roles.

Swami Vivekananda argued that the roles of men and women were complimentary and not opposite. Neither was superior to the other. His views in this respect were shaped by *Advaita Vendanta* which rests on the praxis: evam evadvityam, i.e., one absence and no other'. Metaphysically speaking, the innate sexual differences derive from the Reality; *Purusha* and *Prakriti* are one like the *Yin* and the *Yang*, or *Shiva* and *Shakti.* The apparent manifestations only reveal the Reality in varied forms. As Swami Vivekananda writes 'It is very difficult to understand why in this country so much difference is made between men and women, whereas the Vedanta describes that one and the same conscious Self is present in all beings.

He believed in the argument of the 'perfect balance' and harmony in nature to prove that the living beings, though carved from the same matter, were cast in varied moulds to perform different types of functions, and thus each held a unique position in the cosmological order. He remarked that men and women be judged by the standard of their respective greatness.

To judge men-women in terms of physical strength is unjust. If man can boast of his muscular power, women can rely on her innate patience and the ability to forebear; if he is ingenuous, she is the energy in his back; if he can make reckless use of his vocal cords, she has the power of suggestibility—her twinkling eyes and other gestures convesmassages far more profoundly than any other means. When man operites it the sensory level, she makes use of her extransensory perception. What men discovers through reason, she knows it already through faith. The ruggesness of man is contained only by her purity and selflessness. If man is aggressive in the present, she is convulsive in the future. Man's strength is his weakness, but women's weakness is her strength at the gross, physical level. As Swami Vivekananda put it: 'Each is equaly good in his or her own way. What man can wring up a child with such patience, endurance and love and the women can. The one has developed the power of coing; the other the power of suffering. If women cannot act, neither can man surfer.'

Women is both *Mahamaya* and Mahashakti, and holds the key to the world. Swami Vivekananda believed with Sri Ramakrishna, his spiritual preceptor, that all women are parts of the Divine Mother, and, therefore, they should be looked upon as mother by all. He seemed to be inclined to the view of Yajnavalkya that women were ever pure (Pavitram)- He epressed sympathy even for the fall on woman who put their bodies to unworthy use, under the pressure of circumstances.

The supreme ideal of women as mother had such an appeal to Swami Vivekanada that he even justified the Mother-worship of the Tantras in its purest form and said that a woman's internal manifestations such as knowledge, devotion, discrimination and making man omniscient, of unfailing purpose, and a knower of Brahman.

In her role as mother, a women undergoes the ordeal of maternity and faces a number of problems while nurturing her children. She spends sleepless nights without a groan, feeds children sometimes at her own cost, and is ready to go to any extent of safeguard them. Motherhood is thus as much an assertion of a woman's creativity power as the pinnacle of her glory. The *smriti-karas* declared that the father is a hundred times more venerable than the teacher, but the mother is a thousand times more venerable than even the father. It was this age-old Indian ideal which was emphasised, again and again, by Swami Vivekanand in his speeches and writings.

Swami Vivekanand was of the view that such nation stood for an ideal and strove to attain it. To understand nation one must first understand its ideal, for each nation refuses to be judged by any other standard. The mother, being the epitome of love, service and sacrifices has always commanded respect in the Indian society. In one of his lectures at Brooklyn, he said mother is the representative of God, if God is the mother of the universe. . . Our God is both personal and absolute. The absolute is male, the personal female. And thus it comes that we now say : The first manifestation of God is the hand that rocks the cradle.

In another speech at Pasandena, California, he emphasised the aforesaid ideal again. 'Now the ideal woman in India is the mother, the mother first, and the mother last. The word "Woman" calls up to the mind of the Hindu, motherhood, and God is called Mother. That was not the case in the west where the sensual aspects of a woman's personality were given precedence over her inner virtues. The soul is sexless, and woman representing the energy aspect of the Lord, cannot be viewed in an insular way, in her physical dimension alone. The name mother has been called holy once, and for ever; for what name is there which he lust can ever approach, no carnality ever can come near than the one word, mother? That is the ideal in India.

Linked to motherhood is wifehood. The Indian wife purifies herself through fasts, prayers and penances before conceiving a baby. The conjugal union marks the greatest prayer between man and wife, the prayer that is going to bring into the world another soul fraught with a tremendous power both for good and for evil. Swami Vivekananda was convinced that the pre-natal influences determined the psychology of children, and that those who were born by chance, in moments of coarse passion, or in unholy circumstances were sure to prove 'a curse to humanity'. He was of the view that Indian eugenics tradition which prescribed certain *samskaras*.

His idea to establish a woman's monastery was aimed at creating a class of *brahmacharins* who were so fired 'with the strength of that virtue of chastity' is to die for a cause that was dear to them. He was sore with Jesus as he had not assigned woman an equal place with men. He also disapproved of the act of Lord Buddha in placing the *Bhikshuni Sanghas* under the supervision of the male monks.

The ideal woman of Swami Vivekananda's conception was the one who combined in her the purity and chastity of Sita and Damayanti, the saintly disposition of *brahmavadinis* like Vachaknavi, Vadva, Pratitheyi in Vishavavara, the intellectual acumen of Gargi and Sulabha, the spiritual powers of Savitri or Anusuya, and the physical strength and courage of Lakshmi Bai, the queen of Jhansi.

The realm of the ideal is in the subjective world; that of the real, in the objective. The former is ostensible in nature and relates to the future; the latter is authentic and caters to the present. The *ideal* is important for it is like a goal to be attained; the *real* has value as it forms the bedrock of any future development. Although Swami Vivekananda putforth the idealistic conception of Indian woman before western audiences, he was not ignorant about their problems and needs. He often recalled that women, during the early vedic period, enjoyed a high social status, and had access to the holy scriptures.

He quoted Manu to show that gods blessed those families where women were happy and well-treated. "Can you better the condition of your women?" he asked. Then there will be hope for your well-being. Otherwise, you will remain as backward as now.

Swami Vevekananda regretted that the Indian women had been 'trained in helplessness, servile dependence on other', and so they were good only 'to wipe their eyes out at the slighest approach of a mishap or danger'. They had become oblivious of the fact that they were *shaktis,* carrying a huge reservoir of inner strength, which if put to use, could change the face of mankind. He exhorted them to acquire a heroic spirit, and to learn even the self-defence techniques. They, too, like men, should have muscles of iron and nerves of steel, besides being sure in word and deed.

Unlike many of his contemporary social reformers, Swami Vivekananda did not lay social evils, including those which degraded the status of women, at the door of religion. It may be noted that Swami Vivekananda's concept of religion was not confined to 'books and dogmas'; it was practical to the core, and aimed not only at self-development but also at the welfare of mankind.

Swami Vivekananda was aware that number of historical and socio-economic factors such as the influx of foreign invaders, the predominance of priestly classes, the rigidity of social system, the scurrilous comments on women in the post-vedic literature, the birth of the cult of *devadasis*, the growing incidence of the cases of *sati* and infanticide, etc., had led to a decline in the position of women. But, he thought the most important factor which hampered their progress was that they were deprived of the right kind of education. By education, he did not mean the stuffing of the mind with information or pedantic ideas; but a system by which character is formed, strength of mind is increased, the intellect is expanded', and which helps one to stand on one's own feet'. He regarded religion is the innermost core of education, is it alone could enable one to realise one's inherent divinity. He suggested that the girls must be taught the rudiments of science, arts, house-keeping, cooking, sewing etc., but they must not be allowed to read novels, as these might pollute their minds. Besides, they ought to learn drawing, modelling, painting and other fine arts, fruit-modelling with hardened milk, painting, photography, the cutting of designs on paper, gold and silver filigree, and embroidery, so that they can earn a living in case of need.

Swami Vivekananda believed that women could excel in all fields of human activity, if treated at par with men, and given proper education and training. He rejected the idea that they were incompetemnt to take up intellectual or spiritual pursuits.

He wanted women to think for themselves to diagnose the malacy afflicting their social position, and to come forward to root it out. Women need not depend on the crutches of men, or suffer from inferiority complex. They should also not try to imitate men in all walks of life. On the other hand, men too should not be allowed to unduly meddle in women's affairs.

Abominable social customs like *Sati* and child marriage appeared to Swami Vivekananda as the fossilized forms of irrational beliefs and he condemned them in the strongest terms. He argued that the inhuman practice of *Sati* had nothing to do with religion as such, and must not be viewed that way. It was born of superstition, glorified by the priestly classes for their own advantage, and meekly followed by the people who were led to believe that it had a religious sanction. The custom of child marriage was no less reprehensible, and could not be justified on moral or social grounds. Child marriages led to an increase in the number of child widows, as sometime the difference between a man and his child bride was so great that she became a widow in her teens, and without adequate means to sustain herself, leading miserable life in accordance with the injunctions laid down by the early Hindu law-givers, and the accretions which came to be associated with them, with the passage of time. Child marriage also deprived them of education, and turned them into mothers when they were not physically prepared for that role.

As regards the question of the remarriage of widows, Swami Vivekananda stuck to the ancient Indian belief that 're-marrying is not remarriage' as it is bereft of natural charm and grace. He emphasised the virtues of chastity, fidelity and self control, and regarded the obsession of contemporary reformers with the issue of the remarriage of widows, as utterly meaningless. Besides the problem had different dimensions in different societies. Swami Vivekananda also disapproved of granting freedom to men and women in matters of marriage, as in the west.

Swami Vivekananda's glorification of the Indian women in the West stemmed partly from his patroitic zeal, and partly from his feeling that the position of women in other countries was not better. He thundered before the American audience thus. 'It is a strange fact that Oxford and Cambridge are closed to women today; so are Harvard and Yale, but Calcutta University opened its doors to women more than twenty years ago.

One of the tasks of Swami Vivekananda in the West was to remove the gross misconceptions about the Indian women; for example, that all female children were thrown before crocodiles in the rivers or that all widows were burnt to death. Although he never tried to rule out isolated instances in this regard, he did not quite appreciate the role of Christian missionaries in blowing them out of proportion.

While in India, Swami Vivekananda exhorted women to be bold, mobile, courageous and self-sufficient, and acquire the ability to take initiatives, like their western counterparts. But he did not, at the same time, want them to be vain, prurient, temperamental or materialistic. They were not to profess the ideals of the male world, but to grow strictly in terms of their own nature, and follow the dictates of their own being. They were to develop a strong character to become the catalysts of social change.

Gandhi on Untouchability and Women

The accusations of inconsistency and formlessness in ideology that have been brought against Gandhi have not been completely borne out by what I have attempted to show hitherto. Although Gandhi himself never made a fetish of consistency, I have suggested in the previous chapters that certain fundamental metaphysical and religious beliefs underlie all his teaching and that the apparent ambivalence of his position on certain issues should not be allowed to obscure this fact. Indeed it is possible, as I have indicated, to maintain that far from showing embivalence on certain issues Gandhi held on firmly to his fundamental beliefs concerning Truth and ahiṁsā while to the same time recognizing that in certain situations of moral dilemma he had to act in ways contrary to the beliefs.

It has been said that he was an intensely practical man unconcerned with philosophical ideas or with any systematic presentation of his ideas. To some extent this is true, but my contention is that both his practical activity and his unsystematic presentation of his ideas spring from certain basic presuppositions concerning the nature of Truth or God, man, and the world. It was because of these beliefs that he acted and behaved in the way he did; his life reflected his beliefs. That is, his practical activity was grounded in views concerning the meaning and purpose of life; it was motivated by fundamental metaphysical and religious beliefs which he derived from the Hindu way of life. It is not without significance that he asked to be judged on the way he lived his life.

'You must watch my life, how I live, eat, sit, talk behave in general. The sum total of all those in me is my religion.

If on the face of it this looks like a presumptuous thing to say, feelings of antipathy might be mitigated if it is recognised that Gandhi regarded the way a man lived his life to be of greater significance and a better witness to his beliefs that what he might verbally profess to believe. He made this point clear in his comments on Christian missionary activity. On the other hand it could be argued that it is quite possible for a man to have a genuine belief and to give a very inadequate account of it. His account might be open to criticism for being inconsistent, or formless, or philosophically confused, but the fact that the account he gives of his belief is suspect does not mean that his belief is suspect. In such cases we have to look at the account of man gives of his faith in the way he lives his life.

Gandhi's beliefs concerning the nature of Truth and its inter-relatedness with ahiṁsā, and his beliefs about the nature of the true Self and the unity of all existence, find expression through the techniques of satyagraha and sarvodaya. His sense of kinship with all men and his concern for the welfare ofall men is revealed particularly in his attitude towards, and his treatment of, the untouchables. The term he uses to describe them is *Harijans,* the children of God. By the use of this term he is suggesting that untouchables derive from *Brahman* in the same way as the twice-born Brāhmins, Kṣatriyas and Vaiśyas, and the once-born Śūdras. That being the case they are in no way different from them and they are clearly not to be regarded as outcasts. As Harijans, they partake of the nature of God or Truth and must, therefore, be considered at one with caste members of Hindu society in particular, and with mankind in general.

To understandfully the implications of Gandhi's treatment of the untouchables it is necessary to examine the traditional attitude to caste in India. Though it is difficult to be precise about the origin of the caste system it might be suggested that the Āryans who 'invaded' India distinguished themselves from the original inhabitants of India as twice-born as distinct from once-borne. The appellation twice-born means that they were entitled to study the Vedas and to be invested with a sacred cord at puberty. Three classes of twice-born are distinguished: The Brāhmins who upheld the cultural order and fulfilled sacerdotal functions,; the Kṣatriyas, who maintained the political order and performed military functions; and the Vaisyas, who supported the economic order and performed the necessary functions in agriculture. It is maintained that: 'The superior linguistic, cultural, and social cohesion of the Āryans *vis-a-vis* the various non-Āryan tribes and peoples insured Āryan domination—political, social, and cultural—over the greater part of India even more than their military victories. The once-born are the non-Āryans and are classified as Śudras. They are not permitted to hear the Vedas let alone study them, but they have their prescribed duties and functions, the performance of which ensures their promotion to a higher caste in their next reincarnation.

Outside this four-fold division of society fall the outcastes. They perform menial tasks such as scavenging, and contact with them in any form is deemed to have a polluting effect. No outcaste could ever hope to enter the caste system of Āryan society. Once an out-caste always an outcaste; he would always remain socially excluded.

It will be seen that caste was originally related to functional distinctions within Āryan society. It is possible that differences of colour as well as cultural differences may have played a part in the first instance in distinguishing the Āryans from the non-Āryans for there are references to āryavarṇa and dāsa varṇa where varṇa has the connotation of colour, but the distinctions were primarily functional. Later they ceased to be simply functional and came to be related to birth (jāti). Social divisions and the different stations in life related to functional distinctions were considered to be of divine origin and found mythical expression in the hymn to Puruṣa, (Rig Veda x 90):

'When they divided Puruṣa into how many parts did they arrange him? What was his mouth? What his two arms? What are his thighs and feel called?

The *brahmin* was his mouth, his two arms were made the *rajanya* (warrior), his two thighs the *vaisya* (trader and agriculturist), from his feet the *sudra* (servile class) was born.

The Gītā echoes this hymn when it attributes the four-fold caste system to God but at the same time the emphasis is on functional distinctions and not on distinctions of birth (jāti).

'The four-fold order was created by Me according to the divisions of quality and work.' (4: 13)

A similar mythical expression of functional distinctions is to be found in Plato where social divisions within the ideal state are related to different states of the soul. A predominance of wisdom in the soul produces philosopher kings; a predominance of courage produces soldiers; and where vigour abounds workers are produced. This three-fold division within the state corresponds to distinctions within the soul which were created by God and mythically expressed as gold, silver and bronze. '. . . but God as he was fashioning you, put gold in those of you who are capable of ruling, . . . silver in the auxiliaries, and iron and copper in the farmers and other craftsmen.'

Luther also claimed that classes were ordained by God and he distinguishes three classes namely, the teaching class, the class of defenders and the working class. Man's duty was to serve the ranks of his calling and to perform the tasks appropriate to his class.

The growth of rigidity and inflexibility in the caste system is illustrated by injunctions concerning mixed marriages which are to be found in the Laws of Manu, the ancient law book of the Hindu tradition. The degree to which the offspring of mixed marriages were despised depended on the difference in caste between husband and wife. The most despised of all issue of mixed marriages was the chandala, who resulted from the union of a Brāhmin woman and a Śūdra man; he was automatically excluded from all considerations of the dharma or law.

By taking up the cause of the untouchables, therefore, Gandhi was challenging much of the traditional sanātanist or orthodox teaching concerning the caste system. He was flying in the face of centuries of Brāhmanical teaching and deeply-rooted customs He was questioning the rigidity and inflexibility of the caste system. It needs to be pointed out, however, that Gandhi defended social divisions in the sense of varṇāśramadharma, that is, in the sense that there were certain social functions or duties which were related to one's order or status in society. So in the first instance he approved of a society with functional distinctions based on the different abilities of different members as a way of preserving the stability of social life. He maintained that varṇa had to do with man's duties or vocation in society and did not in any way imply the notion of untouchability. Divisions of the kind he envisaged were to be regarded as natural in society and no notion of superiority or inferiority was involved in any way. A man was expected to develop his hereditary skills, and thereby follow the vocation of his forefathers as a matter of course, though he was not expected to stifle his innovative spirit. It is evident from this that Gandhi assumed a person might inherit the natural tendencies and particular characteristics necessary to enable him to take up the same vocation as his forefathers and also that one form of occupation should not be considered superior or inferior to another. The law of varna, as he called it, resulted from a realistic appraisal of the fact that men are not born equal in the sense that they do not all have the same abilities. Some are born with definite limitations which they can not be expected to overcome and what the law of varṇa does is to ensure that each man is provided with a sphere of activity which establishes for him a place in society and guarantees that his labours are rewarded. In this sense the law of varṇa was a good thing and it was Gandhi conviction that the ideal social order would evolve only when the implications of the law were fully understood. He also maintained that a man's acceptance of his hereditary calling would necessarily limit or prelude the development of ambition and serve instead of release surplus energy for spiritual development. In putting forward this view he was probably too sanguine and undoubtedly presenting an extremely idealistic picture of society. He may have been correct to maintain that, as originally conceived, varnāśramadharma did not imply notions of superiority or inferiority based on one's status at birth, and had nothing to do with the idea of untouchability. Nevertheless it could be argued that if work determines one's place or status in society, and if the work one does is decided by one's birth, then birth becomes the most important factor in determining one's place or status in society. It is only a short step from the functional distinctions Gandhi approves in the case of varnāśramadharma to the divisions he disapproves of in the case of caste and which led eventually to the development of the notion of untouchability.

According to Gandhi's opponents it was his failure to recognise the underlying similarly bertween varṇa and caste that led to the bitter attack on his views by B.R. Ambedkar, the leader of the All India Depressed Classes Federation, who was himself an outcaste. There is little doubt, of course, that had Ambedkar accepted his hereditary status as an outcaste he would never have become such a distinguished lawyer, and Gandhi recognizes this fact when he commends Ambedkar for his intellectual distinction and eminence and shows how silly it was for orthodox brāhmins to count him untouchable simply because he was born a Mahar or an untouchable. Here Gandhi explicitly condemns the rigidity of a caste system which would condemn a man of Ambedkar's intellectual abilities to menial tasks and an inferior status in society. Ambedkar's contention however, is that the idea of varṇa is simply the foreruner of the idea of caste and that both ideas are evil. 'And what is Mr. Gandhi's *varna* system? It is simply a new name for the caste system and retain all the worse features of the caste system.

Ambedkar's arguments were typical of those opposed to Gandhi on this issue, and the latter realised that the system of social, functional divisions he approved of had degenerated into a system of caste which, in his view, was the very antithesis and a perversion of the original idea of varṇa. When unjust social distinctions came to be attributed to differences of divine origin and when the in-equitable stratification of society received religious sanction, then a system of divinely ordained superior and inferior beings had emerged. It was because of this that Gandhi proclaimed the view that the caste system had to be abolished since it was contrary to basic, elementary, moral and religious principles and positively harmful to the spiritual and moral growth of the nation.

'Birth and observance of forms cannot determine one's superiority and inferiority. Character is the only determining factor. God did not create men with the badge of superiority and inferiority; no scripture which lebels a human being as inferior or untouchable because of his or her birth can command our allegiance, it is a denial of God and Truth, which God.'

Indications of the depth of Gandhi's feelings on the question of untouchability are evident from his many references to the subject. I have already referred briefly to his opposition to it in relation to his recognition of the imperfections and weaknesses of Hinduism, and his conviction that it untouchability were to be considered an integral part of the Hindu way of life, he would have to stop calling himself a Hindu. He goes further, however, when he maintains that he 'would far rather that Hinduism died than that untouchability lived.' Untouchability could be compared to arsenic in milk and to a poison that destroys the life of Hindu society. It is grounded in ancient prejudices and is the greatest blot on Hinduism. It cannot claim the sanction of religion because it is contrary to Truth. To say that God has deliberately set one section of society apart as untouchable is nothing short of blasphemy. If Hindus maintain they have the sanction of religion to segregate the pariah then it is possible for the white man also to maintain that he has a similar sanction to segregate Hindus or Indians. So it is necessary that we 'first cast out the beam of untouchability from our own eyes before we attempt to remove the mote from that of our "masters". Gandhi feels so strongly about the iniquity of untouchability that he expresses the desire, should he not attain mokṣa, or liberation from the realm of samsāra, to be reborn as an untouchable in order that he might identify himself with their sufferings and sorrows. In the light of these remarks it is difficult to agree with some of the accusations levelled against him by some of his critics. It could be argued that he may have been confused in seeking to defend varna and oppose caste. But it could also be argued that his conception of the ideal social order, in which every man fulfils his social functions in accordance with his abilities and is content with the status in society his sphere of activity provides him with, corresponds to his conception of absolute Truth. As absolute Truth is beyond realisation within empirical existence and one has to hold on to relative truth as a 'beacon' and 'guide', so it is that the ideal socail order cannot be embodied in any particular form within the empirical realm and one has to hold on to those forms of society that approximate to the ideal. This does not mean that one settles for less in the sense that one dispenses with the ideal. The concept of the ideal still informs the way in which one looks at particular forms of society. This may provide an explanation for Gandhi's strong and vigorous opposition to the practice of untouchability within the Hindu way of life. He was not content with passively accepting the fact that it was a crime; he actively opposed it and sought to undermine it by means of satyāgraha since it was contrary to Truth and to his conception of the ideal social order.

While he was incarcerated in Yeravda jail he undertook a fast on behalf of the untouchables. He regarded fasting as a weapon of satyāgraha and, as we have already indicated, his main aim was to identify himself by means of self-imposed suffering with the despair and suffering of those on whose behalf it was undertaken. It was not, as Fischer suggests, a protest against Hindu maltreatment of the untouchables, because that might have made if a form of coercion, which as a form of violenies would have been unacceptable to Gandhi. But although the fast was undertaken for the good of the Harijans rather than as an explicit protest against unfair orthodox Hindu treatment of them, it did have the effect of producing a spirit of penance and reform throughout India and consequently a certain improvement in the treatment and the conditions of the Harijans. It did not abolish untouchability, but it was effective in the sense that it made the practice of untouchability less socially acceptable.

Gandhi's opposition to caste expressed itself also in his attempt to abolish the caste labels that Hindus applied to themselves. He wished that all members of society would regard themselves as Śūdras, which would mean that there would be no restrictions on marriage or any other issues of caste which tended to weaken Hindu society by turning men's minds from more important affairs. He relates the question of untouchability to his basic beliefs concerning Truth, ahiṁsā and sarvodaya when he states: 'The observance (of the vow of untouchability) is not fulfilled' merely by making friends with 'untouchables', but by loving all life as one's own self. Removal of untouchability means love for, and service of, the whole world, and it thus merges into *ahimsa.* The immorality, injustice, iniquity, inhumanity and soul-destroying nature of the practice of untouchability is both implicit and explicit in Gandhi's thought and, despite his critics, he has every right to maintain that it was the passion of his life to be of service to the untouchables of India.

'What I want, what I am living for, and what I should delight in dying for, is the eradication of untouchability root and branch. What this indicates among other things is not only Gandhi's desire to form a society that approximates to the ideal, but also the inextricable relation that he convinces to exist between religion and morality. Hinduism had ignored this relation and had departed from its lofty ideals and its unequivocal declaration concerning the unity of existence. The whole purpose of the anti-untouchability campaign, therefore, was to restore the purity of the Hindu way of life. If it were argued that the lot of the untouchables could only be alleviated by sowing seeds of dissatisfaction among them and thereby creating the conditions necessary for revolutionary action, Gandhi's reply would be that in the long run, the cause of the Harijans could only be served by means of ahiṁsā and satyāgraha.

What Gandhi is suggesting by his rejection of revolutionary methods for improving the lot of the untouchables is that changes in the life of Harijans could only be effectively accomplished by bringing about a change of attitude among the members of Hindu society as a whole. So making friends of untouchables was not enough, nor, it might be argued, could the abolition of caste labels be regarded as an adequate solution to the problem. As Gandhi indicates, nothing short of a restoration of the purity of the Hindu way of life would suffice. This would involve an inner change and a return to the religious and ethical ideals of Truth and ahiṁsā. If this is so, then the question that might be asked is why social changes of the kind Gandhi refers to should be advocated at all since they do not go to the heart of the problem. One possible answer might be that the inner change Gandhi is proposing is not meant in any pictistic sense; it is not an individualistic affair having no social implications. It involves a change of attitude to human relationships and to states of affairs. Social change is a corollar of inner change and, therefore, although social change is not a sufficient condition, it may be regarded as a ncessary condition for the amelioration of the lot of the Harijans.

Gandhi's life-long fight on behalf of the untouchables is matched by his enlightened attitude towards women. In this respect he was well ahead of his time in India. The status of women in the traditional Hindu system was not an enviable one. They had been reduced to the status of second-class citizens by laws formulated and introduced by men. According to Gandhi's basic principle of the essential oneness of huminity men and women cannot be regarded as different in essence: they share the same soul, the same life, and the same basic human feelings. Yet although they complement one another, Gandhi maintains that men have tended to dominate women with the result that women have developed an unfortunate sense of inferiority and have come to believe that they are inferior to men. It is true that there are vital differences between men and women and that the basic purpose in life for women differs from that of men, but this does not mean that women are in any sense inferior. Gandhi's argument is that women require different qualities than men in order to fulfil the obligations of motherhood, for example, and in many ways it is a sad reflection on society when it encourages women to forsake their customary duties as custodians of family life to take up duties normally performed by men, such as taking up arms in defence of one's country. In Gandhi's view, the duties involved in maintaining moral standards and a good home in the midst of bad social influences require as much courage and fortitude as those involved in defending one's country against an aggressor.

Man's tendency to dominate had led him to regard women as playthings and Gandhi deplores the substitution of what Otto would call an I-It relationship for an I-Thou relationship between men and women, and the custom that decrees that even the most inferior and ignorant of men, despite their worthlessness, have been able to dominate women and enjoy an undeserved measure of superiority over them.

'Of all the evils for which man has made himself responsible, none is so degrading, so shocking or so brutal as his abuse of the better half of humanity—to me, the female sex, not the weaker sex.'

In support of the cause of women Gandhi's argument is that they should rebel against man and refuse to be treated as things or as objects of lust. By so doing they would acquire freedom and the ability to show clearly the powerful force they were capable of exercising in the world. Provided they remained true to their nature women could exercise great influence and wield great power. They were the nobler sex, 'the personification of self-sacrifice', 'the embodiment of . . . silent suffering', and 'the incarnation of ahimsa'. They had greater moral power, courage and endurance than men and an infinite capacity for love and suffering as their endurance of the pangs of labour in child-birth showed. They also had the ability to do more for the cause of truth and ahiṁsā than men and were able to teach the art of peace to the world.

'If non-violence is the law of our being, the future is with woman . . . who can make a more effective appeal to the heart than woman? . . . God has vouchsafed to women the power of non-violence more than to man. It is all the more effective because it is mute. Women are the natural messengers of the gospel of non-violence of only they will realise their high state.

Gandhi's praise of women's capacity for ahiṁsā, however, does not mean that in certain circumstances they might not be justified in resorting to Hiṁsā. If a woman is assaulted she has the duty to protect herself even to the point of using armed violence, but her most effective means of resistence is non-violence even to the point of death. The paradoxical nature of Gandhi's attitude is again evident here. Hiṁsā, on the one hand is a primary duty and clearly justified, yet, on the other hand, the most effective resistance springs from ahiṁsā though it might result in death. Even if we were to attempt to reconcil these two injunctions by equating ahiṁsā with non-hatred rather than non-killing, as Gandhi often does, it is still clear that he would insist on equating ahiṁsā with total non-violence.

What is indicated by Gandhi's insistence on the absolute nature of the principle of non-violence, as we have already shown, is that it is absolute in the sense that it informs the spirit and the circumstances in which violence is done. In certain situations a woman must do what she feels she has to do in order to protect herself even though it involves violence. Moral considerations are involved in her action despite the violation of the principle of non-violence. This does not mean, however, that the principal of non-violence has been discarded because it still informs the spirit in which violence is done and can involve feelings of guilt and remorse. It is simply that in situations of moral dilemma certain moral considerations are involved in the 'perspective' of the action, while at the same time one remains committed to the principle of non-violence.

On the question of marriage Gandhi notes that the ideal approach is to regard it as a sacrament. It should be a spiritual as well as a physical union. Human love is 'a stepping stone to divine or universal love.' Friendship and companionship are involved and not simply the satisfaction of sexual desires. Gandhi shows a paradoxical attitude to sex, however, when he claims that in an ideal marriage there is no place for sexual satisfaction. He may mean by this, though the point is not made explicit, that sexual intercourse should only take place when progeny is desired. But does this mean that no pleasure or satisfaction should be derived from the sexual act under any circumstances? It would appear that this may be his attitude because he maintains, for example, that 'The union is not meant for pleasure, but for bringing forth progeny. And union is a crime when the desire for progeny is absent.' If this is the case, then the view that sexual union is the culmination of the act of love between a man and a woman and symbolic of, or 'a stepping stone to divine universal love' would have to be discarded. We may have here also an explanation of Gandhi's attitude to artificial methods of birth-control. Acceptance of the use of contraceptive may imply that some degree of satisfaction is being derived from the sexual act. On the other hand, how can sex be conceived as a fine and noble thing, as Gandhi maintains, in the absence of some degree of satisfaction? In Gandhi's view, however, the use of contraceptives means condoning vice, undermining the virtues of self-control and restraint and results in self-indulgence and 'the dissolution of the marriage bond'. How the latter occurs as a consequence of the use of contraceptive is not made clear, and if may make sense to ask whether birth-control is not made necessary by the fearful consequences of over-population. Gandhi's reply to this argument is that by better management of the land and better agricultural methods it should be possible for India to support twice as many people. Yet he is practical enough to recognise that excessive propogation ot children should be stopped and the methods he advocates are those which derive from proper education. There is need for married brahmacārya as he calls it, that is, abstinence from sexual intercourse within the married bond. Women should also learn to resist the approaches of their husbands. Marriage gives no right to the male member of the partnership to impose his will on the female or to demand her obedience. Should disagreements occur and one partner is unable to submit to the demand of the other then, if there is no other alternative, divorce should be regarded as the acceptable way out.

Gandhi's view of marriage as a sacrament meant that he disapproved of arranged marriages on the basis of monetary settlements or dowries, or on the grounds of caste. He also strongly disapproved of child marriages and drew on his own experiences, full documented in his autobiography, to show the folly of such an institution. He regarded it as a cruel custom and considered it disgraceful that it should be given religious sanction.

'But *brahmanism* that can tolerate untouchability, virgin widowhood, spoliation (*sic*) of virgins, stinks in my nostrils. It is a parody of *brahmanism.* There is no knowledge of Brahman therein.' Child marriages ought to be abolished. This would mean that there would be fewer widows because the restrictions of Hindu society concerning remarriage meant that there were far too many widows. Usually in the higher castes it was the custom for women who had lost their husbands to remain widows for the rest of their lives, but the same custom did not apply to men. Gandhi considered this to be an indictment of the customs of Hindu society and he advocated, on the basis of sex equality, that widows be given the right to remarry should they so desire.

'If we would be pure, if we would save Hinduism, we must rid ourselves of this poison of enforced widowhood.' The reforming zeal of Gandhi presents itself here and in this respect he echoes the teachings of earlier Hindu reformers such as Ram Mohan Roy and Keshab Chandra Sen.

Another restrictions imposed on women that Gandhi vigorously opposed was that of purdah. Originally purdah applied to the Islamic practice of veiling the faces of women, but it was as a form of female segregation that it came to be accepted by the Hindus. The main purpose of purdah was to preserve the purity of women by keeping them confined. At best it was an attempt by husbands to protect their wives from marauding male predators; at worse it was a violation of basic human rights which resulted in wives being treated as slaves, or as the property of their husbands. In Gandhi's opinion it was a barbarous custom and the arguments he levels against it relate to the question why a man should consider himself to have the right to guard his wife's purity. Women had no reciprocal rights in the case of male purity, so if male purity was the prerogative of the male, why should not female purity be the prerogative of the female. In any case it was fundamental mistake to assume that chastity was like some kind of hot-house plant that could be protected by the walls of purdah. Chastity was not something that could be imposed from without; it was something that grew from within.

Reference to chastity as a virtue that a person cultivates within rather than something that can be imposed on a person from without by means of social customs raises questions similar to those considered in connection with untouchability. If chastity is a matter of one's attitude to human relationships and states of affairs the question that arises is what purpose is served by such social customs as purdah. Gandhi seems to be recognizing this point when he refers to it as a barbarous custom. If the advocates of purdah were to reply that the custom provides the necessary conditions for the cultivation of the virtue of chastity then the question that might be asked is whether enforced chastity can be regarded as chastity at all. The point might be made that the necessary and sufficient conditions for the cultivation of chastity rest with the attitude of the person concerned to states of affairs and not with social rules and customs that might be imposed on that person from without. The social custom of purdah would be unnecessary if one's attitude to human relationships were already chaste.

If this is the case with chastity does not the same argument apply to marriage customs? As we have seen Gandhi disapproves of child marriages, arranged marriages, artificial methods of contraception and enforced widowhood. It might be argued that the social changes he advocates in respect of these Hindu customs provide the necessary if not the sufficient conditions for regarding marriage as a sacrament. But if the restoration of the purity of the Hindu way of life is a sufficient condition then what the advocated changes do is to indicate what it means for Gandhi to say that marriage is a sacrament. It could be seen to involve mutual consent (hence no child marriages); self-control and self-restraint (so no artificial methods of birth-control); mutual love (hence no arranged marriages involving caste considerations and dowries); and mutual respect (involving no enforced widowhood). The social changes advocated may not be regarded as sufficient conditions for regarding marriage as a sacrament but they may be seen as the necessary conditions for the social application of the sacramental view of marriage and for the improvement of the lot of women.

Gandhi's attitude to women like his attitude to untouchability springs from his basic conviction that we are all one in that we share the same Atman or soul. The unity of mankind derives from the unity of Truth which is God. People complement one another. One person cannot be degraded without the other suffering, for the abuse of one leads to the abuse of another. Sarvodaya, therefore, in Gandhi's view included in the welfare of women and the untouchables in Hindu society and the restoration of their basic human rights. This in turn involved among other social changes a re-examination of the educational sytem of the country which is the subject of the next chapter.

Lala Lajpat Rai

Remarkable continuity of these ideas exists down to the early twentieth century. The enlightened Arya Samajists as Lala Lajpat Rai also recommend the *Manusmriti* as the 'best despite its corruptions known code of Hindu Law' which ascribes a very high status to women and displays an extraordinary solicitude for their interests, for their chastity, and for their respect.[30] In an article published in the *Modern Review* in early 1920, Lala Lajpat Rai suggests the social reformers to have 'clear grasp of the fundamentals' that due to the 'special adaptation of women's body to maternity' she would 'always be different from men mentally as well as physically'. A girl therefore, required education for her 'complete evolution to womanhood'.[31] He also defends the refusal of property right to woman: the principle is to keep the mother function free of all entities and pecuniary cares. Every woman is a mother in embryo. That is her supreme function in life. That is her social mission' (emphasis in original).[32] In fact, the famous Arya Samajists subscribed by and large to the theory that their programmes for reform and female education should be geared to equipping and training her for wedding and family in the changing situation of British rule.[33] They desired women 'enlightened' but 'dependent; they wished to give her 'dignity' but not 'freedom'.[34]

References

1. Maharishi Dayanand Saraswati, *Satyartha Prakash* (Hindi) Arsh Sahitya Prachar Trust, Delhi 1988 (36th reprint of the 2nd edition revised by Swami Dayanand and published in 1883). It is worth noting that lakhs of copies of the *Satyartha Prakash* have been sold.
2. Swami Dayanand particularly takes into account the contemporary concerns of the social reformers in Bengal: J.T.F. Jordens, *Dayanand Saraswati: His Life and Ideas,* Oxford University Press, Delhi, 1978, 70-98.
3. *Satyartha Prakash,* 36, 51 and 54.
4. *Ibid.,* 49 and 50. Swami Dayanand visualizes compulsory education for both boys and girls.
5. *Ibid.,* 52, 58-61 and 80.
6. *Ibid.,* 24. The Swami uses the word 'Arya-kul' for the schools meant for the twice-born as distinct from the 'Gurukul' where the Shudras went without the *upanayan* ceremony.
7. *Ibid.,* 26.
8. This may be inferred from the minimum age prescribed for marriage which was sixteen years for girls and twenty-five years for boys: *Ibid.*, 32 and 54. However, the full education prescribed for boys is supposed to take 20-21 years : *Ibid.,* 47.
9. *Ibid.,* 51. The essential contents of the education prescribed for girls were grammar, religions, requiring some study of the Vedas, medicine, arithmetic and craft, including some idea of the construction of houses.
10. *Ibid.,* 26, 27, 51, 66 and 71. In passing, however, the Swami refers to the possibility of the Kshatriya girls participating in war and state craft: *Ibid.,* 51.
11. Compare *Ibid.,* 21 and 51.
12. *Ibid.,* 63, 64, 71 and 81.
13. This is Swami Dayanand's idea of Swayamvar: *Ibid.,* 54, 56, 64 and 81.
14. *Ibid.,* 51 and 56.
15. *Ibid.,* 75.
16. *Ibid.,* 64, 71.
17. *Ibid.,* 64, 71.
18. Boys were advised not to marry girls with any sort of deformity, paleness of complexion, large build, brown eyes and the ones inauspiciously named after certain stars, flowers, birds, animals, rivers and mountains : *Ibid.,* 53.

19. *Ibid.,* 52-53.
20. *Ibid.,* 82-83.
21. *Ibid.,* 73, 76.
22. *Ibid.,* 74-79. However, whereas the husband was allowed sexual gratification through *niyoga* during the pregnancy of the wife, she was not allowed gratification for its own sake: *Ibid.,* 79.
23. *Ibid.,* 75.
24. *Ibid.,* 74.
25. See, for example, *Vishuddha Manusmriti* (with Hindi translation, annotation and commentary by Surendra Kumar) Arsh Sahitya Prachar Trust, Delhi, 1990 (3rd edn), 163, 165-78, 181, 184-87, 191, 219, 252-55, 259, 266, 269, 2ℇ4, 447-52, 454, 456-61 and 468.
26. 'Introduction': *Ibid.,* 60, 68-70, 74, 96 and 99, See also, Calarisse Bader, *Women in Ancient India: Moral and Literary Studies,* Kegan Paul, London, 1925 (rep.) 54-68 and 300, for example.
27. *Ibid.,* 9-10.
28. *Ibid.,* 96-97;
29. *Vishudha Manusmriti,* 452, verses 17 and 19.
30. *Ibid.,* 447-51, verses, 3, 5, 6, 8, 9, 11 and 13-15.
31. 'The position of Indian women', (The Tripura), 18 March, 1915, quoted in Madhu Kishwar, 'The daughters of Aryavartya', The Indian Economic and Social History Review, 23, 2 (1986), 177.
32. Social Reconstruction in India. The Relations of the Sexes, in *Lala Lajpat Rai: Writings and Speeches* (ed. Vijaya chandra Joshi, University Publishers, Delhi, 1966, 376, 378 and 381.
33. Quoted in Madhu Kishwar, 'The daughters of Aryavarta', 177-78.
34. For the Arya Samaj debate over the objectives and contents of the women's education, Kenneth W. Jones, *Arya Dharam: Hindu Consciousness in 19th century Punjab,* New Delhi, 1976 106-8, and Madhu Kishwar, 'The daughters of Aryavarta', 173-178.

11

Independence and After

After achieving independence in 1947, India had a tough job of social reconstruction, economic progress and political consciousness to be able to ensure justice and equality to all its citizens. The makers of the Constitution of India, which amongst others, had distinguished women like Sarojini Naidu, Hansa Mehta, Durgabai, Renuka Ray and Malti Chowdhry as its members, were conscious of the prevailing social infirmities and inequalities offered constitution to the nation which bestowed equal rights to all its citizens and that all of them are equal before the law. In this context legal, political and socio-economic status of women has to be investigated.

Legal status (Article 14 of the Constitution) provides that the state shall not refuse any person equality before law of equal protection of the law in the territory of India. Article 15 further illustrates and fortifies the right to equality by saying that the state shall not discriminate against any citizen on grounds only of religion, race, caste, sex, place of birth or any of them. It further provides that nothing in this article stops the state from making any special provision for women and children. Article 16 provides equality of opportunities for all citizens in subjects of employment or appointment to any office under the state.

Besides, Article 42 provides that the state shall make provision for securing just and humane conditions of work and for maternity relief. A uniform civil code is envisaged throughout the territory of India in Article 44 of the Constitution.

Women have the right to obtain education to be able to do any work they selected to do. According to Article 29 (2) of the Constitution "no citizen shall be denied admission to any educational institution maintained by the state or receiving aid out of state funds on grounds only of religion, sex, race, caste, language or any of them."

Despite the liberal provisions made to ensure equality to all citizens and thereby women as well, the latter continue to suffer from oppression in the male dominated society.

New Acts

In the pre-independence period, the woman had no property rights. She was not legally authorised to adopt a child nor could she validly marry her daughter and a mother could also not fix a guardian for her children by will. These and many other infirmities undermined the position of women. Attempt to reduce and remove the infirmities were made by enacting four Acts of Parliament. The Hindu Marriage Act 1955 makes monogamy the rule for both men and women. Divorce is allowed under certain conditions and petition for divorce can be filed either by the husband or wife. The Hindus Succession Act, 1956 empowered the Hindu women to inherit property. The ground of heirship mentioned in the Schedule to this Act is blood relationship and the daughters, widow and mother of the late male inherit equally with the son. According to the Hindu Adoption and Maintenance Act, the woman can adopt a child if she be a widow or divorced or if her husband had become hermit or apostate or has been declared having unsound mind by competent court. In case the husband wishes to adopt a child, permission of the wife is necessary. Under the Hindu Minority Guardianship Act, 1956 a wife is entitled to maintenance under certain conditions and circumstances. She may stay separately from her husband without forfeiting her right to maintenance. Children both legitimate and illegitimate are entitled to be maintained by parents. This right can be applied to those who inherit the estate of the deceased.

Besides, these four Acts, many other laws have been passed to abolish undesirable practices and protect, promote and safeguard the female interests. Some are Dowry Act, Suppression of Prostitution and Immoral Traffic Act, 1958; Plantation Labour Act, 1951; Mines Act, 1952; and Factories Act, 1958. These laws were an advanced measure but for the major part, decorated the statute books, for women always failed to avail the provisions made therein. In many cases illiteracy, lack of information and awareness, costly and long drawn out legal methods discouraged them from going to law courts. The enforcement machinery also was not sufficient to ensure implementation of these laws. Ladies not withstanding these disabilities continued to work for a better deal. In the seventies a fresh look commenced to be taken on the difficulties, particularly after a committee established by the government produced the report of the Committee on Status of Women in India "Towards Equality" (1974). Now onwards the discussion on law and women was a departure from the part in the sense that stress shifted from removing discrimination against women to paying attention on the gender bias in the law and inviting attention to the violence and oppression against women within the home. This attitude and a new concept produced several important amendments to the prevailing laws and initiation of new bills.

The year 1976 watched passing of Bill for Equal Remuneration to men and women for the same sort of work. Another progressive step was adopted by amending the Factories Act which made it necessary on part of employer to provide creches for the children of working mothers in the factories. At about the same time Maternity Benefit was extended to those women who hitherto were not covered under the Act of 1958.

The laws concerning dowry, rape and violence against women were amended to make them more stringent to ensure that the guilty were punished. For example, in case of violence against women, the Criminal Law Amendment Act, 1983 recognised for the first time domestic violence committed by the husband or any of his relations and such a violence became a crime under the Act. The Law was also amended and it provided that if a married women committed suicide within seven years of her marriage, her husband or his relations would be presumed to have abetted the suicide (Section 113/4 of the Indian Evidence Act of 1872).

Similarly, the changes that were incorporated in the Act 1983 regarding rape were in the interest of women. The Act enjoined that the victim should be saved from the glare of publicity during investigation and trial. The definition of rape also changed the element of consent removed. The burden of proving one's innocence was transferred to the accused. Prevention of *Sati* Act was passed in 1987 which was preceded by amendment to the Dowry Act of 1961 in 1984 and again in 1986. The amendments were made basically to plug the loopholes. The crime has been made cognisable and non-bailable. It also provided for Dowry Prohibition Officers at State level.

The other advanced legislations/amendments related to abortion, matrimony, divorce, right to children and right to property, maintenance, family courts for fast settlements of disputes besides many more bills introduced to ensure a strong legal structure towards achieving equality and improving the destiny of women.

The legal framework, even though a step forward and an enabling aspect in the progress of women, the plethora of Acts could not achieve the desired results. For in the case of social legislation it is also mandatory to change the outlook, in the perception of women's role and support services. All these have been very slow to reach. Resultantly even after more than a century of social reforms, the change though discernible is remote from being indicative of equality between men and women.

The overview of the condition is generally distressing. Rape, dowry death, female foeticide, i.e., misuse of sex determination test of the child in the uterus and the abortion of a female foetus are rampant. It was alleged in *The Times of India* dated 12th April, 1991 that between 1978 and 1983, 78,000 female foetuses were aborted after sex determination. This figure is on the conservative side for it is suspicious that each and every case got reported. The Maharashtra Government in reply to the women's groups enacted the Maharashtra Regulation of use of pre-natal Diagnostic Technique Act in April 1988. The misuse of test still prevails. This really indicates the horrible behaviour formula. These may be labelled as psychosicknesses, or uncivilised conduct; but the fact remains that gruesome and a healthy society should get rid of them. A central legislation to remove this crime resided by and once the law is there to implement it sincerely it deserves. The need is all the more urgent due to the provisional figure of sex ratio 929 females for 1000 males made available by the census department in context of the 1991 census. These figures inform us of the existing imbalances in the society.

The melancholy augury of the entire situation is that the offence rates in case of rape, dowry and violence against women are rising. In Delhi alone 132 dowry deaths occured between January 1989 and February 1990 while in the year 1987, rape cases registered in the Union Territory of Delhi were 103, the number increased to 161 in the year 1989 and 26 gang rape cases.

The conditions in the country elsewhere were same. In 1985 the data collected by the Police Research Development Bureau for 22 states displayed 1689 cases of rape, 13,952 cases of molestation, 7,652 of abduct of women and 802 dowry cases registered under different sections of the Penal Code. These figures do not represent the total situation and many cases remain unrepresented.

It has been experienced widely by the social activists and the women's organisations that increase in offence is mainly because there is hardly any deterrent and the accused generally gets away with anything. For example, in the cases of dowry deaths in Delhi over the last four years only one conviction exists and out of 6,500 cases registered with the police on offence against women, there were only 1,500 arrests and all of them were freed on bail. Besides, the Police Research Bureau recorded 3 per cent conviction during the last ten years.

It seems that women had to ask for, agitate, demand and advocate legal remedies to minimise and/or abolish the disabilities inflicted on them. Having acquired this enabling factor, the women have now to fight for the implementation of laws in right earnest. There is still a need for "stringent laws, sensitive judiciary, effective enforcement machinery and vigilant women's groups to deal with such atrocious crime against women". More than anything else, there is a requirement for total revolution in the attitude, their perspective, their thinking that always condemn the women for the crime of which she is the victim and not the perpetrator.

The implementation apart, there are still drawbacks in some of the laws concerning women which should be amended to ensure equality.

Besides the social legislation 'planned change' played a significant role in creating awareness amongst females.

Planned Change

No society is static and as such no two generations are same. Social change is a continuous procedure. Admittedly it is far slower than what is possible in technological progress and scientific discoveries. Social change in some conservative societies is so slow that it remains unnoticed and provides credence to the fact that society is static. Resultantly it becomes significant to induce change to awaken it from the long slumber to which it is accustomed. Over 5,00,000 villages of India where almost 80 per cent of our population lives were no better on the eve of freedom. The leadership and the designs of the country experienced that all around planned change, particularly in the economic sector was necessary. This challenge was met by formulating the First Five Year Plan.

The First Five Year Plan amongst several provisions for development of agriculture and industries required for social education at the Block level with three female functionaries (one at supervisory level and two at the village level) to create awareness and improve their luck and to assist them to manage their houses better, the objective being to make them of development needs so as to ensure that they praised the means and measures that were employed to increase agriculture production.

The planners, however, soon felt that in the entire process of development, participation of the women would be necessary and their welfare and progress had to be alongside the development in other spheres. Two years after the First Five Year Plan became operative, special provisions were framed within the plan to create an autonomous body for the welfare of women, children and the disabled. Thus, the Central Social Welfare Board at the National level and State Social Welfare Advisory Boards at the State level were set up.

The set up of the Boards and Project implementing committees at the project level provide an opportunity to women to link themselves with the designs of programmes and implementing them at the grassroots. Thousands of women appeared to offer their services as volunteers and many of them served on the Boards and assisted in formulating policies. Many more women volunteers worked in the project areas. In many cases these were illiterate women who were perhaps conscious of the problems and were eager to participate to assist in making a better universe for themselves and for womankind in general. It was as if to say that with single stroke the women eager to participate in work outside the home under the strong leadership of Mrs. Durgabai Deshmukh. Mrs. Durgabai Deshmukh remained the first Chairman of the Board for many years. She had the privilege of introducing new programmes and formulating policies and above all observing the voluntary character of the Board. Her leadership in those early days founded sound services. The Board was full of life and always on the march ahead, the zeal and strength of the days of Durgabai became unknown once she deserted the Board.

The Welfare Extension Projects, one of the important programmes of the CSWB (Central Social Welfare Board) had for women and child welfare services aimed at improving the health, adult education, teaching improved skills for the home management, environment sanitation and craft classes with the target of training women in crafts to enable them to increase the family income if they so desired. *Balwadis* for children under six years were a significant component of the project as well. These project centres became women's centres where they could learn new things, meet and discuss and also have some recreation. The welfare extension projects were few but wherever they were started there was a positive effect of the services. In fact the Welfare Extension Projects were the first to have services for women's welfare in the villages.

The later Five Year Plan broadened, the scope of services for women even though for the major portion, the approach remained welfare. In the Second Plan, besides maintaining the welfare services already commenced, the need for implementing the principal of equal wages for equal work was emphasised and provisions for coaching for women to compete for higher jobs was prescribed. This would be seen as a change in the perception of women's topics and recognition of the social infirmities.

The Third Five Year Plan went a step ahead and focussed attention on the female education, promotion of health services with stress on maternal and child health, health education, nutrition and family planning. Under social welfare the largest share was assigned to expanding services in villages, the remarkable feature being the condensed courses for female education which enabled them to pass middle/matric examination in within two years, based on their earlier schooling.

In the next plan, education of women got further impetus. In the sphere of social welfare, the stress shifted from women and children to family welfare. Family welfare centres *(Griha Kalyan Kendras)* were introduced in many places, even though the target group remained unchanged. Larger funds were given for the family planning programme to reduce the birth rate to 40 to 50 per thousand live births. High priority was given to immunisation of pre-school children, pregnant ladies and to supplementary feeding of both these groups apart from the nursing mothers.

The period under the Fifth Five Year Plan collided with the International Year of the Women. The plan as such did not probably have anything innovative, taking hints from the earlier plans it provided weightage to the training factor, saving of women in need, functional education to enable women to perform the duties of a housewife (including, nutrition, health care, domestic economy, etc.).

These years however were significant in the sense that a Report of the Committee on the position of women in India was produced. This committee, after preparing the question relating to the rights and position of women in the context of changing socio-economic conditions and subjects relating to the development of women, said that dynamics of social change and development had adversely affected a large number of women and had created new imbalances and disparities such as shattering sex ratio, lower expectancy of life, higher infant and maternal mortality, low work participation, illiteracy and growing migration.

These disclosures in a way were a disappointed reflection on our development work lasting over two decades. Something had to be done to improve the situation. The Committee on Status of Women in India, (CSWI), Report was put before the Indian Parliament and it was discussed with a great interest shown by the members, particularly the women members. Resultantly women appeared as critical inputs for national development rather than as goals for welfare polices. Their participation was felt to be of great importance in the whole gamut of progress work. It also became known that the process of economic change adversely affected the women. Women's economic liberation was a remote dream. It was strongly felt that the equality envisaged in the Constitution would be of no value unless the right to economic freedom inherent in it becomes a reality.

The recommendations of the CSWI Report accompanied the climate produced by the International Plan of Action for women. The National Plan of Action identified the fields of health, family planning, nutrition, literacy, employment legislation and social welfare for implementing action programmes for ladies. The plan also indicated planned implementation to improve the fate of women.

During these years, various women's organisations became more active, and women activists emphasised the infirmities with which the women constantly suffered. Not only this, a number of meetings, seminars, workshops, etc. were arranged apart from the publication of books, articles in newspapers and research findings which were made public.

The Sixth Plan proved a landmark in the fight for equality. It made important changes in favour of women. For the first time one entire chapter was dedicated in the Sixth Plan to progress of women. The fundamental unit however remained the family rather than the women for development programming.

The Plan also provided for joint titles to men and women. This was one way to access resources which probably would contribute to their growth.

As a follow-up of the National Plan of Action, a Women's Welfare and Development Bureau was set up, in fact the forerunner of the Women and Child Development Department organised under the Ministry of Human Resource Development in 1985.

The Department is a nodal point within the government and it has amongst others, the responsibility of co-ordinating, monitoring and introducing policies and programmes.

The Seventh Plan further "operationalised the concern for equity and empowerment articulated by the International Decade for Women". The stress has been on constructing confidence, disseminating information, providing knowledge about their rights and privileges. Training for economic pursuits and opening new knowledge for employment of women were some of the other fields of concern.

Besides, the women started to access the inputs and productive resources, a method which was introduced in the Sixth Plan in the form of Joint titles. Another salient feature was the recognition of the domestic work, like collection of fuel, fodder, water, etc. In addition supportive services for women and children became a part of the package.

Today besides the Human Resource Ministry having a Department of Women and Child Development, many other Ministries such as Rural Development, Labour, Education, Health, etc. have women's cells. There are also nearly 27 schemes catering to the requirements of women. The University Grants Commission had been instrumental in establishing a Department of Development Studies in various universities in the nation.

All these attempts have certainly produced an environment for working more vigorously towards similarity between men and women. This parity is tough to achieve, at the same time there is an increasing knowledge, women now have attempted to assert to some extent, and there has been a visible transformation in their social position. In this direction the part played by the voluntary organisations, especially the women's groups, is no trivial achievement. Women's groups have sprung up all over the nation. Considering the difficulties and the population, these groups meet only the fringe of the requirement. Nevertheless it is a good start.

The key to the progress is education. Renewed attempts have to be made for girls to have time and opportunities for schooling.

Economic Independence

Women have always taken part in the economic activity of the society ever since man placed his foot on this earth. It is however a different matter that her work has been concealed behind a thick veil in the male-dominated society.

The women have been involved in domestic crafts, in the agriculture sector, in the household front, in finding fuel and water for the family and fodder for the animals. Certain agriculture related jobs are performed by women like transplanting, cutting and harvesting, etc. Even in the household industry, whether it is the handloom or the potters wheel, she is present to perform the job of preparing the stuff, colouring it and in the case of pottery, of baking it. This is all apart from the six or seven hours job that is performed by her in the house, like cooking, washing, cleaning, bearing children, etc. Since she get no cash money or wages, she is termed as dependent. She performs the necessary jobs, it may also be that without her contribution, the household expenses are difficult to meet, yet she is neither regarded economically productive nor the bread winner.

However, with the advocacy being conducted for the cause of female, there is greater feeling at least on the women's part, though not extensively, of economic freedom. Economic independence is necessary to ensure parity among women and men. Pandit Jawaharlal Nehru rightly said, "The habit of looking upon marriage as a profession almost and as the sole economic refuge for women, will have to go before women can have any freedom. Freedom depends on economic conditions even more than political ones and if a woman is not economically free and self-earning, she will have to depend on her husband or on someone else and dependents are never free. The association of man and woman should be of perfect freedom and perfect comradeship with no dependence of one or the other."

The data on employment condition leading to economic freedom and overall contribution of women to the economic growth and economic health of the family, is neither accurate nor sufficient, since there are variations in the figures available and this variation is created by the definition adopted by each of the organisations/departments like the Census of India, National Sample Survey, the Labour Bureau, etc. In fact, the female employment is generally underestimated. The concept of employment rotated around the cash wage earners, her labour in the farm and in the house having been taken for granted. As per the 1985 report of the UNICEF about 45 per cent of the total number of employed women were unpaid helpers on family farms or non-farm enterprises.

Statistics disclose that women's employment has in the two decades beginning from 1961 displayed that female work participation was 28 per cent. In the subsequent census in 1971, it lowered to 14.2 per cent and by 1981 it again increased to 20.85 per cent, lower than that of the 1961 figures. The main cause for variation in the figures appears to be as the workers were defined very narrowly in the 1971 census. This was somewhat corrected at the time of 1981 census and the scope of the definition was broadened. The census of 1981 introduced a category of marginal workers which covered many women.

There were 44.97 million, or 13.99 per cent were ladies main workers out of the total population of 321.93 million ladies (1981). In case of villages the percentage of prime workers was 16 while in case of town the percentage was 7.28. Further, of the 44.97 million main workers in the nation (excluding Assam) the majority, that is, 20.77 million or 46.18 per cent were agriculture labour, 14.93 million or 33.20 per cent were cultivators, 20.6 million or 4.59 per cent worked in household industry and 7.21 million or 16.03 per cent were involved in other activities.

Among the women dominated industries in 1981, *bidi* making had the highest proportion as there were 1,549 ladies per 1,000 male *bidi* workers. The ratio of male-female workers was considerably low with regard to women in industries like manufacture of transport equipment and parts, manufacture of electrical machinery, apparatus and machines, etc.

Women, besides being entrepreneurs, are also joining enterprises being run by others for money. This phenomenon is visible in village as wells as in towns. However, in villages the number of self-employed women has lowered from 356 thousand in 1971 to 325 thousand in 1981. In towns the picture is different. There has been a fairly good increase of 33.07 per cent.

The employment of women has also not kept pace with the increase in population. In the last few decades of planning, the women population has increased by 55 per cent while the female work force only by 15 per cent. This decline may remain a decline in the women population as compared to the male population. The literacy rates among ladies are low, there are also some women at the decision-making level. Inspite of these handicaps, there is qualitative improvement, in the sense, that there is diversity of profession and ladies are now found as physicians, nurses, teachers, administrators, bankers, entrepreneurs, in fact there is no such profession where women are not now working. The number of women in such cases is limited.

Women have taken responsibilities outside the home. They have performed equally well if not better than men. It has however been a tough task to leave the home and find jobs outside. It has also been difficult for them to move up the ladder.

Besides, consideration of home and children weigh heavily with her. Her work, howsoever important, is regarded as of secondary significance. Her first duty even today is regarded to be the home and the children. In fact in her case, always it is the family decision where the employment of ladies is concerned—whether she should work or not, where she should work, what sort of jobs she should have, are all issues where he decision is never final.

Another disgusting factor is that women are not paid for equal work despite the legal provisions that exist. It has been the custom that in the agriculture sector they are paid only 40 to 60 per cent of the male wages. As the time passed, the women's earnings are displaying a downward trend. Between 1964-65 and 1974-75 the difference between the earnings of men and women in the farm sector had increased by 50 per cent. The ladies in the self-employed, home-based industry are facing problems for speedy industrialisation is dislocating them. In most of the cases they are being compelled to work on fixed rates just as for traders, middlemen and small industrialists.

In the recent plans, particularly in the Sixth and Seventh Plan, the stress has been to vocationalise education. Regional Vocational Centres, one each at Bangalore, Bombay and Trivandrum, apart from the National Institute at Delhi, have been introduced. In addition many training institutions have been launched all over the country for women.

The economic activity of the ladies continues to receive attention but economic liberation of women still needs acceptance. Some of the constraints to be looked into are:

(i) Absence of enforcement of social and labour legislation.

(ii) Insufficient access to employment advantages like minimum hours of work, minimum wages, maternal health care, day care for their children, etc.
(iii) New and diverse horizons of employment.
(iv) Inadequate managements for skill training, management training, etc.
(v) Knowledge programme also needs to be strengthened to produce social change.

The voluntary agencies can assist in ensuring better status to the lady workers and increase their bargaining power, at least for equal wages, by nurturing unionisation amongst women. SEWA, a voluntary organisation, has done pioneering duty in this direction.

These voluntary agencies can also launch an awareness programme directed towards the facilities available under the law, the employment opportunities, attitudinal changes and acceptance of the new part of women outside the home. The Labour Ministry and the Social Welfare Department have an important role to play in this area. Economic freedom, besides building confidence in women, will also assist them to take an active part in the political life of the nation.

Political and Administrative Role

Women had participated very actively in the political life of the nation, particularly after Gandhiji led the freedom struggle. They participated in various phases of the struggle. Ladies also fought and won elections after the Congress decided to frame the government under the Government of India Act, 1935. Immediately following the announcement of independence, many women alongside the men were elected to frame the Constitution for independent India.

Some women excelled in the international field. Mrs. Vijayalakshmi Pandit became the first woman President of the UN Assembly, a rare honour for the female of the world. Similarly, Raj Kumari Amrit Kaur became the Vice President of the League of Red Cross, Hansa Mehta and Lakshmi Menon occupied offices in the Human Rights Commission and the UN Commission on the Status of Women. Mrs. Sarojini Naidu became the first Governor of Uttar Pradesh. Afterwards her daughter Padmaja Naidu was the Governor of West Bengal.

Women also fought elections and were elected to both the Central Parliament and the State Assemblies. Some of them became Cabinet Minister, Minister of State, etc. Mrs. Sucheta Kriplani became the Chief Minister of Uttar Pradesh, Shashikala Kakedkar the Chief Minister of Goa, Mrs. Nandini Satpathy, the Chief Minister of Orissa.

Mrs. Indira Gandhi possessed the signal honour of becoming the first woman Prime Minister of India, a position she held for about nineteen years except for a short period when the Janata Party came to power in 1977.

Born on 19 November 1917, in a very comfortable home, Anand Bhavan, Allahabad, Indira Priyadarshini Nehru was the daughter of Pandit Jawaharlal Nehru, the first Prime Minister of free India and a distinguished leader of the freedom struggle. Indira's political association started at four years of age. She watched the trial of her grandfather, Pandit Motilal Nehru, sitting on his lap. Later as a young girl she organised the *Vanar Sena*. Its members, the little children, were to offer water to the marching *Satyagraghis.* They also assisted in distributing literature and carrying messages.

During the Quit-India movement Indira Gandhi became actively engaged in the freedom struggle. She violated the law by taking out processions. The police *lathi* charged, the courageous young Indira continued to hold the tricolour despite the *lathi* blows. Indira rose in the Congress (Indian National Congress) ranks and became its President. She became Prime Minister in the year 1966 after the death of Lal Bahadur Shastri, the then Prime Minister. Her Prime Ministership years have been very eventful. She assisted Bangladesh achieve conquest in its independence war. She provided new direction to the policies and programmes and was internationally honoured as a politician of high calibre. After serving the nation for over three terms, she met with a tragic death in the year 1984.

These women were the exceptions being the children of the circumstances; once the opportunity knocked their door, they exploited it completely and earned a name for themselves.

First elections held in 1951-52, 27 ladies were elected to the Parliament, at the state level only 16 states out of the 25 states (category A, B & C) had ladies MLA's (Member of

Legislative Assembly) with the State of Bihar electing a maximum of 13 female members followed by Uttar Pradesh and Madhya Pradesh with seven each. The position in the next elections remained same. In fact there were 25 ladies members of Parliament in 1957 against 27 in 1951. In the state Assemblies 196 women were elected by 13 states. Bihar again led by electing 33 members. This seesaw war continues even today. There has not been a substantial increase in the number of ladies that have become parliament members. The position as it stands today after more than three decades is that in 1984 elections, 46 seats out of the house of 537 seats were held by women, an improvement over the past years. The Rajya Sabha had 28 ladies in the house of 245 members. There has been greater representation of women in the Rajya Sabha by nomination. In the recent elections (in 1989 there were only 24 women in the Lok Sabha and 24 in the Rajya Sabha), the position is not even comparable with the first elections in 1951.

As far as the political portfolios for women are concerned, these have been slow to approach. Today there is no lady amongst the Cabinet Minister, the courage women State Ministers is negligible. Women are yet remote from participating in the decision-making level.

The participation of female members, both in the state legislative and the central parliament, has been important. They have not only discussed and piloted the bills concerning women's development, dowry, child care, health education, etc., but have taken a deep interest in the debates in specialised topics.

Women, however, have not succeeded to make pressure groups, this may be due to the insignificant number that are returned to the parliament, want of awareness, the voting formula, which is for the major part based on caste and socio-economic position of the candidate, rather than on political ideology, lack of decision-making power. And as such participation of female at the district, state and national level is not commensurate with their numbers. It is also tough for women to participate in the political life in view of the stringent social usages besides the socio-economic barriers.

Participation of women in the *Panchayati Raj* Institution has been low. There has hardly been any engagement of women in the *Panchayati Raj* Institutions. Their participation was sought to be ensured by nomination of one or two female members wherever they could not be elected. There has been in the recent years intention for providing 30 per cent representation to women. Andhra Pradesh and Karnataka already have 30 and 25 per cent seats respectively for women.

Political parties have really shown the interest required to organise the women power. The which has many women members had had only one female President of the Congress in Mrs. Indira Gandhi after freedom. The Bharatiya Janata Party (BJP) has one woman Vice-President. Mrs. Vijayraje Scindia. Despite the fact that each of the political parties now launch their programme for women and exhibit concern for them, in actual practice very few female candidates are fielded in the elections.

Non-Governmental Sectors

Women's contribution in the non-governmental sector also had been appreciating. Besides championing the cause of women and seeking improvement in their position, they have launched programmes of protection and development.

The women's cause apart, there have been many organisation launched by women for the welfare of weaker classes of the society. Some of these are the Indian Council for Child Welfare, the Family Planning Association, etc. In recent years women have also participated very actively in the Blood Donation programme, particularly in inspiring the public. All this is being done as a labour of love and for no personal·gains.

The Indian Council for Child Welfare has had distinguished women like Mrs. Indira Gandhi, Hansa Mehta, Pushpa Mehta, Phul Renu Guha, Rajan Nehru, Mrs. Tara Ali Baig and many others as its President.

Mrs. Tara Ali Baig worked for the 'child' for over forty years. Born in Mussorie in 1916, granddaughter of Sir K.G. Gupta and wife of the deceased Mirza Rashid Ali Baig of Diplomatic Services, was a promising workers. She was responsible for introducing and submitting an eight-point National Policy to the government which finally paved the platform for the government to pass the 1974 Policy for Children. Mrs. Baig was the General Secretary of the Council and subsequently became its President. During her tenure new directions were provided to the child welfare work, and it was shifted from its narrow concept to a broader perspective. In fact, she founded the S.O.S. Children's villages in India. Mrs. Baig worked for a transformation in the institutional procedure of children's orphanages and allied institutions.

Mrs. Baig was recognised as an expert on 'child welfare'. She became the President of the International Union for Child Welfare, a world apex body federating 90 nations with child care programmes. Mrs. Baig also had the honour of presiding over the World Congress on the 'child' in Sweden in the year 1969.

Besides being an outstanding social worker, Mrs. Baig was a prolific public orator and an author. She was invited to write the official biography of Smt. Sarojini Naidu. She wrote two books on women and many articles on varied topics.

Another distinguished leader in the cause of women has been Dr. Phul Renu Guha, famous as a worker and educationist. Born on 12 August 1911 in Calcutta, she had her schooling in India and UK. In her initial days she participated in the freedom moment. She was elected to *Rajya Sabha* in 1968 and became the Union Minister of State. She was also Chairman of the Committee established to study the position of women. She has been actively linked with many women's organisations. Her work in Calcutta, both in political and social welfare, is popular and still continues. Even at the age of 80, she remains active, attends meetings and tries her best to solve the difficulties of women.

While Dr. Phul Renu Guha continues her work in Calcutta peacefully, Mrs. Sarojini Vardappan is a name synonymous with social services and women's development in Tamil Nadu. Born in September 1921, in Madras, Mrs. Vardappan's relation with women's work is of over 40 years. She has been Chairman of the Central Social Welfare Board, Chairman of the Red Cross Branch of Tamil Nadu and many similar organisations. Her aim has been to improve the position of women and sponsor programmes for the needy.

Mrs. Vidyaben Shah, born on November 7, 1922, has been a social worker in the area of child welfare. In fact, she began her public career by taking part in the Quit India Movement. Once she was out, never returned and resultantly she has been associated with many organisations involved in child welfare, women and family welfare and other social and relief work. She was also the chair person of CSWB.

As for the child welfare work, it all commenced in Saurashtra, with the child welfare council and later in establishing and developing the famous *Bal Bhavan* at Rajkot. She is today the President of the Indian Council for Child Welfare, a position she has occupied for two terms. During her tenure she has attempted to develop child welfare councils in areas short of them.

Besides these traditional areas, the women have also come into health-related fields and have found new spheres of development. One such sphere is the Voluntary Blood Donation Programme. The need of this programme is urgent, specially in view of the threat posed by AIDS all over the world. Mrs. Kanta Saroop Krishen born in West Punjab, now a part of Pakistan, commenced her social work activities in the pre-partition days. She has been linked with the Red Cross and its Hospital Welfare Section, Women's Defence Council, Bharat Scouts and Guides, and Child Welfare Council. These initial years in the voluntary arena assisted her in developing the Blood Donation Programme. She can aptly be called the founder of this programme in North India and for developing the voluntary feeling all over India. She feels and rightly so, that blood donated by the free desire of the donor for a cause is better than the commercial blood. She has made all out attempts to start voluntary blood donation societies in various parts of the country. Her life's mission has been to spread the concept of voluntary donation and abolish commercialisation of blood.

Mrs. Saroop Krishen can be a proud mother of the movement and says proudly that there is no commercialisation of blood in Chandigarh. After her earlier success in Chandigarh she approached larger areas and along with others founded the Indian Society of Blood Transfusion and Immunohaematology. In 1972, she became its Founder-Secretary General, a position she occupies till today. The ISBTI has had its birth pangs but with remarkable courage, Mrs. Saroop Krishen has steered through tough times.

Her request, her visit, her contacts are not only confined to one area or one class of the society. It may be the school students, the college students, universities, offices and housewives, Mrs. Saroop Krishen has a programme for all of them. She has time for all. For her, a blood donor is a VIP.

There are many other women, who need to be mentioned here but then many more volumes would be required. This short description of women in the work would be incomplete without referring to women in the Family Planning Association, particularly the deceased Lady Rama Rao, the founder of the Association and the current President of the Association, Mrs. A Wadia.

A field where women have to exert completely, are the trade unions. Trade unions have worked as pressure groups. Women workers have co-operated in the activities and programmes of the trade unions. They have taken part in the strikes as well. Unluckily the number of women activists here is small and as such their topics have not been taken up seriously. Despite the expression of concern at various forums, the trade unions have yet to pay adequate attention to women's difficulties. They are issues like equal pay for equal labour, maternity benefits and child care facilities, etc. In fact, no trade union has gone on hartal on these important issues.

It may be pointed out that ladies have supported action and in some cases have initiated action where they felt absolutely wronged. Some of the significant events relate to the Chipko Movement, the politics of alcohol licensing, government water supply in Himachal Pradesh, fight for canal water and public lands by poor ladies in drought-prone Marathwada and battle for self-respect, employment and justice among Tamil Nadu landless workers.

More such attempts are required to restore a place of equality of ladies at par with men.

After more than 40 years of freedom, a change in the position though not dramatic, is discernible, probably because of the social legislation, the development made in education, health or economic area or as a consequence of technological developments, or probably as a process of evolution. There are, though in small numbers, ladies in almost all fields of the national life. They are physicians, engineers, pilots, journalists, teachers and lecturers, administrators, diplomats, head of states, etc. In spite of these achievements, the fact remains that women's condition even today is deplorable. According to the

1981 census there were 933 women for 1,000 men, against nearly 47 per cent educated men only 25 per cent educated women. Dowry deaths, child marriages, perpetuation of widowhood, desire for son in every field of life continues to have social desire.

As for the child marriages, as per the 1981 census out of 321.36 million women, 147.14 million or 45.79 per cent were married; of these 2.63 million or 1.79 per cent were aged 10-14 years. In the villages out of the 115.00 million married women 2.42 million or 2.11 per cent were aged 10-14 years and in the cities out of the 32.14 million, 0.68 per cent were aged 10-14 years.

"The level of current fertility among these girls can be judged from the fact that 20,014 births were reported to these girls. It is quite shocking during the last one year proceeding the 1981 census enumeration were not restricted to first order births but almost 10 per cent of them were of second order. Giving birth to a second child before the age of 14 years is really a reflection on the prevailing social system which needs drastic change."

The condition in the economic front or for her economic liberation is no better. The women's work in the house including collection of firewood, fetching water from remote places, assisting in the family business or in the agricultural fields as it is not remunerative and she is also unpaid for, is not seen as work. The census does not consider it nor is it recognised. It is estimated that of average hours of unpaid duty done by women outside their homes, ranges from 6.1 to 7.5 per day with few women working for 10 hours and more. Besides, 89.51 (1981 census) per cent of the women workers are involved in the unorganised sector. Of these 82.3 per cent are in agriculture allied professions. In the organised sector women form 13.3 per cent of all workers. In the public sector, they account for 11 per cent of the total employment and in the private sector, for 17.8 per cent.

In the senior management employment, women hold 994 posts against 15,993 men in same positions in the All India Services constituting 5.8 per cent. There are only 21 females officers in the Indian Police Service as against 2,418 males

(0.9 per cent). In the Indian Administrative Services, there are 339 ladies against 4,209 men (7.5 per cent).

Besides the concern expressed in other areas, the economic freedom is greatly being championed for women. This in a way, appears to be right course. But has it assisted? The question remains unanswered. The woman is now burdened with two jobs, work within the house and a job outside. Does it really provide her enough free time to enjoy the fruits of her economic freedom? Not only that, she in many cases is probably the custodian of her salary till she reaches home, when it becomes a part of the total family income, the salary having been passed on to the mother-in-law or the husband.

The economic freedom, therefore, is not the total solution; equal stress has also to be on the total development of the woman aware of her rights and responsibilities, recognition of her part and work in the home, awareness amongst the people that ladies are as good citizens as others in this nation. If necessary social system has to change where women do not have to asks for discounts, it is their right and they must get it.

The situation in the political arena is no better. Each of the political parties advocate the principle of women's participation. But do we observe the reflection of their desires in Parliament? The percentage of female members of parliament have been minimising instead of increasing. 27 ladies were elected to the *Lok Sabha* in the first election while 19 were elected/nominated to the Rajya Sabha. Today after 44 years of freedom, there are only 24 females members in Lok Sabha and 24 in the *Rajya Sabha.*

The ladies have to travel a long way before they can be equated with males. Having agreed that they have to travel long way to ensure a place that rightly belongs to them as citizens of India, a concrete action is invited. How do we approach the women in the far and backward areas? How do we make aware, men and women, of the roles and responsibilities of each of the citizens of this nation? How do we introduce acceptance of changed role in the traditional society and how do we ensure that the female child in the family is equally significant if not more as the creator, the producer and the maker? The future lies with her. This is a tough task, it requires both men and women to contribute to this cause. In the past, not only the women who have been in the vanguard of the social reform movement, men have also played distinguished and important roles. It is, therefore mandatory to discard isolation and have men and women participate in this great venture. Let there be a movement, a movement of the sort led by Gandhiji for the national freedom, in which he invited and motivated women to participate. Let the males feel the same concern over the condition of almost 50 per cent of the population which, if not absolutely inhuman, is degrading.

References

Census of India, 1961, 1971, 1981.

Govt. of India, New Delhi, Towards Equality—Report on the Status of Women in India, New Delhi, 1974.

The Tribune, September 23, 1990.

The Times of India, April, 1991.

The Hindustan Times, May 3, 1991.

Indian Management, Special Issue, April, 1988.

Five Year Plan Documents.

Dayal, Rekha (Ed.), *Resource Book on Women and Development*, New Delhi, 1987.

Desai, Dr. Neera, *A Decade of Women's Movement in India,* Bombay, 1988.

Desai, Dr. Neera, *Women in Modern India,* Bombay, 1957.

Hansa Mehta, *Indian Women*, Delhi, 1981.

Mankekar, Kamala, *Women in India*, New Delhi, National Institute of Public Co-operation & Child Development, New Delhi, *Report of the National Workshop on Enforcement Machinery and Women*, Feb 19-20, 1988.

Tara Ali Baig, (ed), *Women of India*, New Delhi, 1957.

Verma, S.C., *Women's Vital Role in Rural Development*, New Delhi.

The Tribune, 23 September, 1990.

The Indian Education Commission Report 1966, Para 53.

Govt. of India, Deptt. of Social Welfare, *Towards Equality – Report of the Committee on the Status of Women in India*, p. 237.

12

The Biographical Notes

Amman, Bee, Abadi Bano Sahiba, popularly known as Bee Amman; mother of the famous Ali Brothers; championed the cause of Hindu-Muslim unity, participated in khilafat movement d. 1924.

Asaf Ali, Aruna, b. 1909; m. Asaf Ali 1928; came in contact with Gandhi and participated in 1930 movement; offered individual satyagraha 1941; was "heroine" of the 1942 struggle, remained underground till 1946; president, Delhi P.C.C. 1947; joined Socialist Party 1948; member, C.P.I. 1955-8; First Mayor of Delhi 1958; joined Congress 1964.

Banerjee, Purnima, offered individual satyagraha 1941; participated in Quit India movement; secretary, Allahabad City Congress Committee; member, U.P. Legislative Council; member, Constituent Assembly 1946; died.

Barua, Kananlata, b. 1926; daughter of Shri Krishna Kanta Barua; as a student, took part in Quit India movement; led a procession to the Golpur police station for hoisting the national flag; shot and killed by the police while hoisting the flag on Sept. 20, 1942.

Basanti Devi, b. 1880; m. C.R. Das 1897; joined politics 1917; participated in non-cooperation movement 1921; withdrew from politics after death of C.R. Das in 1925; d. 1974.

Bhattacharjee, Kalyani, daughter of Beni Madhav Das, principal of Ravenshaw Collegiate School, Cuttack; sister of Bina Bhowmick (nee Das); associated with revolutionary movement in Bengal 1930-8.

Besant, Annie, b. 1847; came to India 1893; translated Bhagvad Gita 1895; established Banaras Central Hindu College 1898 which formed the nucleus of B.H.U.; president, Theosophical Society 1907-33; editor, *New India* and *Commonwealth*;

founded Home Rule League 1915-16; president, Indian National Congress 1917; started Indian Women's Association 1917; eminent educationist, politician and social reformer; d. 1933.

Cama, Madam K.R., b. 1861; daughter of Jijibai and Sorabji Framji Patel; attended the socialist conference at Stuttgart 1907; worked for India's freedom in Europe; closely associated with Shyamaji Krishnavarma as also with Savarkar, Sardar Singh Rana, Viren Chattopadhyaya; returned to India 1935; d. 1936.

Captain, Perin, b. 1888; grand-daughter of Dadabhai Naoroji; educated in Bombay and Paris; political worker since 1910; took to khadi work 1920; one of the founders of Rashtriya Stree Sabha; first woman "Dictator", Bombay Provincial Congress Committee during 1930 satyagraha; suffered imprisonment on several occasions; d. 1958.

Chattopadhyaya, Kamaladevi, b. 1903; educated in London; joined Congress 1922; first woman to contest election 1926; secretary, All India Women's Conference; took part in freedom movement throughout; founder organiser of Congress Socialist Party, presided at its Meerut Session 1936; member, Congress Working Committee, 1946.

Chaudhurani, Saraladevi, b. 1872; grand-daughter of Debendra Nath Tagore, daughter of Swarnakumari and Jankinath Ghoshal; m. Pandit Rambhuj Dutt; taught in Maharani School, Mysore; private secretary to the Maharani for some time; worked in the swadeshi movement 1905; edited *Hindustan*; prominent woman leader, worked for the upliftment of women; d. 1954.

Chowdhury, Malti, m. Nabakrushna Chowdhury; educated at Santiniketan; participated in the 1930, 1932 and 1942 movements; associated with Utkal Navajivan Mandal; member, Constituent Assembly 1946.

Cousins, Margaret Elizabeth, b. 1878; educated at Royal University of Ireland 1902, taught music at school in Dublin; m. James Henry Cousins 1903; founded Irish Women's Franchise League, was its Honorary Treasurer in England and Ireland; imprisoned during the suffrage movement; came to India to join Annie Besant 1915; taught at theosophical schools; associated with Indian National Congress 1917; senator, National University (India); associated with the All India Women's Conference; imprisoned 1932-3; edited *Stri Dharma*; d. 1954.

Cursetjee, Miss Shirinbai Manekjee, b. 1844; founded National Indian Association 1881; founded the work guild 1892; founded the Stri Zarthasti Mandal with Mrs. Pattuck 1903; trustee and member, managing committee, Bai Avabai Petit Parsi Girls' Orphanage since its formation 1911; member committee, Cama Oriental Institute of the Adams Wylie Hospital run by Parsi Charitable Organisation Society; organiser of the Presidency Women's Association; died.

Dande, Kamal, wife of Prabhakar Dande, was shot dead during demonstration connected with Naval Munity in Bombay, 1946.

Das, Bina, b. 1911; daughter of Sarala and Benimadhav Das; took part in anti-Simon demonstration; volunteer, Calcutta Congress 1928; fired at Stanley Jackson, Governor of Bengal on Feb. 6, 1932; imprisoned 1932-9; member, Bengal Legislative Assembly 1946-51.

Das, Santi (nee Ghose), b. 1916; daughter of Devendranath Ghose; came in contact with Jugantar Party; shot Stevens, District Magistrate of Comilla; sentenced to transportation for life; released 1937; m. 1942.

Das Gupta, Kamla, b. 1907; joined Jugantar Party; arrested in connection with Dalhousie Bomb Case 1930; again arrested 1933 in connection with Jackson shooting case; joined Congress 1938; Secretary, Women's Sub-committee of the B.P.C.C. 1941; participated in Quit India movement and sentenced; relief work in Calcutta; Noakhali and Comilla 1946-8; edited monthly *Mandira*.

Desai, Bhaktibehn, b. at Limbdi in Surendranagar District of Gujarat; m. Darbar Gopaldas, ruler of a small state in Kathiawar; participated in Nagpur Flag Satyagraha 1921, Borsad 1923-4 and Bardoli satyagraha 1928; imprisoned several times; significant role in awakening of women in Gujarat.

Deshmukh, Durgabai, b. 1909; her mother was secretary, Rajamundry D.C.C.; started Girls' Hindi School 1923; participated in salt satyagraha; law graduate Madras

University 1942; member, Constituent Assembly 1946-50; chairman, National Committee on Women's Education 1958; associated with many social organizations; m. C.D. Deshmukh 1952.

Gandhi, Indira, b. 1917; daughter of Kamala and Jawaharlal Nehru; educated at Geneva (Switzerland), Poona, Bombay, Santiniketan, Oxford; founded Bal Charkha Sangh and Vanar Sena 1929 – children's organization to help 1930 movement; worked in slum areas among untouchables as a student in Poona; m. Feroze Gandhi 1942; participated in Quit India movement and was imprisoned 1942; worked in riot-affected areas of Delhi 1947; founder chairman, Bal Sahyog 1954; president, Indian Council of Child Welfare, 1958-64; vice-chairman, Central Social Welfare Board 1953-7; president, All India Youth Congress 1956; president, Indian National Congress, 1959-60; member, Executive Board, UNESCO 1960-4; minister for Information & Broadcasting, Government of India, 1964-6; Prime Minister of India since 1966.

Gandhi, Kasturba, b. 1869; wife of Gandhi; identified herself with the work of her great husband; joined Gandhi in South Africa 1897; participated and led women's satyagraha in South Africa; soul of the Phoenix Settlement 1904-14; nurtured ashrams at Kochnab, Sabarmati and Sevagram; worked with Gandhi at Champaran 1917; active part in Kaira Satyagraha 1918; courted arrest 1930, 1932; participated in Rajkot satyagraha 1938; worked with the untouchables; d. 1944.

Ganguli, Kadambini, b. 1862; daughter of Brajakisore Basu; m. Dwarkanath Gangopadhyaya; educated in England; attended Congress sessions 1889, 1890; first woman graduate of Calcutta University, first woman doctor of Bengal and first woman delegate to address the Indian National Congress 1890.

Ghose, Suniti, (nee Choudhury), b. 1917; daughter of Umacharan Choudhury; joined Jugantar Party, shot at Stevens, Distt. Magistrate of Comilla 1931, sentenced to life imprisonment; m. 1947.

Gokhale, Avantikabai, b. 1882; worked as midwife 1904-12; joined Social Service League 1913; met Gandhi 1916;

worked with him in Champaran 1917; started Hind Mahila Society Bombay 1918; member, Bombay Municipality for years from 1926; one of the founders of Desh Sevika Dal Bombay 1930; d. 1949.

Gowarmma (Venkataramaiya, K.A.), b. 1911; trained in Hindustani Seva Dal's training camp 1932; participated in no-tax campaign in North Kanara 1931; subjected to severe police beatings; imprisoned; assisted "Balakashram" home for the children of participants in the no-tax campaign in Kanara 1933.

Ikramullah, Begum Shaista S., b. 1915; daughter of Sir Hassan Suhravardy; m. Jkramullah I.C.S. 1933; member, Delhi Women's League; convener, All India Muslim Student's Federation; member, Constituent Assembly 1946 and member, Constituent Assembly of Pakistan 1948.

Joshi, Kalpana (nee Dutt), b. 1914; daughter of Shobhanadevi and Binodbehari Dutt; participated in college students' strike 1930; joined Indian Republican Army 1931; connected with Chittagong Armoury Raid 1933; closely associated with Surya Sen; sentenced to life imprisonment 1933; member, C.P.I. 1942; m. P.C. Joshi 1943.

Kale, Ansuyabai, b. 1896; member, C.P. Legislative Council 1928; member, International Labour Organization 1929; resigned Legislative Council, joined satyagraha movement 1930; member, A.I.C.C. 1932; president Nagpur Congress Committee 1935; president, C.P. Harijan Conference 1936; president, All India Women's Conference 1947; member, Lok Sabha 1952-7.

Kanitkar, Kashibai, b. 1861; author and novelist.

Kanuga, Nandubehn, b. 1887; wife of Dr. Balvantrai Kanuga, a close associate of Sardar Patel; joined non-cooperation movement 1920-1; leader of Women Volunteers (*Swayam Sevikas*) Ahmedabad Congress 1921; participated in civil disobedience movement 1930-2; elected member, Bombay Legislative Assembly 1937; participated in quit India movement and suffered imprisonment; d. 1950.

Kaul, Rajpati, mother of Kamala Nehru; participated in 1930, 1932 freedom movement in Delhi; imprisoned in Lahore jail; was injured during demonstration organized in front of the courts in Delhi 1932; d. 1949.

Kripalani, Sucheta, b. 1908; taught history at Banaras Hindu University; secretary, Foreign Affairs Department as well as women's section of the Indian National Congress 1939-41; participated in 1942 movement; member, Constituent Assembly 1946; member, Congress Working Committee 1948-51; member, Provisional Parliament 1950-52; member, Lok Sabha 1952-6, 1957-60 and 1967-70; minister, U.P. 1960-2; Chief Minister U.P. 1962-7; d. 1974.

Kundapur, Umabai, b. 1892; participated in non-cooperation movement 1921; hony. secretary, Women's Association 1921; founded Hubli Bhagini Samaj 1922; in-charge Tilak Kanya Shala Hubli 1922; captain, Women's Volunteer Corps at Belgaum Congress 1924; "Dictator" 1932 movement; imprisoned 1932; engaged in Bihar earthquake relief work 1934; member, Provincial Adult Education Board, Bombay 1937; connected with Kasturba Gandhi Memorial Trust.

Mehta, Hansa, b. 1897; educated at Baroda, London, m. Dr. Jivraj Mehta 1924; prominent woman leader; participated in Simon Commission demonstration 1928, civil disobedience movement 1930; president, Bombay P.C.C. 1930; member, A.I.C.C. 1931; imprisoned 1930, 1932; elected to Bombay Legislative Council 1931; member, Constituent Assembly 1946; founder Vice-Chancellor, M.S. University of Baroda, 1949-58.

Mehta, Sharda, b. 1882; daughter of Balabehn and Gopilal Manilal Dhruv; graduated 1901; m. Dr. Sumant Mehta; organised movement against *girmitia* system 1917; associated with Indulal Yajnik in editing *Navajivan* 1919; helped Whitley Commission in surveying Ahmedabad mill-workers 1929; participated in 1930 movement; member, Ahmedabad municipality 1931-5; associated with Baroda Praja Mandal; one of the founders of Jyoti Sangh, Ahmedabad 1934; d. 1970.

Mehta, Usha, b. 1920; connected with underground Congress Radio during Quit India movement Bombay; imprisoned; at present, teachers at Bombay University.

Moodaliar, Vallamah Moonsamy, b. 1898 at Johannesburg in South Africa; participated in the satyagraha led by Gandhi in South Africa; d. 1914.

Naidu, Sarojini, b. 1879 at Hyderabad; daughter of Barada Sundari and Aghornath Chattopadhyaya; educated in England; m. Dr. G. Naidu in Madras 1898; renowned poetess, prominent politician, president, Indian National Congress 1925; attended second R.T.C. in London; Governor, U.P. 1947-9; d. 1949.

Naoroji, Khurshedbehn, b. 1894; grand-daughter of Dadabhai Naoroji, participated in salt satyagraha, 1930; worked with Khan Abdul Ghaffar Khan in N.W.F.P.; imprisoned several times during 1930-45; was associated with Gandhian institution; d. 1966.

Nawaz, Begum Shah, b. 1896; daughter of Sir Muhammed Shafi; m. Mian Shah Nawaz 1911; responsible for getting a resolution passed against polygamy at the All India Muslim Women's Conference 1917; member, Punjab Film Censor Board 1926; first woman on the executive committee of the All India Muslim League; woman delegate to London R.T.C. 1930-32.

Nayar, Sushila, b. 1914; doctor, participated in the freedom movement; attended on Gandhi at Aga Khan Palace 1942-4; member, Delhi State Vidhan Sabha 1952-6; minister, Delhi State 1952-5; speaker, Delhi State Assembly 1955-6; minister for health, Government of India 1962-7.

Nehru, Kamala, b. 1899; daughter of Rajpati and Jawaharmul Kaul; m. Jawaharlal Nehru 1916; participated in national movement; president, Allahabad D.C.C. 1930, suffered imprisonment 1931; established hospital in Swaraj Bhawan; and played an important part in the awakening of women; d. 1936.

Nehru, Rameshwari, b. 1886; daughter of Raja Narendranath; m. Brijlal Nehru; edited *Istri Darpan* for several years; social secretary, All India Women's Conference; member, Age of Consent Committee; president, London Committee of Indian Women's Association; president of Women's Committee of the Indian League 1931-3; d. 1966.

Nehru, Swarup Rani, b. 1869; wife of Motilal Nehru and mother of Jawaharlal Nehru; took part in freedom movement, lathi-charged in April 1932; arrested in 1933 while on her way to Calcutta Congress; d. 1938.

Nikambe, Shantibai, b. 1865; visited Europe and America 1896, 1913; prominent social worker and nationalist; headmistress, Aden Girls' School 1886-90; inspectress, Girls' Primary Schools, Bombay; conducted school for married women 1912-34; assisted Pandita Ramabai in the Sharda Sadan High School 1890.

Nilkanth, Vidyagauri, b. 1876; daughter of Balabehn and Gopilal Manilal Dhruv; m. Ramanbhai Nilkanth 1889; first Gujarat woman graduate; started Ladies Club 1902, *Mahila Mandal* 1914; president, All India Women's Council, Ahmedabad 1926-35, All India Women's Conference 1932-3; president, Women Labourers' Conference Bombay 1933; president, Harijan Sevak Sangh, Ahmedabad; returned her Kaiser-i-Hind medal and resigned her municipal seat in protest against the repressive policy of the Government 1930; d. 1958.

Nivedita, Sister, alias Margaret Elizabeth Noble, b. 1867; in Ireland; eldest daughter of Samuel Richmond and Mary Isabel, a teacher; attracted to Swami Vivekananda's teachings; came to India 1898; was given the name Nivedita by Swami Vivekananda 1889; engaged in plague relief work 1899; worked in the swadeshi movement and national awakening in Bengal 1902-6; designed a "national" flag for India 1905; author, sometime editor, *Karmayogin*; d. 1911.

Pandit, Vijaya Lakshmi, b. 1900; daughter of Swarup Rani and Motilal Nehru; m. R.S. Pandit 1921; participated in freedom movement; imprisoned 1931, 1932, 1941, 1942; member, Allahabad Municipality 1936; minister, U.P. 1937-9; 1946-7; member, Constituent Assembly; member, Lok Sabha; 1952-7; 1962-7; served as Indian Ambassador to USSR 1947-9, USA 1949-51, High Commissioner U.K. 1955-61; president, U.N. General Assembly 1953-4; Governor of Maharashtra, 1960-4.

Pandita Ramabai, b. 1858, daughter of Lakshmibai and Anant Padmanabha Dongre; m. Bipin Bihari Das Medhavi; sudra by caste; gave evidence in Marathi before Hunter Commission 1883; became Christian 1883; founded Sharda Sadan 1889; renowned social reformer, worked for the upliftment of Indian women; d. 1922.

Panjikar, Krishnabai, b. 1906; first m. Gulwadi 1917; became widow after six months; m. Panjikar; a teacher; opened primary school at Dharwar; started Women's Association Dharwar; participated in salt satyagraha; imprisoned 1932; participated in 1942 movement; d. 1959.

Parvati Devi, b. 1901; wife of Chaturbhuj Didwania; prominent member of Delhi Congress Mahila Sangh; organised Bal Sena; worked in Rajasthan along with Jamnalal Bajaj; took part in the civil disobedience movement 1930 and the Quit India movement.

Patel, Maniben, b. 1903; daughter of Vallabhbhai Patel; took part in non-cooperation movement 1920, and actively associated with later freedom movement; imprisoned 1930, 1933-4, 1938-9, 1940, 1942-5; personal assistant to Sardar Vallabhbhai Patel, 1930-50; member, A.I.C.C. 1951; secretary, Gujarat P.C.C. 1953-6; member, Lok Sabha 1952-7; connected with numerous educational and social organisations.

Petit, Mithubehn, b. 1892; met Gandhi in 1915; secretary, khadi section of Women's League Bombay; started an association with Kasturba Gandhi Women's Swaraj League 1930; participated in the Borsad and Bardoli satyagraha and the Quit India movement; died.

Prabhavati Devi, b. 1906; daughter of Babu Kishore Prasad, an associate of Gandhi in Champaran satyagraha; m. Jayaprakash Narayan; worked at Sabarmati Ashram; worked with Kamala Nehru in Allahabad for national awakening and uplift of women; d. 1973.

Raiji, Jaishri, b. 1895; sister of Hansa Mehta; graduate Bombay university, member, Bombay university senate; took part in civil disobedience movement 1930 and Quit India movement; member, Bombay Corporation; member, Lok Sabha 1950-7.

Ranadive, Kusum; sister of the well-known communist leader, B.T. Ranadive; was wounded in police firing during the Naval Mutiny in Bombay 1946.

Rasul, Begum Aizaz, b. 1909; daughter of Nawab Sir Zulfiqar Ali Khan; m. Nawab Aizaz Rasul of Sandila; member, U.P. Legislative Council 1937-53, its Deputy President, 1937-

40; member, Constituent Assembly 1946-50; member, Rajya Sabha 1952-6, U.P. Vidhan Parishad 1958-68; minister, U.P. 1969-71.

Ray, Renuka, b. 1903; social secretary, All India Women's Conference 1934; member, Indian Legislative Assembly 1942-5; president, All India Women's Conference 1953-5; member, West Bengal Legislative Assembly 1952-7.

Reddi, S. Muthulakshmi, b. 1886; bachelor of medicine 1912; member, Indian Women's Association 1917, its president after Annie Besant; president, All India Women's Conference 1930; vice-president, Madras Vigilance Association; secretary, Madras Children's Aid Society 1924-36, first woman member, Madras Legislative Council 1926-30; elected Deputy President of the Council; first Alderman of the Madras City Corporation; member, Hartog Committee 1928; resigned from Legislative Council in protest against the arrest of Gandhi; started Arvai Home and Orphanage 1930; one of the three women who gave evidence before Parliamentary Joint Select Committee 1933; chairman of the Madras State Social Welfare Board 1954-7; d. 1968.

Roy, Lila, b. 1900; participated in non-cooperation movement 1921; assistant secretary, Bengal Women's Suffrage Committee 1921; member *Sri Sangha* 1925-37; opened "Chhatri Bhavan" in Calcutta 1930; participated in the salt satyagraha 1930; formed Dacca Mahila Satyagraha Sangh 1930; edited *Jayasree* 1930; joined Congress 1937; member, Women's Sub-committee of the National Planning Committee; associated with Subhas Bose; member, Central Committee of Forward Block; member, Constituent Assembly 1946; joined Congress 1949; joined P.S.P. 1954; d. 1970.

Sahagal, Manmohini, b. 1919; daughter of Lado Rani and Ladli Prasad Zutshi; educated at Lahore; president, Lahore Students' Union; participated in civil disobedience movement 1930; member, Punjab P.C.C.; general secretary, National Council of Women 1945.

Sarabhai, Ansuyabehn, b. 1885; sister of Ambalal Sarabhai; educated in England; associated with Gandhi in the first labour strike of Ahmedabad 1918; closely connected with Major Mahajan Sangh Ahmedabad; prominent social worker and philanthropist; d. 1972.

Sarabhai, Mridula, b. 1911; daughter of Sarla and Ambalal Sarabhai; organized youth movement in Ahmedabad 1927; participated in salt satyagraha at Ahmedabad 1930, Rajkot satyargaha 1938; helped I.N.A. trials 1946; imprisoned several times; general secretary A.I.C.C. 1946; worked in riot-affected areas 1947; known later for her strong views on Kashmir; d. 1974.

Sarabhai, Sarladevi, b. 1896; wife of well-known industrial magnate, Ambala Sarabhai; came under influence of Gandhi 1930; eminent philanthropist and social worker; mother of Vikram Sarabhai and Mridula Sarabhai.

Satyavati, b. 1907; grand-daughter of Swami Shraddhanand; one of the founders of Naujawan Bharat Sabha in Delhi; participated in salt satyagraha 1930; prominent part in Delhi political awakening; member of the Congress Socialist Party; d. 1945.

Sehgal, Lakshmi (nee Swaminadhan), b. 1914; daughter of Ammu and S. Swaminadhan; private medical practitioner Singapore 1940-3; secretary, women's section, Indian Independence League, Singapore 1942-3; joined I.N.A. 1943; minister, Provisional Government of Azad Hind 1943-5.

Sheth, Indumati, b. 1906; graduated from Gujarat Vidyapith 1926; participated in Quit India movement and suffered imprisonment; minister, Bombay 1946-56; member, Social Welfare Board 1958-62; president, Ahmedabad City Congress Committee 1958-62; education minister, Gujarat, 1962-7.

Sipahimalani (Miss) J.T., b. 1906; principal, Bal Mandir, Karachi; engaged in khadi and hospital work; first woman member, Karachi Municipality; took leading part in the civil disobedience movement 1930-2; suffered imprisonment; speaker, Sind Legislative Assembly.

Subharoyan, Mrs.; daughter of Rai Saheb K. Rangarao, the well-known social reformer of South Kanara; m. Dr. Subbaroyan, zamindar of Kumarmanglam; member, Madras University Syndicate and Senate 1923-6; president, Madras

Women's Conference 1928; chairman, Women's Purdah Clubs, Madras and Ootacumund; engaged in upliftment of women and children; participated in freedom movement.

Sushila Devi, b. 1904; wife of Shamji Mohan; closely associated with Bhagat Singh and his group; took part in the civil disobedience movement 1932-4; and Quit India movement; imprisoned several times; d. 1963.

Swaminadhan, Ammu, b. 1894; daughter of P. Govinda Menon; m. Dr. S. Swaminadhan 1908; treasurer, Indian women's Association since 1924; attended International Women's Conference, Paris 1926; held positions of secretary, vice-president and chairman, All India Women's Conference; member, Madras Corporation 1934-9; participated in Quit India movement; member, Central Assembly 1945 and Constituent Assembly 1946; member, Provisional Parliament and Lok Sabha 1952-7.

Swarnakumari Devi, b. 1885; fourth daughter of Debendranath Tagore; wife of Jankinath Ghoshal; attended Congress Session 1889, 1890; founded "Sakhi Samiti'; edited *Bharati;* was a novelist, poetess and social worker; d. 1932.

Tata, Herabai Ardeshir, member, Bombay Theosophical Society; in collaboration with Mrs. Besant founded Bombay branch of Indian Women's Association; member of Women's Delegation led by Sarojini Naidu which waited on Montagu when he visited India in 1917; went to England along with women leaders to plead for women's rights 1919; d. 1941.

Tata, Mithan Ardeshir, b. 1898; Bar-at-Law; member of Women's delegation sent to England to press for voting rights for women 1919; took interest in social work and women's movement.

Urmila Devi, b. 1883; sister of C.R. Das; participated in non-cooperation movement; organised Nari Karma Mandir and Nari Satyagraha Samiti 1930; toured South India for eradication of untouchability 1933; worked with Gandhi in Noakhali 1946; d. 1956.

Vaidya, Gangabehn, b. 1878; m. Meghjibhai; widow at 16; met Gandhi 1919; helped in collections for Tilak Swaraj Fund 1922; moved to Sabarmati ashram; participated in civil disobedience movement 1930; imprisoned; engaged in social work and village uplift.

Velayudhan, Dakshayani, [m.] R. Velayudhan 1941; member, Legislative Assembly, Cochin State; member, Constituent Assembly 1946-50 and Provisional Parliament 1950-2.

Waddadar, Preeti, b. 1911; member, *Dipali Sangh* (a student's organisation, Dacca); member, Chhatri Sangh, Calcutta; worked with Surya Sen, led an unsuccessful attack on the Pahartali European Club at Chittagong on Sept. 24, 1932; committed suicide on the spot by swallowing potassium cyanide.

Zutshi, Lado Rani, b. 1882; daughter of Janak Rani and Jeewan Lal Tikku; m. Ladli Prasad Zutshi, nephew (sister's son) of Motilal Nehru; founded Mahila Sammelan in Allahabad, founded Kumari Sabha, organized Ladies Recreation Club, Lahore; actively participated in the freedom movement; d. 1968.

Bibliography

I

All India I.N.A. Enquiry and Relief Committee, *The I.N.A. Speaks,* New Delhi: Rajkamal Publications, 1946.

Ahluwalia, B.K. and Ahluwalia, Shashi, *Netaji and Gandhi,* New Delhi : Indian Academic Publishers, 1982.

Ahluwalia, B.K. and Ahluwalia, Shashi, *Netaji and Indian Independence,* New Delhi : Harnam Publications, 1983.

Arya, Manawati, 'The Rani of Jhansi Regiment in Burma,' *The Oracle,* Vol. II, No. 2, April 1980.

Athinahappan, Janaki, 'The Rani of Jhansi Regiment,' *The Oracle,* Vol. II, No. I, January, 1980.

Banerjee, Maya, 'My Life with the Rani of Jhansi Regiment,' *The Oracle,* Vol. II, No. 2, April, 1980.

Bose, Krishna, 'Important Women in Netaji's Life,' *Illustrated Weekly of India,* Vol. XCIII, No. MH9, 13 August 1972 and 20 August 1972.

Bose, Mihir, *The Lost Hero: A Biography of Subhas Bose,* London: Quartet Books, 1982.

Bose, Sisir K. (ed.), *A Beacon Across Asia: A Biography of Subhas Chandra Bose,* New Delhi : Orient Longman Ltd., 1973.

—,*Netaji Collected Works* (Vols. I–V), Calcutta: Netaji Research Bureau, 1980, 1981, 1981, 1982, 1985.

Bose, Sisir K. and Bose, Sugata (eds), *Netaji Collected Works* (Vol. VI), Calcutta: Netaji Research Bureau, 1987.

Bose, Subhas Chandra, *An Indian Pilgrim: An Unfinished Autobiography and Collected Letters 1897–1921,* New York: Asia Publishing House, 1965.

—*Correspondence 1924-32,* Calcutta: Netaji Research Bureau, 1967.

—*Bose, Subhas Chandra Crossroads: The Works of Subhas Chandra Bose,* Calcutta : Netaji Research Bureau, 1962.

—*Selected Speeches of Subhas Chandra Bose,* New Delhi:

Publications Division, Government of India, 1962.

—*Testament of Subhas Bose,* New Delhi: Rajkamal Publications, 1946.

Carr, Gerard H., *The War of the Springing Tigers,* London : Osprey Publishing Ltd., 1975.

Chandra, Jag Parvesh, *Meet Col. Lakshmi,* Lahore : Indian Print Works, 1946.

Chattopadhyaya, Kamaladevi, *Indian Women's Battle for Freedom,* New Delhi: Abhinav, 1983.

Desai, A.R., *Social Background of Indian Nationalism,* Bombay : Popular Book Depot, 1954.

Forbes, Geraldine, 'Goddesses or Rebels? The Women Revolutionaries of Bengal,' *The Oracle,* Vol. II, No. 2, April 1980.

—Mothers and Sisters: Feminism and Nationalism in the Thought of Subhas Chandra Bose,' *Asian Studies,* Vol. II, No. 1, 1984.

Gandhi, M.K., *India of My Dreams,* compiled by R.K. Prabhu, Ahmedabad : Navajivan Publishing House, 1962.

Gedge, Evelyn C. (ed.), *Women in Modern India,* Bombay: D.B. Taraporewala Sons and Co., 1929.

Ghosh, Jitendra Nath, *Netaji Subhas Chandra: Political Philosophy of Netaji History of Azad Hind Government I.N.A. and International Law,* Calcutta: Orient Book Company, 1946.

Ghosh, K.K., *The I.N.A.: Second Front of the Indian Independence Movement,* Meerut, 1969.

Hayashida, Tatsuo, *Netaji Subhas Chandra Bose: His Great Struggle and Martydom,* Calcutta : Allied Publishers, 1970.

Heimsath, Charles H., *Indian Nationalism and Hindu Social Reform,* Princeton, New Jersey : Princeton University Press, 1964.

Ikramullah, Begum Shaista S., *From Purdah to Parliament,* London : The Cresset Press, 1963.

Jain, Devaki (ed.), *Indian Women,* New Delhi : Publications Division, Government of India, 1975.

Jayawardena, Kumari, *Feminism and Nationalism in the Third World,* London : Zed Books, 1986.

Jog, N.C., *In Freedom's Quest : A Biography of Netaji Subhas*

Chandra Bose, New Delhi : Orient Longmans Ltd., 1969.

Lebra, Joyce C., *Japanese-Trained Armies in Southeast Asia,* New York : Columbia University Press, 1977.

—*Jungle Alliance,* Singapore: Donald Moore for Asia Pacific Press, 1971.

—*The Rani of Jhansi: A Study in Female Heroism in India,* Honolulu: University of Hawaii Press, 1986.

Lebra, Joyce C., Paulson, Joy, Everett, Jana (eds), *Women and Work in India: Continuity and Change,* New Delhi: Promilla & Co., Publishers, 1984.

Majumdar, Shanti, 'Netaji's Rani of Jhansi Regiment—Reminiscances,' *The Oracle,* Vol. II, No. 3, July 1980.

Manohar, K. Murali (ed.), *Women's Status and Development in India,* Warangal: Society for Women's Studies and Development, 1984.

Mehta, Hansa, *Indian Women,* New Delhi: Butala & Co., 1981.

Mies, Maria, 'Indian Women and Leadership,' in *Bulletin of Concerned Asian Scholars,* Vol. 7, No. 1, 1975.

—*Indian Women and Patriarchy,* New Delhi : Vikas, 1980.

—'The Social Origins of the Sexual Division of Labour,' in *ISS Occasional Papers,* No. 85, 1981.

Mookerjee, Dr. Girija K., *Subhas Chandra Bose,* New Delhi : Publications Division, Government of India, 1975.

Panikkar, K.M., *Hindu Society at Cross Roads,* Bombay : Asia Publishing House, 1955.

Randall, Vicky, *Women and Politics: An International Perspective,* Chicago: University of Chicago Press, 1987.

Roy, Manisha, *Bengali Women,* Chicago: University of Chicago Press, 1975.

Roy, P.B., *The Glory That is I.N.A.,* Calcutta : Ratneswar Mazumdar for Sreeguru Library, 1946.

Sachchidananda, and Sinha, Ramesh P., *Women's Rights : Myth and Reality,* Jaipur : Printwell Publishers, 1984.

Saqui, A.B., *Facts About the I.N.A.,* Lahore : The National Book Society of India, Ltd., 19 (?).

Sharma, R.K., *Nationalism, Social Reform and Indian Women,* New Delhi : Janaki Prakashan, 1981.

Singh, Mohan, *Leaves From My Diary,* Lahore : Free World Publications, 1946.

Srinivas, M.N., *Caste in Modern India,* New York : Asia Publishing House, 1962.

Srinivas, M.N., *The Changing Position of Indian Women,* New Delhi : Oxford University Press, 1978.

Toye, Hugh, *Subhas Chandra Bose : The Springing Tiger,* Bombay : Jaico Publishing House, 1959.

Carol Hills is an independent television producer in Boston, Massachusetts. She earned a master's degree from The Fletcher School of Law and Diplomacy in 1990.

II

A.B. Keith, *A Constitutional History of India, 1600-1935* (Allahabad, 1961), p. 359.

Aiyer, A. Rangaswami, *Annie Besant—Her Work for Swaraj.*

All India Congress Committee—*Women on the March,* April 1958, p. 7.

All India Congress Committee, *Women on the March*, August 1957, p. 13.

Amrita Bazar Patrika, April 10, 1930; Nehru, J., *An Autobiography*.

Annual Register, January to June, Vol. I, 1942, p. 301.

Annual Register, Vol. I, 1940.

Annual Register, Vol. I, January to June, 1932, p. 24.

Annual Report of Police Administration, Bombay, 1932.

Annual Report of the Administration of Bengal, 1932-33, p. 20.

Annual Report of the Police Administration of the Town of Calcutta and its Suburbs, 1932, p. 11.

Arnold, Edwin, *The Marquis of Dalhousie's Administration of British India,* Vol. II (London), 1865, p. 151.

Athinahappan, *The Rani of Jhansi Regiment.*

August Struggle Report prepared under the aegis of All India *Satyagraha* Council, U.P. Branch (unpublished), A.I.C.C. Office, New Delhi.

Award given by Ramsay Macdonald when Premier in 1932, regarding the political rights of major and minor communities in India.

B.B. Mazumdar, and B.P. Mazumdar, *Congress and Congressmen in the Pre-Gandhian Era, 1885-1917* (Calcutta, 1967), p. 128.

Ball, Charles, *History of the Indian Mutiny,* Vol. I, London and New York, p. 246.

Banerjee A.C., *The Making of Indian Constitution*, Calcutta, 1948, p. 402.

Bapalal Doshi, *Limbdi ni Ladbat* (Ahmedabad, 1974) (Gujarati).

Besant, Annie, *India Bonded or Free,* Second Edition, 1930.

Chandrakant Patel, *Swatantra Andolanma Raas* (Ahmedabad, 1975), (Gujarati).

Chattopadhyaya, K. *The Awakening of Indian Womanhood.*

Commonwealth Relations Office, Vol. 163, pp. 443-45, quoted in *Civil Rebellion in the Indian Mutinies 1857-59,* Calcutta, 1957.

Congress Presidential Address from 1911 to 1934, Madras, p. 772.

Dutta, K., *Chittagong Armoury Raiders Reminiscences*, p. 41; *Annual Register*, Vol. II, 1932, p. 10.

Emerson, *Non-Violent Non-Cooperation in India*, Asia, August 1922.

Followers of Khan Abdul Ghaffar Khan, a leader of the national movement in the North West Frontier Province.

Forbes, Mitchell, *Reminiscences of the Great Mutiny, 1857-59,* London, 1910.

Foreign Political Consultation No. 75 and K.W. March 2, 1 55, (N.A.I.).

Foreign Political Proceeding No. 127, May 28, 1858.

Foreign Political Secret Consultation No. 138, December 18, 1857 (N.A.I.).

Foreign Political Secret Consultation No. 355, July 31, 1857. For details see Appendix D, Part II.

Foreign Political Secret Proceedings No. 1052, February 12, 1859. For details of her letters, see Appendix F.

Foreign Political Secret, A Consultation, No. 34-38 of November 26, 1858, (N.A.I.).

Foreign Political Supplement (Madar Bakhsh), 287, December 30, 1859, (N.A.I.).

Foreign Political Supplement Consultation No. 266, December 30, 1859 (N.A.I.).

Foreign Political Supplement Proceedings No. 280, December 30, 1859; Forest, G.W.

Forest, G.W., *Selections from the Letters, Despatches and Other State Papers, 1857-58,* Vol. IV, pp. 2-3.

From a review of Katherine Mayo's *'Slaves of the God'*, in *The Bombay Chronicle,* 25 April 1929.

From Jawaharlal Nehru, *"The Discovery of India"*

G.A. Natesan & Co., Madras, *Speeches and Writings of Sarojini Naidu*, p. XVII.

G.S. Halappa, *History of Freedom Movement in Karnataka* (Bangalore, 1964), Vol. 11, pp. 440-41.

Gandhi, 'Speech at Gujarat Women's Conference, Dandi,' quoted in Forbes, oddesses or Rebels', p. 1.

Geraldine Forbes, 'Goddesses or Rebels? The Women Revolutionaries of Bengal', p. 1.

Giani, K.S., *Indian Independence Movement in East Asia*, Lahore, 1947.

Gordon, Alexander, Lt. Col. W., *Recollection of a Highland Subaltern During the Campaign,* London, 1898, p. 104.

Gough, General Sir H., *Old Memories,* Edinburg, 1897, p. 19.

Government of Madhya Pradesh, *The History of the Freedom Movement,* (1956).

Horace Alexander, *Gandhi Through Western Eyes* (Bombay, 1969), p. 64.

Independent (unregistered paper edited by Mahadev Desai) December 27, 1921.

India in 1920 (Official Report published every year), p. 238.

India Ravaged–Chimur-Bhansali, Professor, (A.I.C.C. Library, New Delhi).

Indian National Congress Resolutions, 1930-34 (Allahabad, n.d.),.

Innes, Lieut-General J.J. Mcleod, *Lucknow and Oudh in Mutiny,* London, 1896.

Inquilab, monthly journal of the Indian National Congress, Eastern Zone. Edited, Rammanohar Lohia and Aruna Asaf Ali, March 1944, A.I.C.C. Library, New Delhi.

J. Murdoch (comp.) *Twelve Years of Indian Progress, Extracted From the Indian National Congress; the resolutions of its Thirteen Sessions* (Madras, 1898).

J.C. Wilson's *Moradabad Narrative of Events* (Official), dated December 24, 1858.

Jawaharlal Nehru, *An Autobiography* (Loodon, 1941), p. 224.

Jayawardena, *Feminismj and Nationalism in the Third World.* p. 97.

Jhansi had been virtually passed on to the British government during the misrule of Raja Raghunath Rao. It was handed over to Gangadhar Rao, brother of the late Raja in 1843.

Jitendra Nath Ghosh, *Netaji Subhas Chandra,* p. 149.

Jogeshchandra Bagal, *Jattiya Andolane Banga Nari* (Visva Bharati, Bhadra, 1361 B. Sen).

Kaka Kalelkar (ed.) *Bapuna Patro, Bhenone* (Gujarati). Translatior into English by Kaka Kalelkar, *Bapu's Letters to Ashran Sisters,* I (Ahmedabad, 1952).

Kalpana Dutt, *Reminiscences* (Bombay, 1945).

Kantilal M. Shah, *Viramgam Satyagraha* (Ahmedabad, 1974 (Gujarati).

Karnatak Pradesh Congress Committee Report on the happening: in Karnatak, October 11, 1942 to October 31, 1942.

Karnatak Provincial Congress Committee, *Brief Report oı Happenings in Karnatak*, November 1, 1942, to Novembe 15, 1942.

Krishna Basu : '78.

Krishna Bose, *'Important Women in Netaji's Life,'*.

Kulke : '74 : 210-11 and Nanavutty : '76 : 78-79 and 89)

Lal, Pyare, *Mahatma Gandhi, The Last Phase,* p. 37.

Letter from Subhas Bose to Basanti Devi, 20.12.26, *NCW,* Vol. IV, p. 118.

Letter from Subhas Bose to Basanti Devi, 6.7*.25, NCW,* Vol. III, pp. 77-78.

Letter from Subhas Bose to Prabhabati Bose, c. 1912-1913, *NCW,* Vol. I, p. 137.

Letter No. 5950-JL-42/54484, dated October 8, 1942; Letter No. 8245-JL-42/73492, dated December 31, 1942 (in the possession of Amar Kaur).

Lowe, Thomas, *Central India During the Rebellion of 1857-58,* London.

M.K. Gandhi, *Satyagraha in South Africa,* (2nd ed., Ahmedabad, 1950).

Mahadev Desai, *The Story of Bardoli, being a History of the Bardoli Satyagraha of 1928 and its sequel* (Ahmedabad, 1957).

Maharishi Dayanand Saraswati, *Satyartha Prakash* (Hindi) Arsh Sahitya Prachar Trust, Delhi 1988 (36th reprint of the 2nd edition revised by Swami Dayanand and published in 1883).

Mahila Pragati Ke Path Par, September, 1957, (Hindi); *Women on the March*, September 1958.

Major Evans Bell in his *The Empire in India Letters,* London.

Majumdar, *'Netaji Rani of Jhansi Regiment—Reminiscences,'*.

Majumdar, *'Netaji's Rani of Jhansi Regiment—Reminiscences,'*.

Majumdar, R.C., *The Sepoy Mutiny and the Revolt of 1857,* Calcutta, 1957.

Malleson, G.B., *History of the Indian Mutiny, 1857-58,* London, 1858, Vol. I, p. 93; Forest G.W., Vol. III.

Malleson, G.B., *History of the Indian Mutiny, 1857-58,* Second edition, 1879, Vol. II.

Malleson, G.B., *op. cit.,* Vol. I.

Manibehn V. Patel, *Borsad Satyagraha* (Gujarati) (Ahmedabad, 1972).

Mitra, Bejin and Chakraborty, P. (Edited), *Rebel India*, Calcutta, 1946, p. 3.

N.N. Mitra (ed.), *The Indian Annual Register,* Vol. 1, Jan-June 1930, p. 36.

Narrative of Events Mutiny in India, 1857-58, Calcutta, 1881, Vol. I.

Narrative of Events Mutiny in India, op. cit., Kaye, Sir, J.W., Vol. III.

Nehru, Jawaharlal, *The Unity of India, Collected Writing – 1937-40,* London, 1941, p. 401.

Nehru, Jawaharlal, *Toward Freedom*, New York, 1941, p. 432.

Nehru. J., *op. cit.,* p. 334.

P.J. Thomas, *Indian Women Through the Ages* (Bombay, 1964), p. 331.

Panikkar, *Hindu Society at Cross Roads,* p. 39.

Parasnis, *Jhansi Sansthanchya Maharani Lakshmi Bai Sahen Hyanchen Charita*.

Proceedings of the Indian National Congress, 1920, Quoted in Post Wheeler, *India Against the Storm*, New York.

Punjab Congress Committee Report on Disobedience in Lahore, August 9, 1942.

Punjab Congress Committee—*Report on Disturbances in Punjab*, p. 8.

Quoted in Madhu Kishwar, 'The daughters of Aryavarta', 177-78.

Radio Calling, No. II (Papers in possession of Miss Usha Mehta).

Ramnarayan N. Pathak, *Rajkot Satyagraha* (Ahmedabad, 1974) (Gujarati).

Sisir K. Bose (ed.), *A Beacon Across Asia: A Biography of Subhas Chandra Bose,* p. 218.

Report of the Franchise Committee (1918), pp. 4-5.

Report of the Indian Franchise Committee (1932), Vol. 1, p. 166.

Report of the Indian Statutory Commission (Simon Commission), 1930, Vol. I, p. 250.

Report of the Pradesh Congress Committee on the happenings in Karnatak, August 9, 1942 to September 20, 1942.

Report on the Indian National Congress session 1923-24, p. 174.

Roshni, Journal published by the All India Women's Conference. Delhi, May 1947, p. 41.

Rudman, F.R.R., *Central Provinces, District Gazetteer, Mandala District,* Vol. A, p. 255.

Russel, Sir. W.H., *My Diary in India in the Year 1858-59,* London, 1860.

Sangharash Kalin Netaon Ke Jiwanian (Hindi), *op. cit.,* p. 162.

Sangharsh Kalin Netaon Ki Jiwanian (Hindi) published under the auspices of History of the Freedom Movement Board, Uttar Pradesh, 1957.

Subhas Chandra Bose, 'Opening of the Rhani of Jhansi Training camp, 22 October 1943,' Testament of Subhas Bose.

Sitaramayya, Dr. P., *History of the Indian National Congress*, Vol. II.

Sitaramayya, Dr. Pattabhi, *The Nationalist Movement of India*. Bombay, 1950, p. 45.

Social Reconstruction in India. The relations of the sexes, in *Lala Lajpat Rai: writings and speeches* (ed. Vijaya chandra Joshi, University Publishers, Delhi, 1966, 376, 378 and 381.

Special Bulletin issued by the All-India Congress Committee, March 15, 1933, p. 1.

Speeches and Writings of Mahatma Gandhi.

Stri Dharma, Vol. 12, Nov. 1928-1929.

Stri Dharma, Vol. 13 October to December 1930, pp. 336-84.

Stri-Dharma, Vol. 13, December 1929 to October 1930, p. 247.

Subhas Chandra Bose, *'An Indian Pilgrim,'* Sisir K. Bose (ed.), *Netaji Collected Works*, vol. I, pp. 15-18.

Subhas Chandra Bose, *'Netaji's Special Message for the Rani of Jhansi Regiment, May 1944,'* reprinted in *The Oracle* II, (Jan. 1980), p. 42.

Subhas Chandra Bose, *'The Indian Struggle,'* Sisir K. Bose, ed., *NCW,* Vol. II.

Subhas Chandra Bose, *Selected Speeches of Subhas Chandra Bose*.

Suktankar quoted in Asthana 74:8.

Sumit Sarkar, *The Swadeshi Movement in Bengal* (New Delhi, 1973), pp. 287-88.

Susmita Medh (ed.), *Jyoti Vikas Yatra* (Ahmedabad, 1971), p. 290.

Swami Dayanand particularly takes into account the contemporary concerns of the social reformers in Bengal: J.T.F. Jordens, *Dayanand Saraswati: His Life and Ideas,* Oxford University Press, Delhi, 1978, 70-98.

Tantia Tope was born in 1814. His father was in the service of Peshwa Baji Rao II. Tantia was a prominent rebel leader and took part in almost all the stages of rebellion. Ultimately he was taken prisoner on April 7, 1859. He was court martialled and a death sentence was passed on him.

Tara Ali Baig (ed.), *Women of India* (New Delhi, Publications Division, 1958), p. 19.

The author is grateful to Geraldine Forbes, who has interviewed many of the Rani of Jhansi veterans, for her informed and generous observations of the Ranis.

The Cabinet Mission consisted of Lord Pethick-Lawrence, Sir Strafford Cripps and A.V. Alexander.

Usha Chakraborty, *Condition of Bengali Women around the Second Half of the Nineteenth Century* (Calcutta, 1963), pp. 127-28.

W. and R. Chambers, *The History of Indian Revolt,* 1857-58, London, 1859.

Webb Miller, 'I Found No Peace', pp. 190-196; quoted in Jack A. Homer, *The Gandhi Reader*, Bloomington, 1956.

Index